HORRIBLY AWKWARD

AWKWARD

The New Funny Bone

MARION BOYARS
LONDON • NEW YORK

With thanks to

Matt Lucas, Steve Pemberton & Mark Gatiss

Penny

Jamie, Dean

& my editor, Rebecca

HORRIBLY AWKWARD

The New Funny Bone

First published in Great Britain and the United States in 2008 by
MARION BOYARS PUBLISHERS LTD
24 Lacy Road
London SW15 1NL

www.marionboyars.co.uk

Distributed in Australia and New Zealand by
Tower Books, 17 Rodborough Rd, Frenchs Forest, NSW 2086, Australia

Printed in 2008
10 9 8 7 6 5 4 3 2 1

A CIP catalogue record for this book is available from the British Library.
A CIP catalog record for this book is available from the Library of Congress.

ISBN 0-7145-3152-9
13 digit ISBN 978-0-7145- 3152-6

Set in Bembo 11/14pt
Printed in England by Cox and Wyman

CONTENTS

HORRIBLE, AWKWARD and FUNNY TO BOOT

This book is about a new type of comedy. It is the kind of comedy which doesn't just make us laugh, it makes us cringe and squirm as well. It makes us feel uncomfortable. This is the comedy of the horribly awkward.

The development of this new wave of comedy began in the 90s with comics like Steve Coogan, closely followed by Chris Morris and then *The League of Gentlemen*. But the horribly awkward trend is also epitomised by new talent, for example Sacha Baron-Cohen, Matt Lucas and David Walliams, Catherine Tate, Ricky Gervais and Stephen Merchant, Peter Kay and David Mitchell and Robert Webb. Where this type of humour may have once been considered avant-garde, alternative or extreme, it now rests comfortably within the mainstream, with programmes like *Little Britain*, *Peep Show* and *Extras* dominating the prime time slots that were once reserved for game shows, sitcoms and similarly less sophisticated fare.

The new wave of comedians both write and perform the majority of their own material and the new brand of humour that they typify has not only taken the UK by storm, but has gained fans across the globe. That the US is recognising British talent, for example, is proved by the fact that Ricky Gervais won two Golden Globes for *The Office* and has also recently won an Emmy in the US for his role in *Extras* and Sacha Baron-Cohen won a Golden Globe for his role in the movie *Borat*. Or consider the fact that *The Office* has been broadcast in countries as diverse as Argentina, Singapore and Finland, amongst others. The shows created by these people appeal to audiences from all walks of life and are watched by millions, with laughter erupting at dangerous levels. As Alan Partridge bungles his clumsy way through life, David Brent embarrassingly plays up to cameras 'documenting' action in *The Office* and the zany characters of *Little Britain* give us an appreciably alternative view of British society, who wouldn't laugh?

In the past this humour could on occasion be found in programmes such as *Fawlty Towers*, especially the 'Don't mention the war' episode, and the film *This is Spinal Tap*. However, in the UK its use was rare. Whereas the origins of comedy in film and TV may be found in slapstick humour of the kind pioneered by cult classics like Charlie Chaplin, Harold Lloyd, and later Laurel and Hardy, since the innocent variety shows of the fifties saw ratings begin to decline, things have changed. The catchphrase joke-based humour of the 70s sitcoms was laden with innuendo, and 80s comedy such as *The Young Ones* and *French and Saunders* may have been ground-breaking at the time, and certainly alternative, but it is notable, however, that of late our tastes have become more extreme, and more inclined towards the distasteful. The classic aesthetic question of 'Why do we enjoy watching tragedy when it may induce painful emotional responses?' again raises its head. What is it about the visceral experience of recoiling from these recent comic creations that causes us to turn-on and watch them again and again? Why aren't we more annoyed that we are not guaranteed belly-laughs any longer from our comedy heroes, let alone jokes? For instance, on watching a preview of the final episode of Series Three of *The League of Gentlemen*, the creators realised there wasn't a single joke in it, and had to add one in at the last minute.

Finding humour in something relies in part on an intellectual response to the joke. For example, in one of his routines the US comedian Lenny Bruce used insulting names for audience members: 'I see we have three niggers in the audience. And over there I see two wogs, and five spics and four kikes…'[1]

When he began there were gasps and even angry responses, but this changed as the list of insulting and unsettling names grew ever longer. When it became clear he was simply listing all the derogatory terms he could possibly think of, the words lost their emotional impact on the audience. The audience began responding intellectually rather than emotionally and the same people who had been getting annoyed and offended were now laughing.

This intellectual response is vital in regards to horribly awkward humour. You have to be aware of the fact that a joke is being made, and astute enough to pick up on the nature of that joke, to see past the type of material that might otherwise cause offence and find the humour in a situation. With such an abundance of not-at-all-politically-correct content, an audience that reacts with knee-jerk emotional responses is bound to find much that is objectionable. However, because we are analysing the behaviour of characters like Alan Partridge and David Brent on an intellectual level, because we understand that they are fictional characters who provide a simple medium for the message, their bigotry does not offend. Instead, it makes us laugh because we understand the context in which their actions are being presented: through a character who is both detestable and ridiculous and more often than not, bypasses the boundaries of reason.

Through this very deliberate and conscious dismissal of political correctness, cringe-worthy comedy provides a kind of freedom from the constraints this correctness places on our everyday lives. We can laugh at what the characters are saying without fear of recrimination because of the context in which their comments are made. No one is going to beat us up for finding David Brent's

> **Alan Partridge Quote**
> 'Tonight's show is hot. How hot, Alan? Well, imagine Debbie Harry in camiknickers spoon-feeding a beef vindaloo to Pan's People in a sauna in Bangkok. That's half as hot as tonight's show,' Alan Partridge

treatment of his disabled staff amusing. No one is going to rip our telephone number from their phone book just because we enjoy a chortle at the very mention of the word paedophile when watching the DVD of that famous episode of *Brass Eye*.

Again, it is the context which is the key and which sets this group of humorists apart from those who are genuinely bigoted. Their lack of political correctness is centred on flawed, usually dislikable characters. Part of the reason they are dislikable is exactly because they hold politically incorrect opinions. We laugh because of the character's ignorance, not because what they say is true. This reinforces the ignorance and downright stupidity of their opinions.

At the twisted heart of unbearably awkward humour is

comedy aimed at social codes, some of which are enshrined in political correctness. Some comedy theorists say that the greatest incongruity is achieved through violating the taboos of a society and that this violation can provide the greatest laughter.[2] Well, there are many taboos which are well and truly shattered in some of the programmes which will be discussed.

Another branch, practised especially by the *Little Britain* team, involves visual humour. In this instance, it is more concerned with the horrid than the awkward, though it does make us squirm in our seats. It also profiles aspects of our society which are exaggerated for the purpose of the show, such as the upper-middle-class-female character called Maggie Blackamoor, who vomits whenever her sensibilities are offended. She is a caricature of a well-to-do, middle-England housewife who is prejudiced against anything that might not fit her small town view.

> ### *The Office* Quote
>
> 'You grow up, you work half a century, you get a golden handshake, you rest a couple of years and you're dead. And the only thing that makes that crazy ride worthwhile is "Did I enjoy it? What did I learn? What was the point?" That's where I come in. You've seen how I react to people, make them feel good, make them think that anything's possible. If I make them laugh along the way, sue me.' David Brent from *The Office*

Caricatures can also be found in the work of Sacha Baron-Cohen, Catherine Tate, *The League of Gentlemen* and Chris Morris. To a lesser degree their use is also evident in Steve Coogan's work, as well as that of Gervais and Merchant and Peter Kay. Caricatures are a common feature of this kind of comedy. So, we can see that it comments on various aspects of society, whether this be social codes of conduct, the types of people within a society, or the opinions they hold. Its humour derives in part from highlighting these aspects and poking fun at them with a large, red-hot poker.

It is not just the awkwardness on screen that is of significance however; the levels of discomfort amongst audiences themselves is equally important in terms of its appeal. This is palpable when Borat sings about Kazakhstan to the tune of the American national anthem in front of a crowd of increasingly agitated baseball fans – a favourite scene amongst fans of the film. We feel uneasy when David Brent tries to entertain in *The Office* or makes one of his politically incorrect gaffs. We find ourselves unsettled by the darkness in *The League of Gentlemen* and shocked by the controversial content of *Brass Eye*. It seems that the greater the feelings of discomfort amongst an audience, the greater the comedy payoff – because we need to react to our discomfort.

On-screen awkwardness can arise through a character's physical presence, such as that of Alan Partridge or Darren Lamb in *Extras*. It can arise through social ineptitude, as seen in Borat's behaviour as he tours across America and with Vicky Pollard in *Little Britain*. It can also arise verbally, as with the character of Gareth in *The Office*, who is incapable of approaching the opposite sex without making a complete fool of himself, and Jeremy in *Peep Show*, who nearly always says the wrong thing at the wrong time to any attractive woman he may encounter.

All of the programmes discussed contain flawed characters with negative personality traits, such as egotism, arrogance, insensitivity or self-obsession. Or, as with some of the *Little Britain* characters, they manifest their negative aspects physically, such as the vomiting previously mentioned.

course, he wasn't the first to take a comic character and put them into 'real life' situations, nor was he the first to conduct interviews in the guise of an alter-ego. Other characters to have done this before include Dame Edna Everage (aka Barry Humphries), Dennis Pennis (aka Paul Kaye) and Mrs Merton (aka Caroline Aherne). However, thanks to his success in duping the public at an early stage he was encouraged to pursue this angle further.

Another person to have used this form of comedy recently, and to similar extremes as Baron-Cohen, is Chris Morris. In *The Day Today* and *Brass Eye,* Morris interviewed the influential and famous, regularly making them appear extremely foolish. One of the most famous examples of this is the section from *Brass Eye* featuring a discussion about the new, terrible addiction of young people to 'Cake', in which game show host Noel Edmunds was duped into commenting on a fictional situation involving this ridiculous-sounding 'drug'. That Morris also courts controversy (just like Ali G and Borat) is highlighted by *Brass Eye's* 'coverage' of paedophilia, which drew attention to the over-reaction of the media and politicians. This caused a degree of outrage rarely seen, even to the extent that MPs publicly condemned the show despite the fact most of them had not even seen it.

Baron-Cohen was to continue the tradition of comic characters who mock fame, celebrity and power through certain interviewing strategies and techniques. One of the most memorable of these was Dennis Pennis. Both he and Ali G were characters adopted by their creators which enabled them to approach celebrities in a certain way. Both employed slightly ridiculous ways of dressing which immediately caused their interviewees to underestimate them. This was coupled with peculiar mannerisms and forms of speech intended to add to the poor impression they made. These characters were then able to get away with asking questions that other, more serious interviewers would never be able to ask, and this is the foundation of the horribly awkward humour evident in Baron-Cohen's work. He adopts characters which cause people to underestimate him, then asks questions which make us squirm and then laugh as we see the interviewees struggling to make sense of the situation they find themselves in.

It wasn't until 1998 that Baron-Cohen hit the mainstream, when Ali G first appeared on *The Eleven O'Clock Show* on Channel 4. He was told about the interview for the spot on this programme four years and ten months into the five years he had given himself to make it big. At the time he was surviving on virtually nothing in Thailand and was even considering moving there for the foreseeable future.[6] If he hadn't got the job then Sacha Baron-Cohen would probably have ended up as a lawyer rather than a comedian entertaining millions of avid fans — his two possible career paths couldn't have been more different...

On *The Eleven O'Clock Show* Ali G was billed at the 'voice of *da yoof*' and his speech was packed with street slang which many interviewees had trouble understanding. The plethora of slang has even given rise to Ali G translators and online dictionaries which explain what the words mean. It also added a great deal to the humour. For example, when interviewing Rhodes Boyson, a former Conservative cabinet minister:

'Do you believe kids should be caned?'
'Yes'
'You do! Wicked, man. You believe kids should be caned even in school?'
'Yes, I do'

Boyson is of course completely unaware that his interpretation of the word 'caned' was not the one Ali G was using, something the largely young audience fully understood.

It soon became apparent to Channel 4 that Ali G was a rising star and he was given his own show called '*Da Ali G Show*' in 2000 which became an immediate success. Magazines relating to very different areas of interest, such as the celebrity-gossip weekly *Heat* and the (now defunct) rock magazine *Melody Maker*, all agreed that Ali G was the funniest person on television.[7] Some of the people he managed to interview included Jarvis Cocker, lead singer of Pulp,

> ### *Ali G* Quote
>
> Ali G: 'Let's talk about some conspiracy things. Let's go back to the grassy knoll. Who actually shot JR?' R. James Woolsey (former CIA director): 'Don't you mean JFK?'

Paul Daniels the magician, and the former Labour MP Tony Benn. All were submitted to an audience-captivating blend of street speak, seemingly idiotic questioning and a good deal of discomfort. But this is of course where the attraction lies. The audience loved to see the guests squirm in the presence of an interviewer who seemed ridiculous, yet asked questions with great insight and comic value.

One interesting fact that Baron Cohen noticed was that some of the guests tried to gain Ali G's approval: 'They're in the room with a total idiot and yet they're seeking his approval as if it somehow makes them cooler.'[8]

This kind of display can be seen when politicians speak to members of the public and are clearly trying to make themselves appear more down-to-earth in order to appeal to voters. In the case of those who sought approval on *Da Ali G Show* we can assume they thought the host was coolness personified in the eyes of British youth. They wanted his acceptance, believing that audience acceptance would thereby follow. They wanted to be viewed as cool and hip, not realising that in the attempt they would make themselves look the exact opposite.

Dan Mazer, a long-term friend of Baron-Cohen's who went to school and university with him and went on to be a VT producer on *The Eleven O'Clock Show* said, 'We don't try to make a fool of the subject,' adding, 'the point is to laugh at Ali himself.'[9] The latter aspect relates to Ali underlining the absurdity of people trying to ape US black youth culture stereotypes. However, the point Mazer makes seems questionable when it is clear the programme does make fools out of its guests on many occasions.

It is clear that Ali G's form of interrogation is unusual, even bizarre, in comparison with most interviews. His approach will naturally make his 'victims' seem foolish as long as they accept Ali as real and not merely a comic character. Maybe the aim wasn't specifically to make subjects seem foolish, but that has certainly been the result, one which has led to Ali G's stardom. Unfortunately, the immense popularity of the character quickly had a knock-on effect and perhaps lessened the impact of Ali G's absurdity. The use of catch phrases and a schoolboy, sexually-orientated humour has also overpowered the potential impact of the more serious messages, which is also a great shame. It seems that Ali G will be remembered as much for phrases such as '*bling*', '*innit*' and '*bookyakasha*' than for undermining of black stereotypes or pointing out the absurdity of British youths adopting US street and gang culture attitudes.

In 2000 Ali G appeared in Madonna's video for her song 'Music'. He then hosted the MTV Europe Music Awards in

2001 which were held in Frankfurt, Germany. With all this coverage heightening his public appeal it was only a matter of time until he found his way onto the big screen.

Ali G's movie debut was called *Ali G Indahouse* (2002) and followed the course of the title character's political career, one caused primarily by a manipulative Chancellor played by Hollywood stalwart Charles Dance, who has appeared in films such as *Alien 3* (1992) and *The Golden Child* (1986, with US comic favourite Eddie Murphy). The Chancellor's motivation was to oust the Prime Minister, played by Michael Gambon. This Chancellor-Prime Minister opposition is a humorous take on the Gordon Brown–Tony Blair situation as it stood at the time. It is also worth noting that Martin Freeman, who plays Tim in *The Office* (discussed in Chapter Three), was one of Ali G's 'Staines massive'.

> ### *Ali G* Quote
>
> 'That has got to be the best job, no? Watching porno all day. I mean, you've been doing it for twenty-five years, man, and surely no one can keep it hard for that long,' Ali G talking about censorship with James Thurman

Like the television show, the film is packed with juvenile humour which is often crude and sexually based. There are a number of cameo appearances from stars like model Naomi Campbell and British chat show hosts Richard and Judy.

The movie does not contain Ali G's trademark interviews or him fooling people into believing he is a real person and not just a character, representing a departure from the original humour, made possible by the popularity of the character itself. In fairness, by the time of the film's production it would have been virtually impossible to include such things even if the producers had wanted to because Ali was too famous and no one would have been fooled.

This wasn't the case with the Borat movie because the character was still relatively unknown, especially in the American south, and it was easy to convince people he was a real person. In fact, it was the film itself, rather than the preceding series, which shot Borat to fame using the same format that Ali G would have probably used had he not already been in the public eye when he came to make *Ali G Indahouse.*

Ali G Quote

Ali G: 'When is man going to walk on da sun?'

Buzz Aldrin: 'It's much too hot on the sun. We can never go there'

Ali G: 'We could go in da winter, when it's colder.'

Indahouse uses a sexist theme throughout, one blended with plenty of comical slang. This could be, and has been, seen as offensive, but is actually part of the parody of gangsta 'street stylee' that the film portrays. The real gangsta rap/dance music culture is filled with sexism and sexual references, not least in song lyrics. It is also a subculture which turns women into sexual objects, something clearly seen in virtually any advertisement for dance, hip-hop, techno or rave compilation albums in which women are shown gyrating to the music with as little clothing on as possible. *Indahouse* highlights the way in which females are treated as objects. However, this message is somewhat lost because rather than taking Ali G as a ridiculous figure, many have taken him to their heart and actually see him as being cool.

A spin-off from the Ali G film was a hit song featuring the vocals of Ali and singer Shaggy. It was called 'Me Julie' and was about a girlfriend he'd met at a disco in his Goth days. It reached Number 2 in the UK charts. However, despite his British and European coverage by this time, Ali G was still relatively unknown stateside. His only notable appearance across the pond was in Madonna's video and so this made the US a prime location to continue his special brand of comic interviewing.

In the States, HBO commissioned a new Ali G show. Thanks to his lack of exposure he was able to conduct interviews with people including Edwin 'Buzz' Aldrin, second man on the moon, Dick Thornburgh, former US Attorney General and Thomas J. Pickard, former FBI Director. The show ran for two series and also appeared on UK TV. It featured two other characters devised by Baron-Cohen. These were the now infamous Borat Sagdiyev, Kazakhstan's sixth most famous man and a leading reporter with the state-run TV network,[10] and a lesser-known character called Bruno, who is a fashion reporter for a fictional 'Gay TV' in Austria.

Prior to the release of *Borat: Cultural Learnings of America for Make Benefit Glorious Nation of Kazakhstan (2006)* and the storm of controversy it whipped up, there had already been certain complaints concerning Ali G. A number of black commentators, including a few comedians, thought there was a touch of racism to the character.

To understand these allegations you must take into account the fact that Ali G is an 'uneducated, misogynist, black man from Staines.'[11] He employs black stereotypes and claims to be a gang member of the 'West Staines Massive'. However, these elements are purposefully undermined by the fact he is said to live with his grandmother in Cherry Blossom Close.

It is his use of stereotypes which has caused some of the controversy as it is also possible that Ali G's use of such stereotypes helps to reinforce the prejudices of some of the largely white viewing audience. On the other hand, you could claim he is subverting the stereotype, revealing it to be an absurdity and thereby undermining it.

Curtis Walker, who had a BBC2 show called *Urban Heat*, said, 'I don't like the concept of a white guy playing a black guy... and when he is a playing a stupid stereotype it is even worse.'[12] Gina Yashere, who was in the BBC2 series called *A-Force* said that 'a black man pretending to be dumb like that would have seemed too real for white people.'[13]

> ### *Ali G* Quote
>
> 'So, if this show teach you anything, it should teach you how to respek everyone: animals, children, bitches, spazmos, mingers, lezzers, fatty boombahs, and even gaylords. So, to all you lot watching this, but mainly to the normal people, respek.' Ali G

The humour of Ali G arises precisely because he is trying to embody a black stereotype from a completely different culture. In so doing, Ali G points out the absurdity inherent in British youth blindly copying a kind of stateside black youth culture which they know only from their TV screens. This is part of the intelligence behind the character: Ali G is rooted in a cultural phenomena of our times, much as Harry Enfield's TV character, 'Loadsamoney', was in the 80s. Both use trends within British society and make successful parodies of them which create both humour and a critique of the phenomena.

There is one interesting point to make about the clear absurdity evident in the Ali G phenomenon; audience members have copied him. This may not seem strange, but if you consider that Ali G is supposed to be a ridiculous figure then it does seem odd that people have adopted his catchphrases and even imitated his excessive wearing of 'bling.'

In so doing they are adopting his absurdity, making

themselves ridiculous. It seems that some viewers don't get the intended joke and actually believe Ali G is cool. This could be because the impact of Ali G's absurdity and foolishness is watered down by the foolishness of his guests, a factor already mentioned.

Borat was also a creation reliant on absurdity. His popularity on the HBO television programme inevitably led to him following in Ali G's footsteps and making the move into what has become a hit film in spite of stirring up a diplomatic hornet's nest.

Borat and Ali G have another common link which is important to their humour: this is the use of a language barrier when communicating with other people — often to hilarious effect. The origins of this comedic strategy may lie in Baron-Cohen's lifelong admiration of the work of British comic actor Peter Sellers, who he cites as his greatest influence.[14] He is a fan of the Pink Panther movies, which centre

> **Borat Quote**
>
> 'This is Natalya. She is my sister. She is number-four prostitute in whole of Kazakhstan.' Borat

around the clumsy and mentally challenged French character Inspector Clouseau. In these films Clouseau's language acts as a barrier and also leads to amusing misunderstandings, something reflected with both Ali G and Borat.

Ali G's language barrier is formed by his exaggerated use of slang, whereas Borat's is more traditional; the sort of language barrier seen in comedy programmes such as *Allo, Allo* and Clouseau. There is also a more important difference between the two language barriers that Baron-Cohen utilises.

Ali G works in conjunction with a 'generation barrier'. His guests belong to older generations and because of this they do not understand the slang terminology that he is using.

This lack of understanding is then used to humorous effect, as we saw clearly in the 'caned' example previously given in this chapter and may also be seen in those excruciating moments when his celebrity guests try and join in with the slang.

This 'generation gap' highlights another significant difference between the characters which arises from the kind of misunderstandings their language barriers create, and it is these misunderstandings which are intrinsic to the comic effect of both characters. Ali G's language barrier creates misunderstanding on the part of the interviewee, while Borat's creates such misunderstanding in relation to the character himself rather than those he is interacting with.

Borat's portrayal of his supposed homeland caused a degree of outrage in Kazakhstan's political circles. The row over his portrayal actually began in 2005 after the character followed in Ali G's footsteps and hosted MTV's Europe Music Awards in Lisbon. The Kazakhstan Foreign Ministry spokesman Yerzhan Askykbayev told a news conference that Baron-Cohen's behaviour was 'utterly unacceptable'. Cohen's response was to post a video as Borat on the character's official website in which he said, 'in response to Mr Askykbayev's comments, I'd like to state I have no connection with Mr Cohen and fully support my Government's decision to sue this Jew.'[15]

To counteract the negative image Borat was considered to portray of the ex-Soviet country, the Kazakhstan government took out adverts in US papers in order to show the American people the 'real' country. Borat's Kazakhstan website was also shut down by people who opposed his displays of anti-Semitism and his false representation of Kazakh culture.

The belief that *Borat* the movie contained an unfair portrayal of life in Kazakhstan was underpinned by such things as the assertion that inhabitants were making monkey porn, throwing Jews down wells, exporting pubic hair, abusing gypsies and enjoying incestuous relationships. In response, Baron-Cohen says: 'I think the joke is on people who can believe that the Kazakhstan that I describe can exist.'[16]

In spite of this defence, in September 2006 President Nazarbayev of Kazakhstan visited George Bush at the White House and one of the topics they discussed was his country's image and Borat's effect on it.

However, maybe it should have been George Bush and US politicians getting upset about the film. The section on Kazakhstan is clearly intended as parody and is completely ludicrous. It is important to note that some of the scenes during the rest of the movie which are set in the States are also staged with actors, rather than genuine members of the

> ***Borat* Quote**
>
> 'Kazakhstan is more civilised now. Woman can now travel on inside of bus and homosexuals no longer have to wear blue hat' Borat

public playing some roles. Nevertherless the film reveals a society struggling with deep set prejudices. Put simply, the US is shown in the film as a bigoted nation of largely ignorant people, its underbelly exposed in a successful critique carried out with comic flair, a critique that was hinted at in the title of the movie: '*Cultural Learnings of America*'.

One of the possibly worrying aspects of this factor is that many of the people shown in the film didn't seem to notice that their responses were distasteful and neither has the film caused the kind of national soul searching that one might expect after such a damaging exposé. Baron-Cohen comments: 'I think it's an interesting idea that not everyone in Germany (during WWII) had to be a raving anti-Semite.

They just had to be apathetic.'[17]

Baron-Cohen's concern with public responses under Nazi Germany may well stem from his Jewish background. His grandmother was a highly regarded ballet dancer who fled from Germany during the Third Reich and now lives in Haifa, Israel. When *Borat* was released she went to a midnight screening and called her grandson afterwards to compliment him.[18]

In respect to both Borat and Ali G, it seems that people were asked to be part of the film and the show under false pretences. Alex Alonso felt as though he were 'tricked' into appearing with Ali G.[19] He was approached to appear on a programme called *The Message* which was said to be aimed at the British youth with the purpose of presenting serious topics in an understandable way.

Alonso was asked to appear in order to discuss Los Angeles gang culture and its destructive influence, believing the programme would present the subject matter in a sensible way. The letter sent to him by TalkBack Productions stated, '*The Message* (working title), is a late-night factual-entertainment programme aimed at a youth audience.'[20] One of the people interviewed in Ali G's HBO network show was Ralph Nader, a consumer activist and former US presidential candidate for the Green Party. A spokesman for Nader stated that 'they [the programme makers] said they were doing an educational special and were going to gear it towards children and introduce them to civic figures.'[21] This means the production company probably used the same tactic with all its requests for people to appear on Ali G's show. None of the people invited would have realised that they were to be subjected to Ali's irreverent questioning, that they would be made to squirm with awkwardness before the shell-suited, street talking king of bling.

In the case of the *Borat* movie a fifteen million pound lawsuit was instigated by the residents of a Romanian hamlet where some of the movie was filmed. They claimed that they had been misled into believing it was a documentary which was being filmed. However, this is not the only lawsuit to help fuel the controversy of both Borat and Ali G.

One woman attempted to sue for slander when she was mentioned in Ali G's HBO show and allegedly described as a 'bitch'. At least three other lawsuits have been brought, all of them in relation to the *Borat* movie, including the one mentioned above. There were also two students in the States who sued for damages after making racist comments, claiming they had been plied with alcohol. The etiquette coach, Cindy Streit, who appeared in a scene in which she was given a bag of excrement by Borat, claimed her business had been ruined by this exposure.[22]

Despite, or possibly helped by, this controversy, both Ali G and Borat remain extremely popular. In fact, *Borat* became number one in Kazakhstan's DVD charts according to Amazon,[23] something which probably would not have happened had there not been so much fuss made of the film

The humour of both characters appeals particularly to teenagers. They show no respect for people, no matter what position they hold.

This irreverence derives, at least in part, from Baron-Cohen's love of *Monty Python*, along with the characters of Derek and Clive, played by Peter Cook and Dudley Moore. The enjoyment of the former began at about the same time as he discovered Peter Sellers. His brother took him to the theatre to see one of the most irreverent and controversial films of all time, *Monty Python's Life of Brian* (1979). The young Baron-Cohen was then introduced to the often rude and irreverent Derek and Clive a few years later and both of these tastes are reflected in his own work.

One of the most important reasons people have taken to the fake gangsta and the Kazakhstan reporter is that we, the audience, are in on the joke. This complicity is also what helped to make programmes such as *Candid Camera* so popular. This is effective partly because we can feel superior to those who bear the brunt of the humour. With Ali G, and Borat to a lesser degree, this is heightened in many cases because the people he is interviewing are in positions of power, have celebrity 'status' or are known to be learned and intelligent, such as MIT Professor Noam Chomsky. Therefore the audience's feeling of superiority is more pleasurable because we are wiser than the wise when it comes to understanding that a good leg-pulling is actually taking place.

> ### *Ali G* Quote
> 'Sex can lead to nasty things like herpes, gonorrhoea, and something called relationships.' Ali G

The only problem with this audience–inclusive humour arises when we feel empathy with one of Ali G or Borat's subjects. For example, in *Borat* the title character attends a high society dinner. The other people there are unaware of the deception being played on them and believe their guest to be genuine. Borat then insults one of the men and his wife. Without empathy for these people this can be found funny. However, if you feel they are undeserving of this treatment and empathise with their shock and obvious displeasure, the joke no longer holds any amusement, but becomes discomforting and unkind. The borderline between humour and discomfort is less clear and the awkwardness we feel becomes one no longer laced with laughter. It transforms into a genuine lack of comfort, which becomes unbearable to watch.

Our amusement can also be heightened or diminished according to the choice of interviewees. When speaking to people who are famous, powerful or learned, our sense of enjoyment is increased because we can feel superior and enjoy the experience of watching such people being unwittingly duped and made fools of. However, if the interviewees are normal people both these elements are removed.

Ali G and Borat are surprisingly effective characters on a deeper level than many may suspect. The latter exposed the serious issues within US society, as already mentioned and if we look again at the work of Ali G, especially earlier in his meteoric rise to fame, we find that many of the questions he asked interviewees were not as stupid as they seem at first. Actually, this isn't quite true. They are stupid, but cleverly constructed. Baron-Cohen has applied his intelligence and wit to the directions his questions take. For example, when interviewing Rhodes Boyson he asked, 'Why do clever people go to university? Why don't you send the thick people cos they need it more?' This is both a stupid and clever question. The question is stupid because university courses strive to reach high academic standards and to ensure this have high entry requirements. The question is also clever because the interviewee has to think, and to do so in a way they probably have not done before because no one else will have thought to ask such a daft question. In the case of the example, Rhodes Boyson actually couldn't come up with an answer for Ali.

The question plays with the expectations of both the viewer and interviewee. This is not the type of question we have come to expect from most interviews and is therefore funny in itself. It also serves to put the interviewee off balance, who, after many other interviews with various people, will be expecting certain questions and have answers at the ready, all of which prove useless in the face of Ali G's enquiries.

Due to the success of Baron-Cohen's characters, and in spite of the controversy, he has won a number of awards during his career. In 1999 he won a British Comedy Award for Ali G's role on *The Eleven O'Clock Show*. He was voted Personality of the Year in 2000 at the *TV Quick* awards in London. Following that was a BAFTA for *Da Ali G Show* in the category of 'Best Comedy'. In 2007 Sacha Baron-Cohen won a Golden Globe for 'Best Actor in a Musical or Comedy' for his role as Borat and was also nominated for an Oscar, along with the other writers, in the category of 'Best Writing, Adapted Screenplay'.[24]

> ### Ali G Quote
> 'One time when me woz high, me sold me car for like twenty-four chicken McNuggets.' Ali G

But where is his work going to go next? Ali G's fame is too great to continue convincing people he is real, as is Borat's. So, after all the side-splitting laughter, after the controversy and the numerous red-faced subjects of ingenious interviews, after the 'massif' success of Ali G and Borat, what does the future hold?

Well, the answer may lie with Bruno, the fashion reporter for Austrian *Gay TV*. This character, appearing in HBO's Ali G show, is an air-kissing and vacuous man. His first appearance was on the Paramount Comedy Channel during London Fashion Week and now he is set for the big screen like his two Baron-Cohen predecessors.

Late in September 2005 Universal Pictures secured a deal for a movie featuring Bruno after winning a bidding war. However, at the time of writing this book Sacha Baron-Cohen was unsure as to what form the film would take, whether scripted or reality based. In fact, he was even unsure as to whether the character featured would be Bruno.

This said, you will definitely get the chance to see him in the Tim Burton movie entitled *Sweeney Todd* (2008). This film was filmed in London in 2007 and stars Johnny Depp. Cohen plays the role of a hairdresser called Signor Adolfo Pirelli.

In fact, Sacha Baron-Cohen has already been involved in a number of other films. The movie entitled *The Jolly Boys' Last Stand* (2000) saw him in a role alongside Andy 'Gollum' Serkis. He starred in and wrote the 2003 release *Spyz*. Directed by James Bobin, it featured Ali G as James Bond and Sacha's current fiancée, the Australian actress Isla Fisher, was also cast.[25] He also had supporting roles in the Nascar parody called *Talladega Nights: The Ballad of Ricky Bobby* starring Will Ferrell, and as Julien in *Madagascar* (2005). The sequel to this animated adventure will see Baron-Cohen back in the same role and is due for release in 2008.

> ### *Ali G* Quote
>
> Ali G: 'Is the brain's memory any good?'
>
> Dr. C. Everett Koop: 'The brain's memory is perfect.'
>
> Ali G: 'Then how come I can't remember me pin number?'

Baron-Cohen has said that he has other characters and he intended to start developing them in 2007, though he admitted that doing reality based work was going to be hard now that he is so well known.[26]

We can be certain that we haven't seen the last of Sacha Baron-Cohen yet, and that's something to be very thankful for. There is another thing that is also certain, and this is that he has already created a comic legacy, that has earned him something special from the viewing public: 'big respek'.

ENDNOTES

1. http://imdb.com/name/nm0056187/bio

2. Strauss, N, 'The Man Behind the Mustache,' p.2 (14th November 2006, www.rollingstone.com/news/coverstory/sacha_baron_cohen_the _real_borat_finally_speaks)

3. http://imdb.com/name/nm0056187/bio

4. Strauss, N, 'The Man Behind the Mustache,' p.2 (14th November 2006, www.rollingstone.com/news/coverstory/sacha_baron_cohen_the _real_borat_finally_speaks)

5. Strauss, N, 'The Man Behind the Mustache,' p.5 (14th November 2006, www.rollingstone.com/news/coverstory/sacha_baron_cohen_the _real_borat_finally_speaks)

6. Strauss, N, 'The Man Behind the Mustache,' p.6 (14th November 2006, www.rollingstone.com/news/coverstory/sacha_baron_cohen_the _real_borat_finally_speaks)

7. Harrison, A, 'Goofy Gangsta', p.2 (The *Guardian*, 2nd May 1999)

8. Heffernan, V. 'The Cheerful Confessions of Ali G, Borat, and Bruno' (*The New York Times*, 15th July 2004)

9. Harrison, A, 'Goofy Gangsta', p.4 (The *Guardian*, 2nd May 1999)

10. www.hbo.com/alig

11. Younge, G, 'Is it cos I is Black?, p.1 (The *Guardian*, 12th January 2000)

12. Gibson, J, 'Comics Find Ali G is an Alibi for Racism,' p.1 (*The Guardian*, 11th January 2000)

13. Gibson, J, 'Comics Find Ali G is an Alibi for Racism,' p.1 (*The Guardian*, 11th January 2000)

14. http://imdb.com/name/nm0056187/bio

15. 'Bush to Hold Talks on Ali G Creator After Diplomatic Row,' p.2 (www.dailymail.co.uk/pages/live/articles/news/news.html?in_article_id=404852&in_page_id=1770)

16. Strauss, N., 'The Man Behind the Mustache,' p.2 (14th November 2006, www.rollingstone.com/news/coverstory/sacha_baron_cohen_the _real_borat_finally_speaks)

17. Strauss, N. 'The Man Behind the Mustache,' p.3 (14th November 2006, www.rollingstone.com/news/coverstory/sacha_baron_cohen_the _real_borat_finally_speaks)

18. Strauss, N, 'The Man Behind the Mustache,' p.2 (14th November 2006, www.rollingstone.com/news/coverstory/sacha_baron_cohen_the _real_borat_finally_speaks)

19. Alonso, A, 'Tricked Into Silly Interview With Wanna Be Gangster Ali G of Britain,' p.1 (www.streetgangs.com/topics/2002/031202aligshow)

20. Court, C. 'Interview Request Letter' (www.streetgangs.com)

21. Chittenden, M, 'How Ali G Duped America's Finest,' p.2 (*The Sunday Times,* 9th February 2003, UK)

22. Sherwin, A, 'Woman Sues Ali G Star for Slander,' p.1 (7th February 2007, www.timesonline.co.uk/tol/news/uk/article1444034.ece)

23. '*Borat* Top in Kazakhstan "Hometown",' p.1 (www.hollywood.com/news/Borat_Top_in_Kazakhstan_Hometown/3668449)

25. Strauss, N, 'The Man Behind the Mustache,' p.4 (14th November 2006, www.rollingstone.com/news/coverstory/sacha_baron_cohen_the _real_borat_finally_speaks)

26. Strauss, N, 'The Man Behind the Mustache,' p.6 (14th November 2006, www.rollingstone.com/news/coverstory/sacha_baron_cohen_the _real_borat_finally_speaks)

2. *LITTLE BRITAIN,* BIG LAUGHS: Matt Lucas and David Walliams

Little Britain was the show that shot Matt Lucas and David Walliams to great fame, but their first forays into the world of comedy were considerably less glamorous. The two of them began working together in 1995, performing at the Edinburgh Festival and usually filling late night slots. Their audiences were often small, as were their venues, but it was this early work that cemented the great writing and performing partnership we know today. This work wasn't as grotesque as the second or third series of *Little Britain*, but contained more of the surreal which was evident in the *Little Britain* radio show and the first series after transferring to television.

Like many performers, their comedy roots run much further back than the beginning of their partnership. In the case of Lucas we find his attraction to comedy began in a bizarre manner and at an incredibly early age. After a car accident Lucas lost his hair and although it subsequently grew back, the trouble remained and, at the age of six, after his hair had fallen out once more, Lucas was diagnosed with *alopecia totalis*. He described this as 'the only trick God played on me.'[1]

After suffering at the hands of other children at primary school, Lucas tried wearing an NHS wig, but this only fuelled the jibes in his direction. This caused two things to happen in his early teenage years while attending the secondary school Haberdashers in Hertfordshire (which was the same school that Sacha Baron-Cohen attended) which would lead to his success in later life:

The first was over-eating. By the age of thirteen his weight was becoming so out of control that his mother decided upon various courses of action at home. When these didn't work she resorted to taking her son to Weight Watchers. There he began to observe people for the first time, noting the habits and manners of the mainly middle-class and middle-aged women who attended. This people watching would continue into adult life, forming the basis for some of the less savoury characters in *Little Britain*. These are overblown caricatures and as such display the horrible humour of the extreme. They piss, puke and fill the air with profanity, all of which helps to make us wriggle on our seats in delighted disgust as we watch and laugh.

The second result of Matt Lucas's baldness and consequential bullying was that he became the class joker. He discovered that popularity could be gained by making people laugh and utilised this in his favour, thus laying the foundations for a future career in comedy.

It seems we have this sudden baldness at a very early age to thank for the laughter Lucas has brought to a nation and beyond. If he'd have retained a full head of hair it is quite probable that *Little Britain* would never have come into existence.

Lucas appeared in a number of plays while at school and

relished the chance to wear a wig or hat and temporarily forget about his baldness. In a sign of what was to come in adulthood, many of his roles were in comedies and as female characters. The use of female personas is one often seen in comedy and has been used by such greats as The Two Ronnies, Kenny Everett and Dick Emery. Comics are often cast as women in pantomimes. Of course, in *Little Britain*, with their repulsive fat suits, silly wigs and excessive make-up (not to mention the false breasts and fake eyelashes), Lucas and Walliams take this tradition to the absolute extreme, aware that today's audiences may not be so easily impressed as those of recent years.

> ### *Little Britain* Quote
> 'You is fat! Oooh man, you is fat. You one big fat thing. You fatty fatty fatty. Ooh you's a fatty fatty boom boom.' Marjorie Dawes episode which Tim Burton worked on.

Strangely enough, the young David Walliams could also be found wearing women's clothes at an early age. Born David Williams in Banstead, Surrey in 1971, with no theatrical background (his parents were a teacher and transport engineer) he nevertheless developed a fondness for dressing up when his sister used to make him wear clothes from her dressing-up box. Rather than trying to avoid such occasions, David encouraged them and soon became comfortable wearing women's clothes. This is summed up by an incident when visiting his sister at guide camp and posing for photographs in a bikini. He also owned a silk dressing gown spurring his father to call him Davina whenever he wore it.[1]

This behaviour caused his parents concern, so they decided their son needed to toughen up or would risk serious bullying at school. With this plan in mind they got the young David to sign up for the Navy Cadets, though he now admits he only agreed to this because he wanted to dress as a sailor once a week.

However, his parents' ploy didn't stop him being bullied due to his obvious campness, so he tried a ploy of his own, very similar to that which Lucas also used. David became the class fool, something which made the most of his theatrical nature and turned the bullying on its head to a degree by making him the centre of attention through choice rather than being picked on. He did this under the adopted persona of a character called 'Daphne', rather than his earlier incarnations as 'Davina', and his classmates would chant his name. The young Walliams enjoyed this strange kind of limelight.

Like Matt, David took part in school plays. He loved drama and always volunteered to be in productions in which he played female roles and always tried to look as convincing as possible.[2] Perhaps unsurprisingly, David was a big fan of Barry Humphries, who infamously dresses as a woman to become Dame Edna Everage. In the late 1980s she was hugely popular and he studied the elements of her character, language, and actions which made audiences laugh. He even went to the live London show at the age of seventeen, saying of the trip that 'it was an absolutely inspirational moment to see the show.'[3]

One of the things that has meant the most to David since the success of his and Lucas' partnership was when Barry Humphries told him *Little Britain* was pure comedy gold, though praise from other heroes, such as Ronnie Corbett (who appeared in a Bubbles DeVere sketch in the 2006 Christmas special), has also meant a great deal.

So, as with Matt Lucas's baldness, David Walliams's campness actually served to bring him into the comedy fold. They both share a background of having been bullied, struggling with their weight when young, watching a lot of TV (especially comedy shows like *Monty Python's Flying Circus*) and growing up in middle-class suburbia. They also both managed to get through their schooling by becoming child comedy acts which set the tone for the future. The fact that both of them enjoyed dressing as women also set them in good stead for their roles in *Little Britain*.

> ### *Little Britain* Quote
> 'I very much wanted to be a serious actor, but then I grew up short, fat and bald, so my fate was sealed.' Matt Lucas[4]

Lucas and Walliams first met at the National Youth Theatre in 1990[5], but didn't team up until 1995. When Lucas and Walliams first started working together they performed material which was sometimes quite anarchic by Lucas' own admission: '...we were young and fearless. We used to perform at the Edinburgh Festival at midnight and we had all sorts of hecklers, but we always took them on.'[6]

This fearlessness clearly made an impression. When Bob Mortimer spotted Lucas performing in the show *Sir Bernard Chumley and Friends*, he was impressed enough to offer him a slot as 'baby George Dawes giving the scores' on the popular comedy quiz show *Shooting Stars,* hosted by Bob and his partner Vic Reeves. Because Lucas's screen time was short he learnt how to deliver a laugh in seconds, something which greatly improved his understanding of comedy and timing. He also got to play the drums, which was something he'd enjoyed previously as a member of a band at school.[7] In the last two series of the quiz show he got to write and perform his own songs, one of which was about one of the show's team captains Ulrika Johnson.

Thanks to this friendship with Vic and Bob, Lucas went on to appear in *Catterick* (2004). This was Reeves and Mortimer's first sitcom and was about a couple of idiotic club workers.[8] Matt also appeared in Boy George's musical *Taboo*, about which he has said, 'I adored doing that.'[9] He has made numerous other appearances in films and programmes, including roles in the BBC drama *Casanova*, starring David Tennant, who plays Doctor Who in the recent series, and in the Cornish horror film *Cold and Dark* (2005). He also toured with Britpop group Blur in 1995, appearing in their video for the song 'Country House'.

In fact, the duo have clocked up a fair amount of screen appearances between them. Both were featured in *Plunkett and Macleane* (1999), starring Jonny Lee Miller and Robert Carlyle. Lucas also made a cameo as 'Cousin Tom' in Simon Pegg's smash hit zombie movie *Shaun of the Dead* (2004), which we will be discussing in Chapter Eight. Something which is not well known is that David Walliams was also in this Brit flick, well, his voice was at least. In this uncredited role he was the voice of a news reporter. However, the lack of credit when working with Simon Pegg and the crew from his TV series *Spaced* is made up for by the fact that Walliams played the extremely strange artist called 'Vulva' in an episode of that cult series (also to be discussed in Chapter Eight).

Also independently of his partner, Walliams was in the BBC drama series *Attachments* (2000), which was about the lives of a group of young professionals working for an internet company. He acted alongside Steve Coogan and Rob Brydon in the television drama *Cruise of the Gods* (2002). When commenting about *Little Britain,* Brydon said, '...there is a delicious quality to it. There's a hint of something seedy, which I quite like. What they're doing has a warmth and bizarreness.'[10]

In addition, Walliams was in the two episodes of *EastEnders* shown on Christmas Day 2003, playing a character called

Ray. He also stars alongside Hayden 'Anakin Skywalker' Christensen in the movie *Virgin Territory* (2007), which is set in Italy during the middle ages.

Their first televisual joint effort came when they created the spoof show *Rock Profile* for the satellite channel UKPlay, which aired from 1999 to 2001. Two seasons of this programme were made and they featured Jamie Theakston interviewing various pop and rock stars who were all played by Lucas and Walliams.

> ### *Little Britain* **Quote**
> 'David made me feel so unfunny because he's so bloody funny. I came back from filming Cruise of the Gods with him saying he's the funniest man in the world'
> Rob Brydon [11]

When Lucas and Walliams first started working on a new comedy show, one which would become *Little Britain*, they looked at the other comedy shows which were popular at the time. Walliams says, 'We looked at the big hits, like *Phoenix Nights* and *The Office*... We really thought, "We'll go the other way. Let's make it absurd. Let's evoke the spirit of the Two Ronnies.' Lucas agrees: 'You can't top *Phoenix Nights* or *The Office*, so why try?'[12]

So they went the way of the extreme, warping stereotypes of the stroppy teenager, the doddery old lady, and the upper-middle class snob. However, the characters still remain recognisable, something which adds to the humour.

What they finally arrived at was a radio show called *Little Britain*. This programme first aired on Radio 4 in 2001 and ran for two series, the first with five half-hour episodes and the second with four. Due to its good reception the BBC decided to commission a television version of the show which would be shown on one of the newer digital channels: BBC Three.

In relation to the transfer from radio to TV Lucas says: 'We always hoped the show would make it on to TV and it was always conceived as both a radio and TV show...'

However, some of the sketches wouldn't transfer between the two mediums because of the expense of sets, including those about the witch's house and the Britannia Cat Club, which is like a book club, only they send you a cat a month, not a novel. To make other sketches work on TV there had to be a degree of compromise and this is what eventually happened with the Kelsey Grammar sketches. They became more frequent in the television show so as to justify the cost of creating the set.[13]

The first television series of *Little Britain* consisted of eight-parts and was shown in 2003, meeting with a positive response. In fact, it would end up doing so well that it is credited with having saved the then struggling BBC Three. Two further series followed, both consisting of six episodes.

The second series of *Little Britain* was shown in 2004. It was so popular with the viewing public that scheduled repeats were shown on BBC One, something which followed in the footsteps of the first series, which had found itself repeated on BBC Two thanks to its popularity.

The third series arrived on our screens in 2005 and from the start it was aired in a prime time slot on BBC One. Though this type of elevation was rare for a comedy programme, it had been seen before. Following the success of Series One of *The Blackadder* (starring Rowan Atkinson) for example, the programme was swiftly transferred to BBC One, where larger audiences were guaranteed.

In the third series of *Little Britain* it appeared that some of the characters were 'wound up,' given endings from which it would be hard to return. This seemed to put pay to any chance of a fourth series. However, when quizzed about this

Lucas and Walliams respond that they only killed off certain characters to allow new ones to be brought in[15] and a fourth season was announced at the British Comedy Awards in 2006.

Little Britain Quote

'I look thinner on radio, but it's nice to take the show on to TV simply because it means we reach more people' Matt Lucas[14]

The comedy duo created a special, one-off show for Comic Relief in 2005 and called it '*Little, Little Britain*'. It featured the likes of Elton John, George Michael and Robbie Williams, the participation of such huge stars being a sign of just how established the show had become. The following year they also performed a live show for Comic Relief at the Hammersmith Apollo and it was also in 2006 that Dawn French appeared in a two-part Christmas special as barmaid 'Myfanwy' in the fictional pub of Llandewi Breffi, Daffyd Thomas' home village. Also appearing was the popular comedian Peter Kay, who played the brother of Dudley Punt, the man with the Thai bride (for more on Peter Kay see Chapter Six). There was another outing for a live *Little Britain* in 'Comic Relief 2007: The Big One', with Walliams also raising money for Sport Relief in 2006 by swimming the English Channel.

Lucas and Walliams decided to take the live stage version of *Little Britain* on tour around the UK in 2005-6. This was so popular that new dates were added and what had been an eighteen date tour became a ninety date extravaganza that lasted six months, a tour for which the tickets were virtually sold out within a week. *The Sun*'s review of the opening night was one of many positive ones: 'there wasn't a dry seat in the house – fans were wetting themselves with laughter.'[16]

This was followed by a tour of Australia in 2007, which

proved to be a huge success, no doubt partly due to the fact that Lucas and Walliams like to be 'quite naughty and spontaneous, getting the audience involved'.[17] It was while touring in Australia that they made a surprise appearance as Andy and Lou in the Ramsey Street soap opera *Neighbours,* the episode was aired in the UK in September 2007.

The pair got to meet Dame Edna for the first time while touring Australia and this meeting was shown in a BBC programme about the tour called '*Little Britain* Down Under,' which was narrated by Rob Brydon. Tony Head managed to join them for some of the tour, much to the delight of audiences. Nearly one million people turned out to see them, showing what a large following they have in other parts of the world.

It was during this tour documentary that David Walliams talked about his style of humour, saying that he likes to use it to shock. He cites Monty Python's vomit king, Mr Creosote, as a memorable influence from his youth, this character having appeared towards the end of the movie *Monty Python's The Meaning of Life* (1983). In the relevant scene the bloated Mr Creosote is nearly constantly vomiting into a bucket, onto the floor and onto the head of the poor soul who's trying to clean up the mess. He then explodes after eating a wafer thin mint and the other diners all begin to vomit, a clear precursor to the *Little Britain* style.

Another influence Walliams mentions is the brash 80s sitcom *The Young Ones.* He recalls a particular storyline when Vyvyan (Adrian Edmondson) thinks he may be pregnant because his stomach is enlarging, though it turns out he's just brewing a very large fart. For David, nothing is off limits, 'There is no subject you can't make a joke of.'

As well as the comedy connections created through other

celebrities appearing in *Little Britain*, such as the aforementioned Dawn French and cameos from people like David Baddiel, Rob Brydon and Ewan MacIntosh (who played Keith in *The Office*) there are also other notable connections within the contemporary comedy scene. One of the members of the team which helped to bring *Little Britain* to our screens was Mark Gatiss from the series *The League of Gentlemen*. He was *Little Britain*'s script editor and Walliams says, 'it felt natural to get someone we were friendly with and who'd done a superb show,' which alludes to the fact that Lucas and Walliams had befriended the team behind *The League of Gentlemen* while performing in Edinburgh years before.[18]

The director of the *Little Britain* television show was Steve Bendelach, who had also worked on *The League of Gentlemen*, as well as *The Royle Family*. A further link with other comedy shows arises due to Lucas and Walliams naming council estates that feature in the sketches after people who have appeared on *Whose Line is it Anyway?*, such as Richard Vranch and Sandy Toksvig.

Like *Whose Line is it Anyway?*, *Little Britain* was usually filmed in front of an audience. This means the laughter isn't dubbed, even on location work, which was shown to an audience at a later date. Lucas says, 'sometimes we have to turn the laughter down or it gets a bit intrusive.'[19]

This highlights just how funny the show is – audiences are heard to be literally cracking-up in the background – and this ability of Lucas and Walliams to tap into our personal sources of amusement is the key to its great success. The third season of *Little Britain* clocked up an astonishing 9.5 million viewers when it was first shown on BBC One.

Little Britain is a character-based sketch show which follows in the footsteps of others like *Harry Enfield & Chums* and *The*

Fast Show. As with both of those programmes, catchphrases, are employed to allow the audience to be in on the joke in a very different way to the work of Sacha Baron-Cohen. With Baron-Cohen's comedy we are complicit in understanding that his characters aren't real people, but also know that interviewees believe they are real. With *Little Britain* we are

involved in the joke because we know the catchphrase or action which is going to come when a particular character appears on screen. For example, when a Vicky Pollard sketch is shown we know she'll say, 'Yeah but no but yeah but...', and when Maggie Blackamoor comes on we know she'll vomit when her sensibilities are offended.

> ### *Little Britain* Quote
> 'Last week we had a man in Barbados who lost a flip-flop. We were able to send a replacement flip-flop out to him first class. All he had to do was cover the cost of the flight...and the flip-flop'. Carol Beers

This simple understanding allows us to be part of the humour and to enjoy the expectation of what is to come. The fact that there is little element of surprise is not important here.

These catchphrases have permeated British society as so many have done before. We all know Larry Grayson's 'shut that door', Kenny Everett's 'in the best possible taste' and Del Boy's 'lovely jubbly'. These and many more besides have become widespread in everyday speech and now we find the same to be true of *Little Britain* catchphrases, a clear mark of the show's popularity. Some of these catchphrases have even started to be used abroad, the use of Carol Beer's phrase 'computer says no' in the Australian soap *Neighbours* being a prime example.

However, catchphrases are not enough to make a show popular. There needs to be additional depth to the comedy and in *Little Britain* this is provided by a satirical look at British people and the larger-than-life characters who have been created by Lucas and Walliams. There is also a further element which singles this show out from other sketch shows: the use of a narrator. This is a highly original and quite peculiar touch, and the bizarre content of this commentary adds much to the overall humour and tone.

This may be an unusual comparison to draw, but the narration in *Little Britain* is in many ways reminiscent of Stanley Kubrick's classic film *A Clockwork Orange* (1971). In this film, the lead character's narration was made all the more bizarre thanks to the use of a made-up language (created by the author Anthony Burgess). The way in which the film aimed to assess British society and its values of the time, is something also reflected in *Little Britain*. Moreover, the content of *A Clockwork Orange* was greatly exaggerated – not only in terms of characters and plot but also the way in which it is depicted – as is the content in Lucas and Walliams show, which is similar in its boldly controversial material.

The narrator of *Little Britain* is Tom Baker, who played the fourth Doctor in the extremely popular BBC science fiction series *Doctor Who*. With his characteristic unrestrained enthusiasm Walliams describes Baker as 'a god to me.' He has an instantly recognisable voice that adds a distinct, surreal touch to the show.

Baker had appeared with *Shooting Stars'* hosts Vic Reeves and Bob Mortimer in Charlie Higson's remake of *Randall and Hopkirk Deceased* (Charlie Higson having been a member of *The Fast Show* team). In that remake Baker played a rather quirky spirit guide called Wyvern. Incidentally, both Lucas and Walliams appeared in different episodes of *Randall and Hopkirk Deceased* in 2001 entitled 'Revenge of the Bog People' and 'Whatever Possessed You?' respectively.

There are quite a number of *Doctor Who* references in *Little Britain*, for instance: in the pilot episode there was a picture of Tom Baker as the Doctor hanging in Jeremy Rent's office. There have been at least three characters named after actors who have played *Doctor Who* 'companions', these being Matthew Waterhouse, who played Adric with the fourth and fifth Doctors, Michael Craze, who was the second Doctor's companion, and Mark Strickson, who was with the fifth Doctor. In Series One, Tom Baker's narrations directly reference *Doctor Who*, as well as *Blackadder*, in which he also appeared. The Tardis can be seen in *Little Britain Live* and yobs shout 'Oi, Davros!' at Andy in Series Two – Davros being the wheelchair-bound creator of the Daleks.

The effect of the narration at the start of *Little Britain* and between the sketches is to unify the show. This unity is created when the programme moves from one sketch to another and Baker says: 'Business is brisk at this fancy dress shop. Fancy dress parties were invented in 1971 by Professor Ian Fancy-Dress-Party,' and 'Rugby is very popular in Britain as it allows men to act out sadomasochistic, homoerotic fantasies in the safety of a sporting contest.'

Tom Baker narrates in the same way as many presenters of TV documentaries and this factor, when added to the fact that the sketches are like a study of different people of the British Isles, creates the impression of a satirical mockumentary.

Lucas and Walliams have drawn on the characteristics of people who actually exist to create the many personalities that populate *Little Britain*. They are therefore satirising people. Because the narration strengthens the idea that we are looking at a skewed version of British society the documentary feel is further solidified.

The Lucas/Walliams view of the British isn't limited by class or gender. Nothing can stop them donning female fat suits, women's clothes, chav voices or 'posh' attitudes in order to bring their blend of humour and observational satire to our screens. In fact, their appearance itself is often part of the comedy, not least in relation to Vicky Pollard's pink shell suit, Daffyd's incredibly camp costumes and Bubbles DeVere's overweight nakedness, saggy boobs and all. You can hear the audience moan with disgust as Bubbles flings open her clothes to reveal the extremely wide curves of her ample body and laugh at the outrageous skin-tight clothes sported by the ever flamboyant Daffyd proving that the appearances – however revolting - of both characters add a great deal to the horrible humour.

> **_Little Britain_ Quote**
> 'Britain... We've had running water for over ten years, an underground tunnel linking us to Peru, and we invented the cat' _Little Britain_ narrator, Tom Baker

This visual element was, of course, missing from the original radio show but has added a great deal of humour to the TV version. Not only are some of the characters' looks funny in themselves, but specific visual gags are also employed, some with the regularity of catchphrases so they become 'catch-activities'. Maggie's vomiting is a case in point as she brings up her lunch in every sketch she appears in, the audience wrinkling their noses at the repulsive sight, but also forced into laughter by the ridiculousness of her middle class sensitivities. Another regular visual gag, and one of the audience's favourites if a vote for the best comedy sketches of all time is anything to go by, is contained in the pieces featuring Andy Pipkin and his carer Lou Todd. The recurring visual joke is Andy getting out of his wheelchair when his carer, Lou, isn't watching. He can be seen climbing trees, running around, throwing himself on the floor, any number of physical activities. But it is the swimming pool scene involving the two characters which was voted the best sketch ever in a poll by Channel 4 with an astounding thirty-two thousand viewers voting for this clip.[20]

The only danger with using regular visual gags and catchphrases is that they can become overly repetitive and lose their impact. Essentially every sketch involving Lou and Andy is designed so that the latter can get out of his chair without the former realising. Though this allows the audience to be in on the joke through understanding the characters' relationship with each other, it could also have the effect of boring audiences if overdone. However, to date this has not happened and audiences are just as amused by the antics of such characters as when they first appeared on our screens.

One thing which has certainly helped to allay any chance of audience boredom has been the introduction of new characters and even the re-introduction of old ones. The 2005-6 live stage show was a prime example of this. Kenny Craig, the hypnotist from Series One, was reintroduced to packed theatres across the UK, as was ex-children's TV star Des Kaye, both of whom were greeted with enthusiasm. Also included, partly to test audience responses, were new characters such as Dudley Punt and Ting Tong Macadangdang, his Thai internet-order bride. They then went on to appear in the third TV series of *Little Britain* after they were well received during the stage show.

This continual changing of characters means the show remains fresh. Audience interest has also been kept strong through changes in the humour itself. This development can be quite easily identified in the transition between radio and television due to the inclusion of visual humour. The change between the first TV series and the second was more subtle.

Series One contained humour of a more generally surreal nature and this was partly because much of it was developed from the radio show, which tended to consist of surreal concepts taken to their logical conclusion, such as a witch having to employ contractors to construct her gingerbread house. The second and third series progressively moved away from this radio show heritage, becoming more visual and more gross. This increased vulgarity includes the aforementioned vomiting of Maggie and the waterfall peeing of Mrs Emery.

> **_Little Britain_ Quote**
>
> 'Look into my eyes. Look into my eyes. The eyes, the eyes. Not around the eyes. Don't look around the eyes. Look into my eyes... You're under!.' Kenny Craig

It is this vulgar and crude element and its noticeable increase which has attracted increasing criticism. This has come from a number of different organisations and people, including The Royal College of Physicians, Age Concern, Fergus Sheppard, a reporter for *The Scotsman*, and Rupert Smith, the television writer for the *Guardian*.[21] Some of this criticism is due to the fact that despite *Little Britain* being aired after the watershed, many children watch the show, *Radio Times* research finding that children as young as four were watching the third series.[22] It has also been claimed by people like Johann Hari, an award winning journalist for the *Independent*, that seeing minorities and disadvantaged social groups being made fun of isn't actually funny. In fact, Hari takes offence at such humour, saying that the people picked on by Walliams and Lucas are simply easy targets for ridicule.

It could be argued that by highlighting these people in such an overblown and ridiculous manner Walliams and Lucas successfully distance the characters from reality. However, this does not seem to be the case. Matt Lucas says: 'You don't need a spin-off show for Vicky Pollard – just step out of your house – she's everywhere!'[23]

So it would seem that, at least in the case of some characters from the show, Walliams and Lucas believe they reflect real people. Maybe we are not laughing at the bizarre and the extreme in this case – maybe these unappealing characters really are the norm. In this light *Little Britain* could be viewed as a kind of critique of contemporary British society. They are pointing at the troublesome, the ignorant, and the ridiculous within our society (though this isn't the case with all of the characters, as can be seen with the Scottish hotelier Ray McCooney, who is simply a strange individual who talks in riddles).

This critique does apply to Vicky Pollard, Carol Beer the bank assistant and travel agent, Maggie the puking Women's Institute member, Lou and Andy, Daffyd, Edward 'Emily' Howard the 'rubbish transvestite', Sid Pegg the Neighbourhood Watch leader, Marjorie Dawes of Fat Fighters, and even Bubbles, who represents a kind of liberated, but sexually predatory woman. The portrayal of such characters could be seen as comic finger-pointing on the part of their creators. In the third series in particular, Lucas and Walliams may be considered to be pointing fingers at these kinds of people, making fun of them.

The most prominent of these characters is Daffyd, 'the only gay in the village'. Three points can be taken from his characterisation and the sketches in which he is central. The first is that homosexuality is now accepted without prejudice. The second springs from the first and relates to the minority character assuming that others are prejudiced towards them. The final point is that there is no need to look or act differently from other people purely because of your sexual orientation.

The first point is made by the way that everyone in Daffyd's village accepts him and his sexuality. In fact, many other villagers are also gay and aren't hard-pushed when it comes to having had more gay experiences than Daffyd, who has actually had none. His constant feeling of being singled out as different is therefore ridiculous.

> **Little Britain Quote**
> 'You're probably not gay at all, you're probably just a little bit poofy.' Daffyd Thomas

This, however, does not reflect British society, especially in rural areas. Homophobia *is* still present in Britain in many areas, and in such a village it is unlikely that an outspoken, flamboyantly dressed and extremely camp gay would be generally accepted. Maybe this is Lucas and Walliams' intent; to highlight just how much prejudice still remains by showing a humorous version of how things would be if it were no longer present.

This leads on to the second element. Daffyd expects to be singled out by the other villagers. He perceives himself as different and this creates his own prejudice against those around him, one which causes him to insist he is the only gay in the village despite the fact that he isn't.

The final point is made very clear: there isn't any reason for homosexuals to act or dress differently purely because of sexual orientation. This is underlined by the other villagers who are gay dressing considerably more conservatively. This also has the effect of implying that there are many gay people leading 'normal' lives and that the British shouldn't think all gays are stereotypically camp, standing out from the rest of society. It is this 'standing out' that helps to make Daffyd so humorous, along with his often bright and skin-tight clothes, and his attitudes towards the other villagers who he assumes will be prejudiced towards him.

Ultimately Lucas and Walliams' show simply makes points about certain kinds of people within our society. In this sense it operates much like Sacha Baron-Cohen's film *Borat,* which was a comedic critique of US society.

Supporters of the show also point out that Lucas and Walliams are simply following a fine British tradition, and this is comedy which breaks the boundaries of political correctness. Previous examples include *Monty Python, Benny Hill* and *Kenny Everett.* This element in itself creates viewer enjoyment because of its risqué nature and challenge of the status-quo. We like to see the upper-middle classes exaggerated. We revel in these views of society and enjoy seeing the twisted representations created by Lucas and Walliams in their horrible spotlights. In a sense, by breaking the boundaries of normal society Lucas and Walliams are forcing us to discuss the issues raised rather than letting society ignore them behind the politically correct veil.

Johann Hari also attacks the show in another way, stating, 'It's hard to escape the conclusion this is a gay man's woman-hatred with a laugh track, a sketch-long recoil from breasts and vaginas.'[24]

In response it should be pointed out that there is only one gay man in the Lucas-Walliams comedy partnership and the idea that *Little Britain* contains any 'woman-hatred' on the part of Lucas is a rather extreme accusation. There are plenty of male characters who are not shown in a good light, such as Edward 'Emily' Howard and Sebastian Love. In fact, both Sebastian

Love and Daffyd Thomas are rather negative portrayals of gay men, disproving Hari's point. Further undermining it is the fact that many of the characters are effectively critiques of different people presented in an overblown and exaggerated way, whether they be male or female.

Despite attacks on the show, especially the more vulgar and crude third series, it has won a number of prestigious awards. These include a Sony Radio Academy Award in 2003, the same year in which David Walliams won the 'Best Newcomer' award at the British Comedy Awards. Also in 2003 came the first of three BAFTAs. This was for 'Best Comedy Programme or Series', and they won the same award in 2005, also receiving 'Best Comedy Performance'. In both 2004 and 2005 they won Best TV Comedy award at the British Comedy Awards, beating Ricky Gervais' *Extras* for the latter honour. In light of these accolades it's clear that Lucas and Walliams were obviously hitting people's funny bones, with a sledgehammer. This success was down to their talent at writing and performing memorable characters.

When creating the characters there is a specific process that Lucas and Walliams go through. They often arrive at ideas independently and then work on them together. As Walliams states, 'We sit in a room for months trying to think of funny things. We write everything together though one of us will normally have provided the germ of the idea.'[25]

Some of the ideas for characters have a genesis far removed from the way they finally arrive on our screens. For example, the idea behind Lou and Andy was actually based on the partnership of musician Lou Reed with artist Andy Warhol, but they developed into the wonderful pairing we have come to enjoy.[26]

An extensive background is written for each of the

characters which includes details like their parentage and siblings. Though much of this material may not be used in the show, it creates a greater sense of reality and makes the characters more than mere vehicles for gags.

Lucas and Walliams have different favourites amongst the numerous characters from the show. Lucas enjoys being Andy because Walliams has to push him around in the wheelchair and he also likes Bernard Chumley due to the fact that this was the first character he ever played. Walliams says: '...for me (it's) Sebastian. It's so much fun working with Tony Head (who plays the Prime Minister).'[27]

Lucas and Walliams have become as popular out of character as they are in character thanks to various chat show appearances. One of the most memorable of these was their inclusion as guests on *The Dame Edna Treatment.* Barry Humphries' creation returned to our screens in 2007 and you could see the comedy duo loved every minute of their time on the show. This was especially true of Walliams, who just couldn't stop smiling and laughing as he shared the stage with one of his biggest heroes. There was even narration from Tom Baker following each ad break. After Baker's introductions Lucas announced, 'Ladies and gentlemen, please welcome our idol...' and Walliams continued, '...Dame Edna Everage!' With this public declaration they cemented our recognition of how much they admire Barry Humphries and his alternative incarnation.

The popularity of Lucas, Walliams and *Little Britain* has led to a great deal of merchandising, even to the extent that fans can buy plush talking dolls of Daffyd and Vicky and a computer game. The popularity has become so widespread that HBO, the same company that created an American Ali G show, is now also looking to create a US version of *Little*

Britain (there's already an Israeli version called *The Israelis* which began in 2007). Though American writers have been drafted in to help, this new show will still remain true to the character-based sketch format seen in the UK. And whilst on the subject of writing and Ali G, it is interesting to note that Lucas did some writing on *Da Ali G Show* (2000).

> ### *Little Britain* Quote
> 'If you have been affected by any of the issues in this programme you may like to know that a special helpline has been set up. I think it's O something and then some other numbers. There may be a 7 in there somewhere, if that's any help' *Little Britain* narrator, Tom Baker

Another way in which this pair of comedy heroes is following in the footsteps of Sacha Baron-Cohen is through the creation of a film version of the series. Possible avenues for this movie include American citizens meeting characters from *Little Britain* (much in the same way as they met Borat) or a film about Vicky Pollard or Lou and Andy.

One further medium in which we are going to see Lucas and Walliams is that of cartoon animation. This is because *The Simpsons'* creator, Matt Groening wants them to appear in an episode of the show, something which Ricky Gervais has already done, as we shall see in the following chapter. In relation to this appearance Groening has said, 'Matt Lucas and David Walliams are like living cartoons anyway.'[28] Since their success it is clear that Lucas and Walliams have been very busy. They've made appearances in numerous films, comedies and dramas while also being in demand for chat shows. Their popularity hasn't waned even though the last series of *Little Britain* was made in 2005. If anything they have become even better known thanks to their additional television work, not least their Comic Relief versions of the show that brought them fame and fortune.

Because of this we can count on them producing more work in the years to come. It is certain that Lucas and Walliams will continue to entertain us, whether they're dressing in women's clothes, vomiting on the floor or simply being themselves, with smiles on their faces as they bring smiles to ours. So, if you're wondering whether we'll see more of this great comedy pairing I have to say, 'Computer says yes!'

Ten Questions & Answers with Matt Lucas

Question 1: Which other comedians have you most enjoyed working with?
Matt Lucas: Vic and Bob. Barry Humphries.

Question 2: If you could meet any comedian alive or dead who would it be and why?
Matt Lucas: Andy Kaufman. A true genius. And Laurel and Hardy because they make me laugh my head off.

Question 3: Would you ever consider playing a non-human character?
Matt Lucas: I was recently a toad.

Question 4: What's David's worst habit?
Matt Lucas: He's very punctual, which shows up my persistent lateness.

Question 5: If you hadn't pursued comedy as a career what do you think you might have done?

Matt Lucas: Any job that involved working inside a giant cake.

Question 6: Who's your favourite comic character of all time, excluding those you and David have created?

Matt Lucas: Gerard Hoffnung.

Question 7: Have you and David ever considered making a sitcom together?

Matt Lucas: We did a pilot for a sitcom years ago called 'Crazy Jonathans' but it failed miserably. Maybe one day we'll try again. I could see a Lou and Andy sitcom.

Question 8: Would you consider creating another comedy for radio?

Matt Lucas: Definitely. It's cheaper to make, quicker, easier to edit and the imagination has no budget constraints.

Question 9: Who are your heroes, comic or otherwise?

Matt Lucas: Charlie Chaplin, Freddie Mercury, David Rocastle.

Question 10: What's the most important advice you could give anyone wishing to pursue a career in comedy?

Matt Lucas: Every joke is a gamble. Failure is an inevitable part of success.

ENDNOTES

1. Viner, Brian, 'Matt Lucas: Pride and Prejudice' (*The Independent* 16th December 2006).

2. Simpson, N, *Kings of Comedy,* p. 29 (2007, John Blake Publishing Ltd., UK)

3. Simpson, N, *Kings of Comedy,* p. 29 (2007, John Blake Publishing Ltd., UK)

4. Simpson, N, *Kings of Comedy*, p. 31 (2007, John Blake Publishing Ltd., UK)

5. Simpson, N, *Kings of Comedy,* p. 33 (2007, John Blake Publishing Ltd., UK)

6. Gage, S, 'How We Met: David Walliams & Matt Lucas,' (The *Independent on Sunday*, August 3rd 2003)

7. Crook, J. '*Little Britain* Re-Crosses the Pond,' p.2 (tv.zap2it.com/tveditorial/tve_main/1,1002,271%7C96853%7C1%7C,00.html)

8. 'Matt Lucas and David Walliams Discuss...' p.5 (www.bbc.co.uk/comedy/littlebritain/interviews/interview1.shtml)

9. Simpson, N, *Kings of Comedy*, p. 23 (2007, John Blake Publishing Ltd., UK)

10. Raphael, A, 'So it's hello from him – and hello from me,' (*The Observer*, 31st August 2003)

11. 'Matt Lucas and David Walliams Discuss..,' p.5 (www.bbc.co.uk/comedy/littlebritain/interviews/interview1.shtml)

12. Raphael, A, 'So it's hello from him – and hello from me,' (*The Observer*, 31st August 2003)

13. Raphael, A, 'So it's hello from him – and hello from me,' (*The Observer*, 31st August 2003)

14. 'Matt Lucas and David Walliams Discuss...' p.2 (www.bbc.co.uk/comedy/littlebritain/interviews/interview1.shtml))

15. Simpson, N, *Kings of Comedy*, p. 6 (2007, John Blake Publishing Ltd., UK)

16. Taylor, C, '*Little Britain* Stars Make Surprise Appearance on *Neighbours*,' p.2 (www.entertainmentwise.com/news?id=28751)

17. Simpson, N, *Kings of Comedy*, p. 6 (2007, John Blake Publishing Ltd., UK)

18. Taylor, C, '*Little Britain* Stars Make Surprise Appearance on *Neighbours*,' p.1 (www.entertainmentwise.com/news?id=28751)

19. Bowman, A, '*Little Britain* Has Spoken' (www.davidwalliams.com/Interview19)

20. Matt Lucas and David Walliams Discuss... p.1 (www.bbc.co.uk/comedy/littlebritain/interviews/interview1.shtml)

21. A good face for radio (www.davidwalliams.com)

22. '*Little Britain* tops sketch poll' (http://news.bbc.co.uk/1/hi/entertainment/tv_and_radio/4406377.stm)

23. Sheppard, F, '*Little Britain*'s in trouble...no buts about it,' p.2 (*The Scotsman*, December 1st 2005)

24. 'Matt Lucas and David Walliams Discuss...,' p.3 (www.bbc.co.uk/comedy/littlebritain/interviews/interview1.shtml)

25. Hari, J, 'Why I hate *Little Britain*,' p.2 (www.johannhari.com/archive/article.

php?id=729)

26. 'Matt Lucas and David Walliams Discuss..,' p.1 (www.bbc.co.uk/comedy/littlebritain/interviews/interview1.shtml)

27. Hoggart, P, 'Mad dogs and Englishmen' (*The Times*, 29th November 2003)

28. 'Matt Lucas and David Walliams Discuss..,' p.3 (www.bbc.co.uk/comedy/littlebritain/interviews/interview1.shtml)

29. '*Little Britain* in *The Simpsons*' (www.davidwalliams.com/LittleBritainSimpsons)

3. RICKY GERVAIS:
The Office &
Lots of *Extras*

When Ricky Gervais walks onto the stage at the start of his live show called '*Fame*' he is wearing a plastic crown and a regal robe. The man some have dubbed the British king of comedy never misses a chance to employ his idiosyncratic brand of irony, a trait which has proved invaluable in creating the hit sitcoms *The Office* and *Extras* along with Stephen Merchant. The title of his live show refers to all that has happened to him in the years since the first series of *The Office* aired on the BBC back in 2001.

Like Sacha Baron-Cohen, Ricky Gervais has become a household name, not just in the UK, but also across the Atlantic. *The Office* has garnered countless awards both sides of the pond, including six BAFTA's and two Golden Globes. In fact, the sitcom was the first British show to have been nominated and won the latter awards beating such shows as *Sex in the City*. *The Office* is also a record-breaking DVD, having outsold all other TV DVDs, it has now sold millions of copies in the UK and has been translated into eighty different languages. Quite an incredible feat considering the very ordinary subject matter.

The format for the show was heavily influenced by the 1984 Rob Reiner film, *This is Spinal Tap* as well the nineties American sitcom, *The Larry Sanders Show* starring Garry Shandling. Like both these comedies, the humour in *The Office* is created through a number of devices, especially the fly-on-the-wall documentary style. This is intended to create a kind of realism, as if we're watching activities within a real office environment — in fact many viewers thought the environment and characters were for real during much of the first broadcast, something which was helped by the regular scenes of people simply working or of the copier running, both tropes adding to the realism of the show. This sense of realism is further reinforced by the short interviews in which the members of staff take part during each episode. We also see staff members giving looks directly to the camera, especially memorable among these are the looks which one of the main characters, Tim, gives us, the audience, when David Brent is attempting to entertain or be humorous. As well as being a fairly unique feature, this is key, as much of the communication in the programme is non-verbal. Through posture, expression, and looks both to the camera and within *The Office* environment we are able to read depth into the characters and their interactions.

The character of David Brent is the lynch pin of the show. He views himself as 'a chilled-out entertainer' and his clumsy and often ridiculous attempts to befriend and entertain his employees create the central comedy. His style of humour is offensive to most of his employees and his attempts to ingratiate himself with colleagues are so embarrassing it is excruciating to watch. Most of the staff are not entertained and do not regard themselves as Brent's friends. This makes him rather a tragic figure, as his approach towards forming friendships is largely ineffectual. However, Brent's absolute failure to appreciate his colleagues distaste for his work ethos, his jokes, his treatment of staff and his general approach to life combine to create an atmosphere of pure tension in places. It is painful to witness, but this is the very source of the humour. His outrageous unpleasantness is what makes him so compelling, and so very funny.

This humour is added to by the fact Brent is clearly putting on a front, trying to pretend he has no ego and is of an equal standing to his employees. Both of these elements are blatantly not the case, as can be seen when he desperately takes centre stage with his guitar on training day and when he completely disregards his staff when accepting promotion in the final episode of Series One.

His attempts to put on a front are primarily due to the presence of cameras in *The Office*. He is always acting up to them, putting on a deliberate show of humour and friendliness. He also wants to appear even-handed, politically correct and clever, though his words and actions undermine this falsehood. Despite claiming that he thinks pornography degrades women it is clearly implied that he has been using the computer in his office to look at internet porn sites in Series One. We also see him saying he wouldn't stoop so low as to make fun of a Wernham Hogg employee's claw hand in the first episode of Series Two, only to find this is exactly what he has been doing when the cameras are not on him. His front is also underlined by the fact he tries to pass off quotes from great thinkers as his own during his staff appraisals in Series Two.

The Christmas Specials see Brent attempting to defend himself, claiming that the BBC documentary makers deliberately showed material which would make him appear a fool. These two programmes take on a slightly different format from the two series, one which both continues the sense of realism and reinforces it, giving it additional depth. In them we find the documentary makers returning to paper merchants Wernham Hogg in order to catch up with the people featured in the original documentary series. We hear them asking the characters a variety of questions, which is an element that was not present in the series. We in turn see the characters responding to things that happened in the two series of the show, such as Brent talking about head-butting one of the candidates for the position of PA.

In *The Office*, the realism of the documentary style is added to by the fact that the sitcom was filmed in an admin block next to the television studios at Teddington, so the workplace that features in the programme was not merely a set.[1] As Gervais wanted viewers to enjoy the deliberate illusion that David Brent and his colleagues were real people, unknown actors were cast, though many have now become instantly recognisable due to the success of *The Office* and roles they have since taken – Mackenzie Crook and Martin Freeman being prime examples. The former, who played Gareth Keenan, has gone on to appear in *The Pirates of the Caribbean* films and also enjoyed success on the stand-up circuit as school teacher Mr Bagshaw. The latter, who played Tim Canterbury, appeared in the movie *Love Actually* (2003), played Arthur Dent in the film version of *The Hitchhiker's Guide to the Galaxy* (2005), and was one of Ali G's crew in the 'Staines Massif'.

Also adding to the realism of *The Office* is the lack of a laughter track, something which helps to distance it (and *Extras*) from many of the other comedy shows appearing at the time. If the awkward silences that follow Brent's hideous slip-ups in the workplace were replaced by roars of 'audience' laughter the impact of the humour would be far less extreme. Nobody would be laughing whilst their boss belittled his overweight employees in a real situation. Whilst staff squirm silently in their seats in *The Office*, the lack of laughter helps us believe in the authenticity of the situation. In fact, by encouraging recognition of certain situations and characters which not only arise within office environments, but also in most workplaces, Gervais broadens the possibility of audience empathy. Most people can find something in

> **The Office Quote**
>
> 'Now guys, we're about to enter a warehouse environment, now I must warn you that some of the people in here will be working class, so there may be ass cleavage. So just find a partner, hold hands.' Tim

The Office that they are able to identify with – and in many cases dislike. Easy viewing is not the intention here.

The frequent use of silences in the programme is a vital part of its cringe-worthy nature. When Brent takes some of his staff for a lunchtime drink in Series Two, in order to prove to those who have transferred from the Swindon branch that he is a great laugh, it is the awkward silence which makes the situation almost unbearable. The silence which greets his supposed motivational speech in the same series is also horribly awkward, along with the dumbfounded silence which occurs when this terrible exhibition of ineptitude comes to an end with the irony of Tina Turner singing 'Simply the Best.'

There have been rumours that *The Office* was based on a documentary about a company in Chessington called 'Northamber'. However, Gervais and Merchant denied this and said that the series was based on their own experience of working in offices.[2] They have also said that the fact it was based in a paper merchants in Slough is essentially coincidental, as life in *The Office* was far more important than the business with which it happened to be associated. Therefore we hear and learn very little about the workings of such a company. ·

To all intents and purposes Gervais and Merchant, who briefly appears as the 'Oggmonster' in Series Two, have cleverly removed *The Office* from any particular business background, so that it becomes a generic office environment. Even people who don't work in offices can identify with character types like the 'I'm-your-friend' type of boss, the ridiculous jobsworth like Gareth, and the practical joking, generally good-natured but 'going nowhere fast' Tim. These kinds of people are found in most workplaces and this means the humour of *The Office* is by no means reliant on having worked in such an environment.

There have been numerous other workplace based sitcoms. However, none have adopted the same fly-on-the-wall approach or worked predominantly with the humour of awkwardness and embarrassment in the way that *The Office* has.

Unlike most sitcoms, a scene in *The Office* does not have to end with a joke. This is due to the documentary feel, which allows a scene to end simply by petering out or with a look to the camera which communicates to the audience in a different way to verbal humour. It allows us to discover the characters for ourselves, to understand how they feel and perceive this without them telling us directly. The fact that they look at us to communicate things like, 'Oh god, he's trying to be funny again,' or 'Get me out of here…' means we become much more involved with the action, and the often difficult situations, than we might otherwise. Such thoughts are conveyed to us by a look from the actor in question, and we provide the wording, we share the emotion, the feeling, the joke, creating a greater bond with the characters. In fact, it is almost like a kind of telepathy, in which we engage subconsciously with the show and real life.

The popularity arising from the identification with the characters and environment, along with the comedy created by both of these elements, has meant that *The Office* has been remade in a number of other countries, such as France, Germany, and, most prominently, the US. When it was first revealed that NBC was planning to create an American version there were fears it would be a poor copy, and to begin with this is just what it was.

> **The Office Quote**
>
> 'The Office is just the greatest programme I have ever seen,' Richard Curtis (Blackadder, The Vicar of Dibley, Four Weddings and a Funeral, Notting Hill)[3]

The writers of *The Office: An American Workplace* paid too much deference to the original, copying it almost exactly. Then, with the final episode of the first season they gave themselves more freedom to bring in their own touches to the narrative and characters.

This proved to be much more popular with American viewers and critics and the show then continued in the same vein in later seasons. In fact, the US version has run for over forty episodes and Steve Carell, the actor who plays the American equivalent of Brent – Michael Scott – won a Golden Globe for 'Best TV actor in a Comedy Series'.

The name of the paper merchants in the US version was Dunder Mifflin, and it is based in Scranton, Pennsylvania. Greg Daniels was the man responsible for the show's adaptation from Gervais and Merchant's BBC original and had been a writer for *Saturday Night Live*, *King of the Hill* and *The Simpsons* (to be discussed in Chapter Ten). Gervais and Merchant had their names listed on the production credits and even wrote an episode for the third season of the show.

It is also of note that Gervais earned far more simply being the producer of the US show than he did co-writing, co-directing and acting in the original, UK show.[4]

The first season, like both UK seasons, consisted of six episodes. This changed considerably with following seasons, the second having twenty-two episodes, the third twenty-three, and the fourth twenty-five. It is in the much longer seasons, and partially due to the fact that material from the BBC original was limited, that the US version of *The Office* took on a life of its own and broke away from its British heritage. It was this breakaway that allowed the writers and producers more narrative freedom, as well as a greater scope for characterisation, especially in regards to those characters who had previously been bit-part players in the office environment.

The viewing figures of this show have consistently risen with each series. The first saw an average of 5.4 million viewers, with the second averaging 8 million, the third 8.3 million and the fourth netting an impressive 9 million and more. Due to the ever increasing popularity of the show, which is now being shown in a number of countries, there has even been an *'Office'* convention held in 2007. This took place in Scranton and included cast and crew appearances, Greg Daniels being one of the special guests who appeared.

One of the big differences between UK and US comedy is concerned with the amount of writers working on the shows. In Britain there are usually one or two writers involved, but in the States there are usually far more working on a project. The US version of *The Office* was no exception and three of the show's writers were also cast as regular characters in the programme. There were also cameo appearances made by other members of the production staff, including Greg Daniels himself.

Echoing Gervais and Merchant's original show, Daniel's production has gleaned a number of prestigious awards. These include an Emmy in 2006 for 'Outstanding Comedy Series', two Television Critics' Association Awards, and a Golden Globe for Steve Carell.

Has the phenomenal success of *The Office*, both in the US and in the UK gone to Ricky's head? No. By all accounts Gervais still has his feet firmly on the ground. Though he uses his success as the basis for the stage show mentioned at the start of this chapter (his third stand-up show) he has not let it change him in any major way.

Maybe this is because he did not find fame until his late thirties. Prior to this he had been a university student studying philosophy at University College London and a student union entertainments manager at the same university (where he met his long-time girlfriend and successful TV producer Jane Fallon). Another interesting fact is that Gervais managed the UK based indie band Suede before they became famous. A detail that pops up in many biographies of Gervais involves his alleged stint as a pizza delivery man. This assertion appears in a number of online biographies of the comedian, but is completely untrue. He has eaten plenty of pizzas, but never delivered a single one.[5]

Ricky Gervais eventually found himself working at XFM at the age of thirty-six. This is when things started to happen for him. It was at the radio station he met Stephen Merchant, who was to be a vital ingredient in terms of both writing, directing and acting when it came to future projects. Gervais was actually Merchant's boss at the station until Stephen joined the BBC and went on a producer's training course. Merchant says of that time that Gervais was, 'the worst boss I've ever had. Because Ricky's not like a proper boss; he was officially my boss, but it was ludicrous.'[6]

Gervais went on to be a regular contributor to Channel 4's *The Eleven O'Clock Show,* where, as we have seen, Sacha Baron-Cohen had also appeared as Ali G. Like Baron-Cohen, he went on to host his own show, in his case entitled *Meet Ricky Gervais.* Aired in 2000, it was not a big hit. An unsuccessful mix of sketches, talk-show 'chat' and games, the show was largely ignored.[7]

Opportunity came Gervais' way again when Stephen Merchant had to produce a programme when doing his course at the BBC. This is how the idea behind *The Office* first came to be transposed onto film. It began with a character called 'Seedy Boss' who Gervais acted out while they were working together at XFM. When Merchant discovered he had to produce a sample programme he contacted Ricky and the two of them committed the Seedy Boss character to film. The nauseating boss we all know as 'David Brent' was born.

The BBC saw what the pair had done and liked it. Gervais and Merchant were commissioned to write and film a pilot episode, insisting that they direct and Ricky take the central role. Both these criteria were accepted thanks to the buzz these new talents had created in the BBC with their rough introduction to Brent's office existence.

When the pilot was made, Gervais and Merchant were not happy with it, feeling it had lost some of the fly-on-the-wall documentary feel which was vital. However, the BBC liked what they had done so much they commissioned the first six-part series and allowed the pair to re-film the pilot, bringing it back to the original, rough documentary style.

When Series One of *The Office* first aired in 2001 it was not an instant hit with the general public. However, critics were praising the programme early on and it was named 'pick of the day' in a number of TV guides. Due to its critical success the BBC repeated it on their second channel and before long began to draw in larger audiences, gaining considerably in popularity and regularly attracting four million viewers.

In 2002 the second series aired and met with equal popularity to the re-run of the first. Retaining the six-part format, it also had a documentary feel and Gervais and Merchant once more refrained from adding a laughter track. This series was followed by two specials shown at Christmas 2003, the second episode attracting a 30% share of the audience: a massive 6.5 million viewers. These were the absolute final installments of work life at Wernham Hogg and created closure in the case of Tim's relationship with Dawn the receptionist, while leaving us with a sense of hope for David Brent's future. The decision to stop producing such a popular sitcom was not only a brave move on the part of Gervais and Merchant, it also showed their integrity. It would have been all too easy to continue creating the show for the sake of financial reward. However, they felt they had shown all they could or wanted to of the characters and the environment of *The Office*. So instead of riding on the crest of the show's popularity and creating another series they brought it to a close as they saw fit.

Of course, this was by no means the end of their comedy partnership. *Extras* was the next production that Gervais and Merchant created as a team, the sitcom first arriving on our screens in 2005 with a second series screened in 2006. The show also starred Gervais, this time playing an actor called Andy Millman, a role for which he won a BAFTA. In the first series Millman is hoping to get his own sitcom produced while taking various jobs as an extra in films, TV programmes and even on stage when he plays the genie to Les Dennis' Aladdin.

In Series Two he is successful in getting his sitcom made after making major compromises. These degrade his initial idea, and what could have been a sophisticated, intelligent and genuinely funny show becomes instead a hideous beast of a prime time sitcom, heavily reliant on catchphrases and clichés. This brings derision from critical circles within the context of the sitcom, but the public love *'When the Whistle Blows'*. This could be seen as a slight to other contemporary British comedies which rely heavily on catchphrases and a degree of vulgarity, such as *Little Britain* and the work of Catherine Tate. However, Gervais and Merchant cite *Little Britain* as one of the shows they enjoy. This could be due to the fact it is not simply a sketch show, but a kind of mockumentary of British society. This echoes *The Office*'s mock fly-on-the-wall documentary style.

> ### *Extras*'s Quote
> 'This is typical first night nerves. I know what you're thinking. You're thinking the script's not funny, it's crass, it's lowest common denominator, and, you know, you're right. But don't worry about it because people will watch anything.' Darren Lamb, Andy Millman's agent in *Extras*

'When the Whistle Blows' is a workplace-based sitcom within a sitcom. It is the broad, clichéd and obvious joke-ridden creation *The Office* could have been if Gervais and Merchant had not remained true to their original vision. The boss, Mr Stokes, is an extremely cartoonish version of Brent and it could be said that Andy Millman is akin to Ricky Gervais minus the control he managed to exert over his and Merchant's sitcoms.

We see that Millman wants to create a work of quality and in the first episode of season two he threatens to walk out on the travesty which is being created from his original idea. Both Gervais and Merchant have displayed similar integrity, but they were not pressurised or caught in a 'catch 22' situation of having to create a lowest common denominator show to get anywhere at all.

Extras co-starred Stephen Merchant as Millman's rather useless agent Darren Lamb (who is as socially inept as David Brent) and he and Gervais got the chance to work alongside Hollywood stars such as Orlando Bloom, Robert De Niro, and Ian McKellen. It also saw them working with British TV personalities like Keith Chegwin and Diana Rigg. Though there was never any question of the audience blurring the distinction between the stars 'real selves' and their *Extra*'s personas – because most played parts so far-fetched that there was never any question of the dialogue being genuine – it was nevertheless extremely funny to see scenes such as the one that has Ronnie Corbett snorting coke. The delight that these celebrities took in sending themselves up was also part of the attraction, and moments like the improvised song called 'Little Fat Man' from David Bowie were made all the more funny because of the audience's awareness of Ricky Gervais' personality on and off stage (he apparently worshipped Bowie as a teen).

Extras enjoyed similar ratings to *The Office*, but not the same degree of critical praise or awards. However, due to the success of both programmes, Gervais has been offered a number of parts in Hollywood movies, parts that many actors would have taken without a second thought. It is indicative of his integrity – and his ability to trust his own judgement – that Gervais has turned down many of these roles because he didn't feel he was suited to play them. Rejected offers include roles in the screen adaptation of *The Da Vinci Code* (2006) and *Mission Impossible III* (2006) alongside Tom Cruise. He has even had an offer to front the re-formed 80s band Frankie Goes to Hollywood. Of turning such offers down Gervais says: 'I've never regretted turning money down. I don't do anything for the money. It bores me.'[9]

> ### *The Office* Quote
> 'As television shows go this thing is just about perfect. You're never gonna get a show closer to perfection than this show *The Office*.'
> David Letterman[8]

The most notorious example of Gervais refusing unsuitable work involved an American drinks company asking him to do a television advert for one million pounds (and this would be for only a day's filming). Gervais declined and the company came back with an offer of two million, but he still would not do it.[10]

However, he's declined an even larger amount. The BBC offered him five million pounds for one of their notorious 'golden handcuffs' deals, meaning he wouldn't be able to work for anyone else. Commenting on why he declined this offer, in his characteristically spirited fashion Gervais jokes: 'I don't want to be the BBC's bitch.'[11]

That said, he has accepted some of the offers which have come his way. He appeared in Christopher Guest's spoof *For Your Consideration* (2006), partly because Guest was the creator of *Spinal Tap* and Gervais is a huge fan. He also took parts in the Ben Stiller film *Night at the Museum* (2006) and acted opposite Robert De Niro in *Stardust* (2007). Gervais also made a guest appearance in the series *Alias* due to the fact he was a huge fan of the show.[12]

Gervais has also made two twenty-minute training videos for Microsoft. These were entitled '*The Office* Values' and

'Realising Potential' and were leaked onto the internet. In these two shorts Gervais plays David Brent and Stephen Merchant plays a Microsoft employee as they discuss issues related to the workplace.[13]

He was also honoured by being the first Brit to write and star in an episode of *The Simpsons*. This episode is called 'Homer Simpson: This is Your Wife'. Gervais is a huge *Simpsons'* fan, describing the long-running animation show as, 'The greatest achievement of humankind since putting a man on the moon. Fuck me, it's good.'[14]

> **Extras Quote**
>
> 'I didn't think I had to make a list of things you shouldn't do at work, one of them tossing off over a pen. Do you really think you're earning your twelve and a half percent by doing that sort of thing under the table?' Andy Millman speaking to Darren Lamb, his agent

The episode itself is based on Homer and Marge being on 'Wife Swap'. It was actually Gervais' partner Jane who came up with the idea. In the episode Gervais provides the voice for a character called Charles who shares similarities with office head honcho David Brent. Charles falls for Marge and sings her a song entitled 'Lady,' which was penned by Ricky. Of the whole *Simpsons* experience Gervais says: 'It was fucking brilliant. I had a whale of a time.'[15]

When it comes to his peers in the UK Gervais is neither impressed nor unimpressed, though he does like *Little Britain* and *Peep Show*. His lack of enthusiasm for British comedy in general is because he says it is always the same people involved with the shows. He believes he and Stephen Merchant have more in common with US counterparts, such as Larry David and Mitch Hurwitz, who writes *Arrested Development*.[16] This cynicism extends from the world of British comedy into the realm of celebrity.

Gervais says that celebrity status is 'irrelevant'[17] What he means is that whether someone is a celebrity or not is unimportant, they still have to earn his respect and he still has to like them if he is going to spend any time with them. Gervais is not interested in being seen with famous people purely because they are famous.

> **Pilkington Quote**
>
> 'Were those presents the three kings brought Jesus for Christmas or his birthday?' Karl Pilkington

The subject of fame is utilised for his third live comedy act which followed on from *Animals* (2003) and *Politics* (2004). At the beginning of *Animals* Gervais says: '...this show is sort of *Life on Earth,* the bits David Attenborough left out.'

The theme of *Politics* is evident in the title and both of these shows start with a film shown on a big screen before Gervais comes onto the stage. His third live show, *Fame* (2007), sold out 'in seconds' in the UK and was also a great success in the States.

For his stand-up acts Gervais has developed a special persona who is akin to both Brent and Darren Lamb. So, unlike many such comedians, he is not actually appearing as himself on stage. Instead, he is 'a boorish, right–wing bloke who's clever, but not as clever as he thinks.'[18]

In these shows Gervais uses irony to discuss areas which are often taboo or avoided as subjects of humour, such as bestiality, disability, and even the holocaust and paedophilia. All involve issues which people are largely not comfortable about confronting. The same humour is used in both *The Office* and *Extras*, especially with the socially inept David Brent and Darren Lamb who say the wrong things, but effectively highlight relevant issues by doing so. There are examples in the quote boxes included in this book of Brent and Lamb's ill-advised dialogue and the following is the Ricky Gervais stand-up equivalent from his show *Politics* when talking about charities: 'When I was growing up there was just Oxfam, you knew where you were, know what I mean? Done well if you've got shares in that, that's gone from strength to strength hasn't it, because you'll always have famine.'

> ## *The Office* Quote
>
> *The Office* is bigger than comedy. Look at the Christmas episode with the theme that David Brent is redeemed by love. That's an incredible thing to bring in. *Little Britain* doesn't have anywhere near the profundity Ricky's comedy has.'
> David Walliams[19]

We also find that the vanity displayed by Brent and Millman is present in the stage shows, Gervais mentioning his BAFTA awards in *Animals* and his Golden Globes in *Politics*.

The subject of fame is not only used for Gervais' third show, it's also a theme which arises in his and Merchant's work. When talking about the phenomena Gervais said, 'Socrates said fame was the perfume of heroic deeds. Well it probably was back then. You had to do something. That was before *Heat* and *Big Brother*'.[20]

This sentiment is borne out in *The Office*. The documentary filming could make staff members famous without the need for any such 'heroic deeds,' just as *Big Brother* has brought fame to people who have appeared on it (along with other reality TV shows). It is possible that the character of David Brent is thinking about this factor from the outset, which is why he plays up to the cameras and tries to remain politically correct, though fails without even realising he is doing so, as with his comments about people with disabilities.

In *Extras* Millman is clearly striving for a degree of fame with the creation of his sitcom. He also finds himself alongside truly famous people and the apparent contrast is made extremely clear, not least in the episode featuring David Bowie, who is treated with due respect while Millman is bumped out of the VIP area of a club for the star (who then sings the mocking song, mentioned earlier, inspired by Millman).

> ### *The Office* Quote
>
> 'There are limits to my comedy. There are things that I'll never laugh at. The handicapped, because there's nothing funny about them or any deformity. It's like when you see someone look at a little handicapped kid and go "Ooh, look at him, he's not able-bodied. I am, I'm prejudiced." Yeah, well, at least the little handicapped fella is able-minded. Unless he's not, it's difficult to tell with the wheelchair ones.'
>
> David Brent

The themes of both shows clearly include this element of fame, but they also share a number of other themes. Ego is seen to be a guiding force in regards to Brent and Millman. Their motivations are often ego based, such as Brent basically taking over training day at *The Office* to such an extent that even before lunch it has become a showcase for his supposed musical and song writing talent. This example is not only a clear case of an inflated ego taking over the day's events at the expense of others, but also highlights Brent's hope of possible fame arising from the presence of the cameras. Millman's ego leads him to create his own sitcom and causes him to attempt to make the most of his minor celebrity status, something which invariably goes wrong. That both Brent and Millman are egotistical and conceited explains a lot of their behaviour

Beneath such negative traits we discover a humanity to both

Brent and Millman, which is key in making them believable as characters and is also highly watchable as it creates depth.

Millman wears his heart on his sleeve and his every emotion can be read from his facial expressions; Gervais is a surprisingly good actor. We can see his pain when things backfire, such as at the club when Bowie sings about him or at the awards ceremony. However, we also see him choosing to visit a child in hospital rather than meet Robert De Niro, something which seals the character's underlying humanity and seems

> ### *Politics* **Quote**
>
> 'I think Schindler's List is a fantastic film...I got it out on video...by mistake, 'cause I'd never heard of it and I was in Blockbuster sort of late one night. I was a bit drunk, and I thought it was a porn film. No, 'cause I saw 18 certificate, top shelf. I thought, oh, black and white – dodgy home movie, German sounding – they're the best, and what swung it was that quote on the back from Barry Norman: "Have a box of Kleenex ready." Rubbish, I used about two. There was a shower scene.' Ricky Gervais from the *Politics* live show

to point to the fact that he is no longer letting fame and fortune guide him, but rather the idea of doing the right thing. Therefore Millman's character changes by the end of the second series and he gains redemption for his previous actions.

This redemption can also be found in the tears of David Brent in the finale of *The Office*. They reveal his vulnerability and allow us to see him as a person just like any other, with weaknesses and feelings. As Gervais says, '...one of the most orgasmic themes in film and comedy is redemption,' [21]

This can be found at the end of both sitcoms with regards to the main characters. Their previous actions are redeemed by the humanity they display, by their own realisation of their mistakes. Through this redemption our view of them is changed, something which gives a satisfying sense of closure to both sitcoms, along with Tim and Dawn getting together in *The Office* and Millman choosing to spend time with Maggie rather than De Niro in *Extras*.

The depth of character found in both sitcoms arises partly because Gervais and Merchant created complete histories for their characters.[22] Another reason for this depth is Gervais' belief that empathy is the most important thing in life. When watching his and Merchant's work we empathise predominantly with the office workers who have to tolerate Brent's attempts at friendship and humour. We empathise with Maggie, Millman's long suffering female companion. We also find ourselves empathising with both Brent and Millman's awkwardness.

In Millman's case this arises in situations of unwanted and unwelcome attention, such as the aforementioned situation when Bowie sings about him. We can see how awkward and uncomfortable he feels and understand such feelings. In regards to Brent, we are party to scenes of extreme discomfort like that in Series One of *The Office* when he pretends to fire Dawn and she bursts into tears. We clearly see his awkwardness and understand that he did not want to make her cry and does not know how to cope when she does. In this particular scene we also empathise with Dawn as most of us have been the butt of an unkind joke and with Ricky Howard, a worker from a temping agency who is sitting in and witnessing the whole spectacle, feeling understandably uncomfortable and awkward himself.

Brent is awkward partly because he does not really know how to interact with other people. He tries too hard, he kills conversations dead with misjudged comments, his humour is weak, and the Latin phrases he uses are always used in the wrong context (much like Del Boy with his use of French in *Only Fools and Horses*). Brent does not 'fit in' with others because he lacks the social skills. A prime example of this lack is at the club in Series One. He is accused of just wanting to have sex with a woman and he replies, 'Yeah, and from behind because your breath stinks of onion, and I didn't tell you that, did I?'

> ### *The Office* Quote
>
> 'He proposed on a Valentine's day, although he didn't do it face to face, he did it in one of the little Valentine bits in the paper. I think he had to pay for it by the word, because it just said "Lee love Dawn, marriage?" which you know, I like, because it's not often you get to something that's both romantic and thrifty'. Dawn

This highlights his complete lack of social graces and dire judgement in terms of reacting and interacting with others. It is this element which provides a great deal of humour while at the same time lending Brent a rather tragic feel as he is unable to be part of the social network around him.

This awkwardness is akin to that of John Cleese's character Basil Fawlty in the hugely popular workplace-based sitcom *Fawlty Towers*. As with Brent and Millman, Fawlty gets himself into intensely awkward situations and much of the comedy is generated by his social bungling and ineptitude.

There is no such ineptitude evident when it comes to Gervais and Merchant. They have even become leading figures in the emerging medium of podcasts. These downloadable videos have been created alongside their friend Karl Pilkington, who is the real star and whose strange thoughts and philosophies are mentioned by Gervais in the encores of his shows *Animals* and *Politics*. He was their producer when working at XFM and puts forward his philosophies in the podcasts, many of which are highly amusing. The podcasts themselves are thirty minutes long and were launched by the *Guardian* newspaper in December 2005.[23] With over half a million downloads per episode, they have been a great success. In fact, their success is so great that the podcasts have even spawned an online encyclopaedia dedicated to Pilkington's pearls of wisdom called 'Pilkipedia'.

Gervais has not been limited to television, film, stand-up and podcasts; he also showed his talent in the area of children's books by creating the Flanimals. These are a collection of strange creatures which he first arrived at when drawing cartoons for his nephew years ago.[24]

The creatures which make up the Flanimals feature in three books and include such things as the 'sweaty little waddle-gimp' called a 'Clunge Ambler' and the 'Edger', which is the slowest of all the Flanimals, so slow it sometimes does not move at all.[25] The first book of fifty-six Flanimals has sold over 300,000 copies since being published in October 2004, despite the fact there is very little in the way of narrative. The book is a kind of wildlife guide to the Flanimals, giving descriptions of what they look like, their lives and how they act. This echoes the mock fly-on-the-wall feel of *The Office*, Gervais creating a mock encyclopaedic feel to *Flanimals* the book, which is rife with futility and misunderstanding, themes which can also be found in Gervais' sitcoms.

Gervais hopes to take these strange little creatures to the big screen. However, rather than jumping in at the deep end, he has planned out their development through the stages of books, talking books, merchandise and a short film before they can amble onto movie screens. The build-up is intentional, Gervais is the master of audience manipulation.

He anticipates audience responses to his work and crafts it accordingly, toying with us at will.

This sort of purposeful manipulation can be seen in the Gervais and Merchant's sitcoms. One of the most clear examples is the growing friendship and fondness displayed between Tim and Dawn in *The Office*. We see how unkind and dislikeable Dawn's boyfriend is whilst also noting how she and Tim clearly have a rapport. This naturally means we are going to root for them to get together, especially as both characters are likeable in themselves. Tim looks to the camera when Brent is trying to entertain, thus creating a bond not only of empathy, but also of humour. However, Gervais and Merchant make us wait until the final Christmas Special episode for the 'payoff' in this relationship, when Tim and Dawn finally get together.

Gervais has other projects in the pipeline, such as a film co-written with Stephen Merchant and an idea for a new sitcom called *The Men at the Pru*. The latter is set in the 1970s in a provincial backwater. They came up with it prior to the creation of *Extras*. The idea is to give it a distinctly retro feel as it follows the lives of a number of twenty and thirty-somethings living out their existence away from the hustle and bustle of a big city.

Even if Gervais were to stop working altogether he could retire happy with the quality of work he has produced. Due to the fact he has rejected offers for roles he considered unsuitable, his credits are universally respectable and create quite a CV. However, I for one hope he will keep working for many years to come and that he and Stephen Merchant bring us more entertainment of the quality that has already graced our screens.

ENDNOTES

1. Ricky and Steve on inspiration for *The Office* (www.bbc.co.uk/comedy/theoffice/defguide/defguide1.shtml)

2. Ricky and Steve on inspiration for *The Office* (www.bbc.co.uk/comedy/theoffice/defguide/defguide1.shtml)

3. *The Office*: awards and quotes (www.rickygervais.com/office_awards)

4. Bilmes, A, 'Heeere's Ricky,' p.3 (www.rickygervais.com/gqapr06)

5. About Ricky (www.rickygervais.com/aboutRicky)

6. Rayment, T, 'After Office Hours,' p.3 (www.rickygervais.com/sundaytimesarticle)

7. About Ricky (www.rickygervais.com/aboutRicky)

8. *The Office*: awards and quotes (www.rickygervais.com/office_awards)

9. Bilmes, A, 'Heeere's Ricky,' p.3 (www.rickygervais.com/gqapr06)

10. Bilmes, A, 'Heeere's Ricky,' p.3 (www.rickygervais.com/gqapr06)

11. Davis, J, 'Ricky Gervais: My Life as a Superstar,' p.2 (http://independent.co.uk/people/profiles/articles321354.ece)

12. Barber, N, 'Ricky Gervais: Step into my Office,' p.1 (http://news.independent.co.uk/people/profiles/article2152792.ece)

13. Microsoft unhappy at Gervais leak (http://news.bbc.co.uk/1/hi/entertainment/5298376.stm)

14. Bilmes, A, 'Heeere's Ricky, p.4 (www.rickygervais.com/gqapr06)

15. Bilmes, A, 'Heeere's Ricky, p.4 (www.rickygervais.com/gqapr06)

16. Bilmes, A, 'Heeere's Ricky, p.4 (www.rickygervais.com/gqapr06)

17. Bilmes, A, 'Heeere's Ricky, p.4 (www.rickygervais.com/gqapr06)

18. Billen, A, 'No, I don't fear death – I'm just frightened of dying,' p.3 (*The Times*, 22nd March 2007)

19. Rayment, T, 'After Office Hours,' p.4 (www.rickygervais.com/sundaytimesarticle)

20. Billen, A, 'No, I don't fear death – I'm just frightened of dying,' p.1 (*The Times*, 22nd March 2007)

21. Davis, J, 'Ricky Gervais: My Life as a Superstar, p.4 (http://independent.co.uk/people/profiles/articles321354.ece)

22. Ricky and Steve on David Brent (www.bbc.co.uk/comedy/theoffice/defguide/

defguide6.shtml)

23. Dee, J, 'The Pod Couple,' p.1 (www.rickygervais.com/pilkington_gu_guide)

24. Billen, A, 'No, I don't fear death – I'm just frightened of dying,' p.2 (*The Times*, 22nd March 2007)

25. Rayment, T, 'After Office Hours,' p.1 (www.rickygervais.com/sundaytimesarticle)

4. 'AM I BOVVERED?': CATHERINE TATE REACHES FOR THE STARS

Born in London on the 12th May 1968, Catherine Tate is a Taurean actress and comedian who spent the early part of her life growing up in a flat on the Brunswick council estate in the Bloomsbury district. Her eponymous television show, *The Catherine Tate Show*, is best known for the catchphrases it has given rise to and which can be heard in many a school playground and office. She has also undertaken numerous serious acting roles, especially since the popularity of her sketch show, which ensured a meteoric rise into the limelight after she'd spent many years in the wings.

Retiring & somewhat shy

Tate has always been a shy person who dislikes being in the spotlight herself and so deflects unwanted attention with jokes and by inventing humorous characters, a trait which began at school. Tate is still shy and it is not until she gets into character – often using prosthetics and make-up so she is virtually unrecognisable – that she gains a kind of vitality borne of the freedom found in being someone else. This kind of mask wearing has been found to be very liberating by many actors. It frees them from themselves and the expectations of others.

If it is by donning the masks of various characters that Catherine Tate finds release from her shyness, then she certainly has some good characters to choose from. There is Lauren Cooper, the stroppy teenage girl whose catchphrase, 'Am I bovvered?',

> **Tate Quote**
>
> 'You ever see those women who leave their money to the cats? Oh, that do make me laugh. What do cats want with it? What they gonna do, go on a cruise? They're fucking cats'. Joannie 'Nan' Taylor

has even been uttered by Tony Blair. She transforms into Joannie 'Nan' Taylor, the old woman who turns the air blue with foul language as she criticises others and makes unkind comments, such as 'one eye looking at you, the other looking for you' when talking about an ugly baby. Tate even becomes men, like Derek Faye, the upper-class bachelor who is constantly offended by being accused of being gay, responding with his catchphrase of 'How very dare you?'

One event which highlights Catherine's shyness occurred just prior to the Variety Club awards in 2005. These were being held at the Hilton hotel on Park Lane in London and on the way there Tate was being accompanied in a cab by her mother. As the taxi neared the hotel with its awaiting paparazzi Tate asked if they could be dropped off at the rear so as to avoid all the attention. She and her somewhat disappointed mother entered the hotel through the back and were only seen by three Swedish businessmen who didn't recognise Catherine.[1]

The chameleon nature of Tate, who can transform herself from a shy, unassuming woman to loud, often in-your-face characters is similar to that of other comedians, as is her reason for having utilised humour in the first place. In Chapter Two we saw that both Matt Lucas and David Walliams used humour at school as a way to gain popularity and friends. It is the act of performing which transforms both Tate, Walliams and Lucas and it is due to the early formation of such a strategy that we have the memorable shows and characters they create.

It is possible that the similarities between *The Catherine Tate Show* and *Little Britain* are due to this common use of humour at an early age by all three comedians. Both shows are sketch based and feature outrageous characters. They also contain the same type of humour, something best illustrated by the similarities between Tate's depiction of stroppy teenager Lauren Cooper and Matt Lucas' Vicky Pollard. In fact, Tate has had Lucas' catchphrase 'Yeah but no but yeah but...' shouted at her by members of the public, and in turn he has had people calling out 'Am I bovvered?' at him, which is of course one of Tate's best known catchphrases. Audiences are clearly prone to confusing the characters Lauren and Vicki Pollard.

> **Tate Quote**
>
> Lauren:'Are you disrespecting my family?'
>
> Teacher:'I didn't mention your family'
>
> Lauren: 'Are you ignoring my family?'

However, there are also important differences between the shows. Tate does not always use a punch-line at the end of her sketches and this is because she says she likes to 'let the characters breathe.'[2] Without necessarily having to use punch-lines you can allow for a greater characterisation which is not limited by the need to constantly end on a gag.

Another difference arises in the amount of vulgarity and horrid humour. Tate's show is tamer than *Little Britain*, which has seriously pushed the boat out when it comes to including elements usually regarded as bad taste, such as vomiting and wetting oneself.

The humour of *The Catherine Tate Show* is based on characters which are clear exaggerations of real people within society, like the belligerent old lady and camp, upper-class bachelor (who can be likened to *Little Britain*'s Daffyd Thomas, the 'only gay in the village'). Such exaggeration is comical, horribly twisting reality into caricatures, some of which make us laugh because of their over-blown nature and others because of how close to the truth they are despite their exaggeration. The prime example of the latter is Lauren Cooper. She is not-too-far-removed from the numerous teenagers who have serious attitude problems and we can recognise her traits as those belonging to many young people.

The humour also seems to have a class divide. Those sketches involving people of working class origins are often not as critical as those about the upper or middle classes. They concentrate more on others being at fault and make the characters' words and actions the source of much of the humour. In the case of sketches involving the upper classes we can see that it is the characters themselves who become the source of amusement, that we are laughing directly at them.

One clear example of the working class character being treated with a degree of kindness is the party which takes place in Nan Taylor's old people's home in the 2005 Christmas special after she has dismissed Charlotte Church as 'fackin' rubbish'. We can see that the audience is encouraged to laugh at her words and at Charlotte Church's reaction to them, rather than laughing at Nan Taylor herself.

The characters of Janice and Ray highlight stereotypes of the working class. They are from 'the north' and in this case the stereotype involves a thriftiness and down-to-earth view of everyday living. When these traits are challenged by the over-priced goods on sale in their local stores and what they perceive as 'snobby' or 'exotic' we hear their catchphrase of 'the dirty bastards'.

An example of the upper class being treated with derision is the Aga Saga Woman who is shocked when her exaggerated upper-middle class sensibilities are offended. This character can be equated with Maggie Blackamoor from *Little Britain*, the woman who vomits at the merest hint of something she finds distasteful. These two characters stress the fact that *Little Britain* went further into the realms of vulgarity and distaste than Catherine Tate ventured.

We laugh at the Aga Saga Woman for being so easily offended, for being so uptight that things which should not shock actually do. This, coupled with characters saying such things as, 'Step away from that cinnamon and gooseberry yoghurt children, it's twenty-four hours past its sell-by date,' shows clearly that the upper classes are being treated with derision. The show pokes fun at the perceived attitudes of these people. There is supposed to be less vulgarity and swearing amongst the upper classes, which can make them appear stilted and anal, something that adds to the humour as the audience are familiar with people who resemble such characters.

There is a long and healthy tradition of poking fun at the upper classes and utilising their more stereotypical characteristics to comic effect. This can be seen in *The Fast Show* with the characters of Lord Ralph Mayhew and his estate worker Ted. Another classic example is provided by Kenneth Williams and Charles Hawtry's notorious sending up of the upper classes in many of the *Carry On* films.

Tate successfully applies upper class stereotypes to create humour in her show whilst at the same time applying working class stereotypes of vulgarity, cursing and frugality to Nan Taylor and the like. She also utilises the stroppy teenager stereotype in the case of Lauren and her friends. This use of stereotypes means we are familiar with the characters and allows us to enjoy them without needing serious thought. Tate's show doesn't challenge or satirise, it simply entertains.

This entertainment factor is far from being a negative. It is reflected in Tate's view of theatre where she expresses the opinion that it is supposed to be entertainment for the masses and that 'to produce something that is alienating is as great a crime as to produce something that is not entertaining.'[3] It is her love of theatre which has caused her to jump at the opportunity to become the next patron of the Royal Court Theatre's Young Writer's Festival, an honour which has previously been held by Kathy Burke and Ray Winstone.

The fact that *The Catherine Tate Show* is virtually pure entertainment puts it in line not only with the early tradition of the theatre, but also with a comic tradition in television and in film. This tradition includes such greats as Laurel and Hardy, *The Two Ronnies*, Kenny Everett, Dick Emery and the aforementioned *Carry On* films. In fact, comedians including *The Two Ronnies* introduced sketches where they dressed up as various characters in their shows, and at no time was there more to their antics than a wish to entertain the masses.

None of the acts or films mentioned tried to make a political or philosophical point, there were no hidden depths for others to try and read into them. They were creating comedy for the sake of entertainment and many are thankful Tate chooses to continue this great tradition, as people do not necessarily want their comedy infused with deeper meaning.

The pure entertainment ethos is also found in shows like *Just For Laughs* and *You've Been Framed*. This is why such shows get prime time slots, attract large audiences, and run for a long time. People like programmes which don't confront them with issues and depth. They often simply want to escape the realities of life and Catherine Tate helps them do so with her collection of characters exhibiting her brand of horrid humour in the best possible way. This is not to say that her show is one of those accused of 'dumbing down' to get ratings. In fact her observations are intelligent, wry and always humorous takes on the type of people we encounter on a daily basis. Often the situations that arise are uncomfortable, with the long suffering staff who have to teach Tate's character Lauren Cooper being one example – many are driven to virtual hysteria by her unrelenting diatribes. But the fact is that many people prefer a fairly basic form of 'pure' entertainment, and she caters to these preferences.

> ## Tate Quote
>
> Kate: 'Guess how much my trip to Egypt cost'
> Ellen: 'Err... eighty pounds?'
> Kate: 'I'm going to Egypt, not phoning Egypt!'

Tate has created her cast of characters by drawing on people she has known, though, as she states, 'I exaggerate and twist people's traits for comic effect.' In relation to Joannie 'Nan' Taylor she admits it is a 'merciless caricature' of older female relatives.[4] Perhaps this is one reason why she has proved to be so popular, tapping into the current preference for extremity, she plays-up the traits of her characters to the utmost of her ability.

The inspiration for the charity fund raising character called Geordie Georgie came from a woman 'wearing a Tibetan hat' who one day knocked on Tate's door and gave the clear impression she thought Catherine wasn't giving as much as she should. In the case of Lauren Cooper, the inspiration is non-specific, the character being based on the general idea of a stroppy teenager.[5]

So Tate's comedy provides us with memorable characters from areas of society we can recognise quite easily. But there is a further dimension to the way in which her comedy operates. We are able to recognise that these characters are caricatures from an external standpoint, and the fact that we are aware of the over-blown and often distorted nature of the personas is part of the humour. This recognition is important, as without it we couldn't identify the comedic exaggeration, and would have no frame of reference by which to judge that what we are seeing is a horribly humorous version of real people.

Despite her success at making us laugh with her selection of well-observed characters, Catherine Tate didn't start out hoping to be a comedian. She wanted to be a serious actress, which strangely enough provided the trigger for her developing her own brand of humour. When it turned out that the all-girl convent school that Tate attended did not have the facilities for her to pursue a course in acting, she moved to the nearest all-boys school. As a newcomer and the only girl to boot, she was guaranteed to draw attention in the playground – and lots of it. It was through efforts to escape such attention that Tate really developed her use of humour as an escapist strategy. Then, before completing her A-levels, Tate moved to the Central School of Speech and Drama, the same school which Dawn French and Jennifer Saunders attended.

An interesting note about her childhood is that her home life was spent exclusively with female relatives. Her father walked out when she was very young and she never knew him. Tate was then brought up by her mother and grandmother, which meant that she had little experience of male authority figure until she moved to the all boys' school.

> ### Tate Quote
>
> 'I love astrologer Jonathan Cainer. I ring his phone line twice a week and he's always spot on with me and three million other Taureans. But I know it's MY soul he's looking into.' Catherine Tate[6]

Self Reliant & Firm in Convictions

Much of Tate's personality is influenced by the desire to be in control, which has also influenced the development of humour as a way to deflect people's attention from the 'real' Catherine. The use of humour puts her in control of what people are able to find out about her and what she decides to reveal, when, and to whom. This is reflected in Tate's words about her work; 'None of my work defines who I am.'[7]

Rather, it is Tate who defines and controls her work, not allowing it to control her, but making sure she is always in the driving seat.

Linked to this controlling nature is Catherine's interest in astrology, something which means she is a huge fan of Jonathan Cainer, regularly checking his predictions for Taureans. She even says that if her comedy and acting career were to end now she would probably become an astrologer herself.[7] Tate recalls something from her birth chart which has remained with her ever since reading it: 'Strive to be successful because you'll be a very bitter failure.'[9] This she has done and thanks to her great success she will never have to find out what kind of failure she would have been.

This love of the zodiac stems from her wish to control and her tendency to worry. The future is an unknown quantity over which we can exercise only limited control, and so to allay the worry which arises from not knowing what's to come Tate has turned to the stars and planets. Astrology is one way of lessening fears about what the future may hold and of feeling more in control.

Her belief in astrology is matched by her dedication to her family, career and even her scripts. This latter element is partly due to her controlling nature as Tate does not like her work to be altered. As long as what is spoken is exactly what she has written in the script she is happy.

> **Tate Quote**
>
> 'I asked her to be in my show because not only did I think she was very talented, but also I knew she was going to be at Edinburgh anyway, so I wouldn't have to pay for her accommodation.' Lee Mack [10]

Her commitment to her work was made very clear soon after her daughter was born: Her husband, Twig Clark, a stage manager whom she met while working for a year at the Royal Shakespeare Company, temporarily gave up his job to look after Erin, who was born in 2003. This happened when Catherine was filming the first series of her sketch show and was suffering from postnatal depression after having endured an emergency Caesarean in order to give birth. Erin was only six months old, a tough age for any young family to deal with, and so rather than burdening her husband with how she was feeling, Tate worked through her problems while creating the series.

Working while suffering from the depression proved somewhat cathartic and Tate even managed to turn elements of the bad times in her life into prospective comedy sketches: 'One thing that gets you through even the darkest hour is a tiny voice which puts it through a filter and turns it out as a sketch at the other end.'[10] This said, Tate credits her husband with having got her through that difficult time of her life and the two are clearly very close.

It is also of note that Catherine suffered depression prior to Erin's birth. Tate puts this down to a lack of control during pregnancy, saying 'You've no control because there's something inside which you can't stop growing.'[11]

It is interesting that so many successful comedians – Tony Hancock, Stephen Fry and apparently Catherine Tate also, to name just a few – have depressive tendencies that belie the comedic personas which have made them household names.

Usually patient & will wait a long time for hopes to mature

It has been briefly mentioned that Tate's earliest desire was to be a serious actress. She had tried pursuing this career by taking the usual route of training and then auditioning for small parts in various shows, like *The Bill* and *Casualty*. She had even gained a year's work at the National Theatre, but this did not see her career progress. The career ladder she was attempting to climb was looking so very long and crowded that she eventually decided just to jump off and instead climb a 'shorter ladder' which she hoped might lead to the same destination. The comedy ladder.

Tate put her feet on the first rung by going on the stand-up circuit, her shyness vanishing when she stepped on stage and wore the mask of her humour. This change to comedy proved to be the perfect move for her. Apart from anything else, the nature of stand-up meant she was in much greater control of her schedule. Instead of waiting for offers to come in after attending auditions she took the initiative and took to the comedy circuit. She was nominated for a Perrier Award at the Edinburgh Fringe Festival in 2000 as part of a show called *New*

Bits which had been put together by Lee Mack, who had seen her five minute stand-up routine in a new act competition and thought she was 'very, very good'.[13] That it took her five years to get to this level not only shows perseverance on Tate's part, but also patience and a refusal to give up on her dreams.

Since being nominated for the Perrier, Tate's star has continued to rise. She returned to the Edinburgh Fringe Festival the year after and then was given roles in the surreal British television sketch show *Big Train* and the BBC comedy *Attention Scum* as well as occasionally contributing to an online spoof of the *Radio Times*: *TVGoHome*. The first of these is the most notable because of the impressive credentials of its creators. *Big Train* was written by Graham Lineham and Arthur Matthews, who were also the creators of *Father Ted*. It featured Simon Pegg, co-writer and actor in the sitcom *Spaced* who went on to make *Shaun of the Dead* (2004) and *Hot Fuzz* (2007).

> ## Tate Quote
> 'She has described herself as a lazy control freak, but when the time comes to do it, she changes. Her brain moves incredibly fast when she's performing. She's completely focussed,' Geoffrey Perkins, producer of *The Catherine Tate Show*[14]

Tate was also offered a part in the Dawn French show *Wild West*. It was after this that the BBC commissioned the first series of *The Catherine Tate Show*. This self-titled show continued for a further two seasons and Tate kept it on BBC2 despite requests that she take it to BBC1. This was due to the fact she preferred the greater freedom which the corporation's second channel allowed, preserving the sense of control she had been enjoying in producing the series thus far. She also knew that were she to switch channels the pressure would be much greater for higher viewing figures.

Inclined to dealing with the public
It was early in 2004 when *The Catherine Tate Show* first came to our screens in a six-part format. Tate could barely believe she had a show in her own name and says, 'Even when I saw it on TV part of me didn't believe it was showing on other people's TV sets as well.'[15]

The BBC then compiled three 'best of' episodes using the best sketches from the series and showed them in the build up to the release of the next series.

The second series was shown in the summer of 2005 and was much more popular than the first. In fact, its final episode managed to attract more viewers than the episode of Gervais and Merchant's sitcom *Extras* which had been shown before it[15] – an incredible feat, especially for a woman working within a field traditionally dominated by men (although in recent years the success of female comedians like Dawn French, Jennifer Saunders, Jane Horrocks and Alistair McGowan's partner Ronni Ancona have ensured prime time comedy slots are occupied by both genders).

The third series aired late in 2006 and was the last of *The Catherine Tate Show*, though she has said she would like to do some TV 'specials' and has not ruled out taking it on tour, as Lucas and Walliams did with *Little Britain*. This series secured viewing figures of between four and five million and was BBC2's top show at the time.

The Catherine Tate Show has not only proved popular with the general public. The show has received much critical acclaim and several awards, the most prominent of which are two at the British Comedy Awards. The first was in 2004 for 'Best Comedy Newcomer', a category which David Walliams won the year before. This award came after the release of the first series of the show. The second was for 'Best British Comedy Actress', given for her work in the second series.

In 2007 *The Catherine Tate Show* was nominated for a BAFTA in the category of 'Best Comedy'. When the award was given to *That Mitchell and Webb Look* Tate felt as if she'd been snubbed and thought the judges were out of touch with public opinion: 'I don't like to use the word "fixed," but it should be fair. Only ten people vote, but have they asked the nation? I've lost three times.'[16]

During the course of the three seasons of her show Tate worked with a range of impressive guest stars. Series One saw Brian Murphy appearing with the characters Irene and Vern and Chas and Dave with Nan Taylor. Paul Whitehouse and Peter Kay appeared in the second series and Jools Holland and Paul O'Grady were guests on the final series.

In regards to ending her sketch show Tate said: 'Well, before I'm ensconced forever saying "Am I bovvered?" I'd like to mix things up, work-wise.'

However, the use of catchphrases from the show is a good indicator of how popular it is with the general public (though it is important to note that none of her characters were written with catchphrases in mind). In fact, Tate has been quite surprised at how some of the sayings have caught on: 'It's completely weird the way some people pick up on certain aspects.'[17]

Even Lauren's infamous 'Am I bovvered?' wasn't really meant to be a catchphrase, though when Tate realised how much people loved and expected it she felt she had to include it in every sketch featuring the teenager.[18] It is this character which has not only given rise to the best known catchphrase from the show, she has also been the most performed by Tate and drawn the most letters from members of the public. Teachers have written to her saying they like the show, but asking if she could please kill off Lauren's character because their lives were being made a misery by children aping the teenager's sayings and attitude.[19]

As with *Little Britain*, *The Catherine Tate Show* has spawned official merchandise, including a calendar and a beaker which plays recordings of the different catchphrases from the show whenever it is set down, such as 'What a liberty!' one of Nan Taylor's phrases, though toned down for the purpose. Tate is actually a little embarrassed about items such as the beaker being released, but defending herself from non-existent criticism on the matter states, 'They give some of the profits to charity, so they make it hard for you to say no'.[20] This defence is indicative of Tate's worrying nature.

> ## Tate Quote
>
> 'One thing that people have been saying is that it's like a Comic Relief sketch, but it's not. It's a proper hour-long drama and Catherine Tate has a proper part. She's amazing in it, her and David Tennant together are a joy.' Russell T Davies, lead writer on *Doctor Who* [21]

Tate's anxiety has no doubt been made worse through her choice of career. As she recalls, there was a time while she was still striving to be a serious actress when she went for an audition for a part in a Royal Court play. When a friend got the part instead, she began to panic that her career in acting would never take off and says, 'I was very worried, restless and discontented.'[22] This type of let-down is hardly going to have been reassuring to someone of a nervous disposition.

Talented & energetic

Since the success of *The Catherine Tate Show* many doors have been opened for its star, including requests for further appearances as characters from the show, but also offers for serious acting work, something she had always hoped her comedy career would lead to. She has made a number of appearances for charity. In March 2005, for example, she appeared with the band McFly on Comic Relief. The band were being interviewed by Simon Amstel and were surrounded by adoring fans when Tate, in the guise of Lauren Cooper, came in and asked the band why they were so rubbish, then going on to confuse them with Busted before being asked to leave the set.

In November of 2005 came Tate's second charity sketch. A special was filmed for the BBC's *Children In Need* programme and in it we saw Lauren on the set of *EastEnders*. In the sketch she had travelled to Walford in order to confront Stacey for stealing her boyfriend. Peggy Mitchell, played by Barbara Windsor, also appeared in this special and Lauren argued with her in the Queen Vic pub. Along with Lauren's own catchphrase, the teenager also spoke some famous lines from the soap opera before storming out of the establishment.

That same month Tate was one of the performers at the 77th Royal Variety Performance. She again appeared as Lauren, though this time accompanied by her friends Liese and Ryan. The sketch she performed on stage is now infamous for the moment she looked up at the Queen and Prince Philip in the Royal Box and said

> **Tate Quote**
> 'I'm a fiery Taurean with my own Uranus. Careful! I'll do the jokes'. Amanda

'Is one bovvered?', mocking the Queen's own voice and manner of speech. The Queen was seen to be smiling and seemed to take this turn of events in good humour. However, amongst other things, Lauren went on to add, 'She is bling, but the old fella next to her is asleep.' It is this comment which some say offended Prince Philip, though these reports are unconfirmed.

As 2005 drew to a close, Tate took on an acting role in *Bleak House*, the award-winning BBC adaptation of the Charles Dickens novel, and with a Christmas special of *The Catherine Tate Show* featuring Richard Park and Charlotte Church as guests. Then in 2006 she had a role in one of the most popular series of the time, the BBC's *Doctor Who*. She played Donna Noble, a bride complete with wedding dress who suddenly appeared in the Doctor's TARDIS at the end of the final episode of that series, entitled 'Doomsday'. She then went on to play a main role in the 2006 Christmas special of that series which was called 'Runaway Bride'. When quizzed about her work on *Doctor Who,* Tate said the whole experience 'was a blast', especially as she hadn't previously worked on a production that employed special effects to such a great extent.

In 2007 Catherine could once again be seen on Comic Relief. This time she didn't just appear as Lauren, but also as Elaine Figgis, Geordie Georgie and Nan Taylor. However, it was the Lauren elements which were especially memorable for two reasons. Firstly, David Tennant played her teacher after Catherine Tate had acted alongside him in his role as *Doctor Who*. Secondly, Lauren did work experience at Number 10 Downing Street and the then Prime Minister, Tony Blair was in the sketch, saying the words, 'Am I bovvered? Does my face look bovvered?'

The success of *The Catherine Tate Show* has also led to serious film roles. These include those in *Starter for Ten* (2006), *Sixty Six* (2006) and *Love and Other Disasters* (2006). Catherine also had a role in *Scenes of a Sexual Nature,* which, like the other films just mentioned, was released in 2006. That she enjoyed the experience was probably down to the lack of studio interference, which meant that control was retained over the script.

With regards to her appearances in so many films in the course of a single year Tate says:

'The films that are coming out this year are very different. Each character is very different to the one I played in the last film. They're nice small roles.'[23] However, it would not be long until she secured a main role and this happened in *Mrs Ratcliffe's Revolution*.

Released in 2007, Tate played the central role of Dorothy Ratcliffe in this Billie Eltringham movie. The film is based on a true story about a family selling their Yorkshire home and moving to communist East Germany in the 1960s. Catherine found she received a good response from the local people when filming in the north of England. 'I was really touched and a bit overwhelmed,' she states in relation to how much people said they liked her sketch show.[24] Her delight is echoed by the real family behind the story told in the film, who were very happy Catherine Tate chose to take the role.[25]

Not only has Tate managed to do all the work listed above, but she has also found time to tread the boards as well. She played Smeraldina in a 2001 Royal Shakespeare Company production of *A Servant to Two Masters*. In 2007 she acted alongside *Friends'* star David Schwimmer, who played Ross Geller in the long-running and highly popular US sitcom. This opportunity arose when she secured a role in *Some Girl(s)* in the West End. While she was playing this role there were reports that she did not get along with co-star Schwimmer.

Tate had written a piece for the *New Statesman* about her excitement in regards to working with Schwimmer and said how she had found it hard to control such feelings. She found it so difficult to conceal and control her excitement that after a couple of months she became a little strained, to say the least, and Tate wrote, 'It's as much as I can do to smile at the man.' This last sentence was used in isolation from the rest of the piece and deliberately spun by some sections of the press into a story about how Tate did not get along with or like David Schwimmer, which was clearly far from the truth. However, Schwimmer, having experienced the sometimes less than savoury practices of some newspapers, rang Tate and said, 'Please don't be worried about any of this – that's just what they do.'[26]

Some argue that there is still a bias towards male comics and that comedy is a little like an all-boys club to which women find it very hard to gain entry. Tate thinks there are too many excuses made for the fact there are not many female comedians, saying: 'Whether you're male or female, if you're not funny, you're not funny. I don't think making people laugh is a particularly gender-specific thing.'[27]

As previously mentioned, with shows like Dawn French's *Vicar of Dibley* proving immensely popular in the UK and also in the US, and with comedians like Ronni Ancona striking out on their own (a new show called *Ronnie Ancona and Co* has been commissioned by the BBC) she may just have a point.

There is one thing we can be certain of, however. As an actress, comedian or both, Catherine Tate looks set to enjoy success for some years to come. Her name has been firmly established as one of the country's leading female comic performers and despite her shyness, her star has continued to rise. Perhaps paying attention to those early astrological readings was not such a bad idea after all.

ENDNOTES

1. Viner, B, 'Catherine Tate: The shy star,' (The *Independent*, 23rd December 2006)

2. Sawyer, M, 'Catherine the Great,' (The *Observer,* 15th October 2006)

3. 'Catherine Tate makes plea for populism a she takes up key Royal Court role,' (*The Guardian,* 6th December 2006)

4. '*The Catherine Tate Show*: Catherine Tate Interview,' p.1 (uktv.co.uk/g2/item/aid/555680)

5. Teeman, T, 'An intimate tete-a-Tate,' (*The Times,* 23rd December 2006)

6. 'Heard the One About Women and Comedy?' (arts.independent.co.uk/theatre/news/article308803.ece)

7. Sawyer, M, 'Catherine the Great,' (*The Observer*, 15th October 2006)

8. Sawyer, M, 'Catherine the Great,' (*The Observer*, 15th October 2006)

9. Teeman, T, 'An intimate tete-a-Tate' (*The Times*, 23rd December 2006)

10. Viner, B, 'Catherine Tate: The shy star,' (*The Independent*, 23rd December 2006)

11. Teeman, T, 'An intimate tete-a-Tate (*The Times*, 23rd December 2006)

12. Gibson, O, ' The *Guardian* profile Catherine Tate,' (*The Guardian*, 23rd December 2005)

13. Gibson, O, 'The *Guardian* profile Catherine Tate,' (*The Guardian*, 23rd December 2005)

14. Sawyer, M, 'Catherine the Great,' (*The Observer*, 15th October 2006)

15. '*The Catherine Tate Show*: Catherine Tate Interview,' p.1 (uktv.co.uk/g2/item/aid/555680)

16. '*The Catherine Tate Show*: Catherine Tate Interview,' p.1 (uktv.co.uk/g2/item/aid/555680)

17. Kilkelly, D, 'Catherine Tate angry over BAFTA snub,' (www.digitalspy.co.uk/tv/a58287/catherine-tate-angry-over-bafta-snub.html)

18. Sawyer, M, 'Catherine the Great,' (*The Observer,* 15th October 2006)

19. Wright, K, 'An interview with Catherine Tate and Adrian Lester,' p.3 (www.handbag.com/gossip/celebrityinterviews/adrian-lester-catherine-tate)

20. Wright, J, 'Monster smash,' (*The Guardian*, 22nd December 2006)

21. Wright, K, 'An interview with Catherine Tate and Adrian Lester,' p.3 (www.handbag.com/gossip/celebrityinterviews/adrian-lester-catherine-tate)

22. Sawyer, M, 'Catherine the Great (*The Observer*, 15th October 2006)

23. Teeman, T, 'An intimate tete-a-Tate,' (*The Times*, 23rd December 2006)

24. Wright, K, 'An interview with Catherine Tate and Adrian Lester,' p.2 (www.handbag. com/gossip/celebrityinterviews/adrian-lester-catherine-tate)

25. Thorpe, V, 'Proletarian utopia? Am I bovvered? (*The Observer*, 24th September 2006)

26. Mangan, L, "'I'm a lazy control freak.'" (*The Guardian*, 12th July 2005)

27. Mangan, L, "'I'm a lazy control freak.'" (*The Guardian*, 12th July 2005)

NOTE: The sub-headings within this chapter were all taken from the description of Taureans given in *Zolar's Encyclopedia of Ancient & Forbidden Knowledge*, Zolar, F, (1984, Arco Publishing, Inc.)

5. THAT MITCHELL & WEBB EFFECT: *Peep Show*, the BBC and Beyond

David Mitchell was born in Salisbury, England in 1974. His parents were hotel managers initially, but the family moved to Oxford in 1977 where his parents became lecturers. When he was at school he wanted to be one of two things; either a comedian/actor or Prime Minister, though this wasn't common knowledge. In fact, he didn't tell anyone he wanted to be a comedian until attending university when he met others who shared his ambition.[1]

However, Mitchell did perform during his time at prep school, though primarily because he enjoyed playing cards backstage. There were so many students involved that most people were on stage for very short periods and got to spend a lot of their time playing cards. Not until he was asked to play the part of Rabbit in a production of *Winnie the Pooh,* the story goes, did he get a taste for being in the limelight. During his performance he discovered that the way in which he delivered his lines made the audience laugh, and this reaction gave him a sense of the pleasure to be found in performance.[2]

Like Ricky Gervais, Mitchell is a big fan of *The Simpsons*. He does not watch much other comedy because he finds it inhibits rather than inspires. However, he does think *Little Britain* is 'excellent' and likes *The Office* and *Extras*, though he also says he feels more comfortable watching older comedies.[1] Of these he says *Morecambe and Wise*, *Monty Python* and *The Two Ronnies* are his favourites.[3]

Mitchell has been compared to comedian and quiz show host Stephen Fry, but finding it difficult to accept such praise he says: 'It's a very flattering comparison, but I don't think I'm anywhere near as clever as he is.'[4]

Both comedians have appeared together when David was a panellist on Fry's fact-based quiz *QI*.

Robert Webb was brought up in rural Lincolnshire. As early as the age of fourteen he decided he wanted to be a performer. The idea of following this sort of career path came to him when watching the sitcom *Home Sweet Home,* which starred a young Martin Clunes (star of *Men Behaving Badly*), amongst others. Webb says: 'They were having a laugh and I thought, "I could get paid for this!"'[5]

However, Webb had been naturally leaning towards performance and comedy long before. Much like Walliams, Lucas and Tate he was 'the funny one', the entertainer at school. Unlike these others, however, Webb did not do it to deflect attention away from other aspects of himself, he did it because he loved to entertain, to make the other kids laugh. Confident and outgoing, he simply revelled in the attention.

Webb sees his early start in comedy as being quite lucky because he managed to get some 'terrible TV parodies' out of his system through creating them for school reviews at the tender age of fifteen. These parodies included one of the long-running children's programme *Blue Peter*, which was called 'Pink Peter' and was an effeminate version, and a parody of the 80s action series *The A-Team*, which was entitled 'The Gay Team'.

Mitchell and Webb both went on to study at Cambridge University, where the former took history and the latter took English. It was at the famous Footlights venue that they first met during a production of *Cinderella* in 1993. The Footlights is where comedy greats such as Stephen Fry, Hugh Laurie, John Cleese, Graham Chapman, Peter Cook and Griff Rhys Jones could be found in their early days while attending the same university. Webb, a year older than Mitchell, was playing Prince Charming while Mitchell's part was considerably smaller, playing a palace official whose character was intentionally dull and boring. So it seems that even at this early time their stage personas were beginning to take shape as Webb tends to play the more charismatic and social characters while Mitchell's are often more straight-laced, conventional and socially inept.

It was during rehearsals for *Cinderella* that their friendship began, Mitchell making Webb laugh from the outset. Finding that they had such a good rapport, both on and off stage Webb then proposed that the following year they do a two-man show. This show would end up being the first of many they took to the Edinburgh Festival. It was a farce about the First World War which Webb describes as 'fucking terrible'.[6]

After graduating from Cambridge, Webb moved to London in 1996 and spent his first evening there in the cinema trying to keep warm because he could not figure out how to use the key on his new flat's electricity metre. Mitchell was soon in the capital as well and they were both trying to make ends meet, but not to the extent that they had to take just any job.

Since moving to London the pair have done their writing in David Mitchell's flat. 'We sit next to each other and bang it out,' says David. They also get annoyed by daytime TV which they can't help but turn on every now and then – both the programmes themselves and the adverts – while getting distracted whenever the snooker is on.

Because the two of them spend so much time working together they don't often arrange to meet socially. According to Webb: 'On weekends, if we run into each other by accident that's a happy bonus, but we don't particularly go out of our way to say, "What are you doing on Saturday night?"'[7]

They remain great friends, but are conscious that other comedy partnerships of the past have become strained or even collapsed because of too much time spent in each other's company.

They were both members of the BBC sketch show called *Bruiser* before going on to make a low budget show called *That Mitchell and Webb Situation* for the now defunct digital channel Play UK in 2001. They also wrote material for *The Jack Docherty Show* while managing to get crumbs of acting work.

By early 2002 it looked as though the pair were heading nowhere fast. Their ideas were getting rejected and too many of the files of ideas on Mitchell's computer were being moved into 'Former Projects'. But then an opportunity came along which has catapulted them straight from the shadows and into the public eye. As Mitchell says, 'Then *Peep Show* gets commissioned, a six-part sitcom on Channel 4, thank you very much'.[8] They never looked back.

As with Sacha Baron-Cohen, Ricky Gervais and Catherine

Tate, it was a long time before their boat began to come in. In fact, they were on the comedy circuit for nearly ten years before being cast in *Peep Show*, the programme which finally saw them break through.

Peep Show is about two friends, Mark and Jeremy, sharing a flat after Jeremy's relationship with a woman called 'Big Suze' has come to an end prior to the beginning of the series. The trope of the show is to use point of view (POV) shots throughout so that all events are seen through the eyes of a character. This allows the character's thoughts to be included as voiceovers, so the audience is essentially in the mind of whoever is the observer at the time.

The point of view element is often achieved by strapping cameras to the actor's heads, allowing as close a representation of what they're actually seeing as is possible. It is due to the use of this trope

> ## Webb Quote
>
> 'I've never really had to do stuff I actually hate. When I started I was turning down crime reconstructions on Crime Watch. Even when I started I was quite snotty. I've never done anything I thought was rubbish.' Robert Webb.[9]

that the working title of the sitcom was originally POV.

The inclusion of POV, along with the audience hearing interior thoughts, not only makes the show both original and innovative, it also involves the audience in the humour in a very different way to the other comedy discussed in this book. Instead of being onlookers we are asked to put ourselves in the characters' shoes. We are not watching from the outside, we're watching and listening from the inside, are party to their viewpoints both physically and mentally.

Thanks to the POV used in *Peep Show* we become complicit in the actions and thoughts of Mark and Jeremy.

This means we are more immersed and involved than is usual with sitcoms. In a quite unnerving fashion, other characters look directly at 'us' and react towards 'us' so that we become part of the show.

> ### *Peep Show* Quote
>
> '*Peep Show* could be described as a sharper, darker version of *Men Behaving Badly* only, crucially, with laughs for people who don't fantasise about living in a Lynx advert.' Gareth Edwards, producer *That Mitchell and Webb Look*[10]

The humour is a mix of the horrible and the awkward, and is heightened by the use of POV and voiceover thoughts. The 'horrible' element arises through such extreme elements as Jeremy's inappropriate sexual suggestions to women, Mark pretending he's got a brain tumour in order to excuse himself from giving a presentation at work and Jeremy killing, burning and then eating a woman's much-loved pet dog. The extreme discomfort that we share as both characters experience intensely awkward situations is created by the fact that we can hear the thoughts of Mark and Jeremy, giving us an insight into their predicament that we would not otherwise have.

The thoughts of these two characters are often attempts to justify their actions through a peculiar kind of logical reasoning. The audience feels awkward because we know in truth their actions are most definitely not reasonable, that they are quite often the complete opposite. The feeling of awkwardness is further accentuated by the fact that we can witness the results of such actions from the characters' points of view. All too close-up, we see the horrified looks on women's faces when Jeremy makes his sexual suggestions, we see the expressions of Mark's colleagues when claiming he has a brain tumour and we also see the incredulous looks of the woman, her sister and their father when they find out that Jeremy has wrapped up their family dog and disguised it as BBQ leftovers, to cover up the fact that he ran over the poor animal in an earlier scene.

Though we can understand their paths of reasoning, unlike Mark and Jeremy we know their course of action is highly immoral and are aware that a very twisted kind of logic is at work – a logic that won't necessarily be effective. Therefore our sense of awkwardness is increased when events reach a climax and we sit under the direct gaze of the 'victim' of whatever Mark or Jeremy has said or done.

The friendship between Mark and Jeremy (or 'Jez') is kept alive by the fact that they rely on each other and agree on many issues. Jeremy acts as a sort of security blanket for Mark, who is often in a state of interior chaos as regards love and relationships. Their friendship also echoes reality in that the two of them met at university, though at Cambridge and not Dartmouth as Mark and Jeremy did within the context of the show.

Mark is pessimistic whereas Jeremy is generally more optimistic. Mark is a loan manager and considerably more financially successful and intellectual. Jeremy's whole approach to life is more casual and creative, he wants to be a successful musician. He knows he is the intellectual inferior, but thinks he is more popular and attractive than Mark. Because of these latter traits Mark tends to look to Jeremy for guidance when it comes to social and relationship matters, something the audience soon realises he is ill-advised to do and which adds to the humour, especially as they are both prone to disasters when it comes to women. Jeremy is also a sexual predator and very politically incorrect, something reflected in other contemporary comedy such as *Little Britain* and the characters of David Brent from *The Office* and Darren Lamb in *Extras*.

Mark's main and continuing love interest is a work colleague called Sophie Chapman, who he ends up marrying at the end of Series Four. Sophie is played by Olivia Colman and her character's outlook is considerably more sunny and far less cynical than that of Mark.

Alan Johnson is a colleague of Mark's and is played by Paterson Joseph. He and Mark become friends as loan managers at JLB. Jeremy doesn't get along with him and one of the long-running jokes of *Peep Show* is Jeremy opening doors to find Johnson standing behind them. An early draft of the final episode of the show's third series had Johnson committing suicide, but the idea was dropped after it was deemed too dark. However, the show does not play-down its dark element ordinarily, as both Mark and Jeremy are continually involved in ridiculously extreme situations, and are often heard to be thinking ridiculously extreme thoughts. To take another example, in Series Four we see Mark accusing the fitness trainer at his health club of sexual abuse, all to remove him from the vicinity where Jeremy's ex-girlfriend works. Or consider the episode where Jeremy practically prostitutes himself in order to keep a job as 'personal assistant' to an ageing musical hero of his. Underlying the darkness of the show is the fact neither Mark nor Jeremy can find happiness and have personal lives verging on the disastrous.

> **Peep Show Quote**
>
> Jez: 'Stop pissing on my bonfire'
> Mark: 'There is no bonfire!'
> Jez: 'That's because you keep pissing on it.'[11]

The first series of *Peep Show* was broadcast on Channel 4 in 2003 and drew a steady 1.3 million viewers, as did the following three series. Surprisingly enough – considering how convincing the two actors are in their parts – it was not written by Mitchell and Webb, but by another comedy writing partnership, that of Jesse Armstrong and Sam Bain.

Throughout this series the object of Mark and Jeremy's desire is their neighbour. Her name is Toni and her husband's name is Tony, something which causes a degree of humorous confusion. Both of the flatmates want to get to know Toni better and Jeremy in particular is extremely fond of the idea of having a 'fuck buddy' next door, something which highlights his attitude towards women. By the end of the Series One Mark nearly sleeps with Sophie and Jeremy manages to coax a hand-job out of Toni, but only after telling her he is terminally ill. This last element perfectly illustrates Jeremy's predatory and extremely politically incorrect approach to women, which contributes to the often distasteful humour.

> ### *Peep Show* Quote
> 'They're all a bunch of Marks, sitting behind their desks with their ties done up to 11, clicking their fingers to the Lighthouse Family whilst getting their dicks sucked by Alsatians.' Jeremy's friend, Super Hans

In the second series Jeremy fell in love with Nancy, an American spending time in the UK to escape her highly conservative background. Her character is quite bohemian whilst also being a Christian. Jeremy actually ends up marrying her, but then admits to an affair with Toni, leaving the marriage in tatters – the likelihood of the main characters finding happiness in *Peep Show* is slim. Early in 2006 there were rumours that *Peep Show* would not return for a fourth series due to the ratings remaining static ever since the first series despite the show's cult following. The reason why the fourth series was eventually commissioned is thought to be the strong DVD sales for the previous seasons.

Series Three aired later in 2006 and received a British Comedy Award for 'Best Television Comedy'. Despite this, the viewing figures for the next series in 2007 did not improve. However, Channel 4 commissioned the fifth series before the fourth had even been broadcast, again because of the aforementioned DVD sales, which had topped 400, 000 and because of Mitchell and Webb's constantly increasing profile through their successful BBC career with *That Mitchell and Webb Sound* on Radio 4, *That Mitchell and Webb Look* on BBC TV, and the then upcoming live tour entitled *The Two Faces of Mitchell and Webb*. There were also the internet advertisements for Apple Mac which helped to increase the visibility of the comedy duo.

> ### *Peep Show* Quote
> 'Good old Mr Patel, he never says a word whether you're buying cornflakes, fabric softener, or gay porn'. Mark

Something which is of note in regards to the other cast members from *That Mitchell and Webb Look* is that James Bachman, Mark Evans and Olivia Colman were all members of Cambridge Footlights at the same time as Mitchell and Webb.

The fifth series of *Peep Show* is due to air early in 2008 and the duo think it could run for a long time to come. As Webb states: 'It could carry on and on. Sam and Jesse are nowhere near running out of ideas.'[12]

Mitchell also sees no reason why the sitcom cannot continue to run providing new seasons are commissioned by Channel 4. He points out that in the US they get two hundred episodes out of their successful ideas and speaking in 2007 commented, 'We've got twenty-four from *Peep Show* so far, so I think there's a few more in it.'

It has been mentioned that the characters in *Peep Show*

rarely find happiness and even when they do it is always short-lived. This is because *Peep Show* uses diffidence and disappointment as a major part of the humour. We watch the characters go through brief periods of hopefulness and happiness only to see it come crashing down. This is part of the horrible humour present in the show. We know that whatever good things may happen there will always be worse to come, that the hopes and dreams of the main characters will always come to nothing and the frustrated, lost, fumbling status-quo of their lives will return. Perhaps *Peep Show* brings out an element of the *schadenfreude* in us. Perhaps we enjoy watching others' failures because it makes us feel better about our own shortcomings.

Ricky Gervais has described the programme as 'the best sitcom since *Father Ted*' and berated the organisers during his acceptance speech at some comedy awards, saying they shouldn't have ignored *Peep Show* in their choice of nominations.[13] The Fox network commissioned a pilot for a US version of *Peep Show* in 2005, but it did not meet with success when aired. This didn't stop the US based production company Spike TV commissioning its own version, which is to be written and directed by *Curb Your Enthusiasm* producer Robert Weide.

It was thanks to their roles in *Peep Show* that Mitchell and Webb were cast in the roles of a PC and a Mac for the Apple Mac adverts which were highly visible on UK sites on the internet in 2007 (there were also US and Japanese versions with different actors). The ads were written in California, though they did encourage Mitchell and Webb to ad lib additional material. In these advertisements their personas are basically toned down versions of those seen in the sitcom, Mitchell the sensible and constrained one and Webb the more casual and creative personality.

When asked if the money from the adverts has made life more comfortable Webb responded by saying, 'If you're an actor, then definitely, a ludicrous amount of money means you don't have to worry too much about the next gig.'

He also said that he is not allowed to do any adverts for other companies.[14] Mitchell, on the other hand, has already advertised another product in the UK and the TV adverts also utilise an element of *Peep Show*. In these pizza ads we can hear Mitchell's voice and the ad is shot from the point of view of his character; a man interviewing the owner of a pizzeria in a supermarket. This POV element has clearly been taken from *Peep Show* and transposed to this advertisement.

Their appearance in the Apple Mac ads has not led to accusations of the pair selling out as we are now used to film and television stars appearing to promote various products. They also follow in the footsteps of a number of other comedians who have happily put their names to a brand, such as Stephen Fry advertising Twinings Tea and Rowan Atkinson appearing in Barclaycard adverts. This said, they are the only ones that I can recall who appear as doppelgangers of already established characters.

Though there has been no backlash in regards to selling out, there has been a voracious debate caused between PC and Mac users online. Webb describes this situation as 'a holy war': 'You look at some of these internet sites and they're really going for each other.'[15]

Which is no doubt good for the campaign...

On the August 28th 2003 *That Mitchell and Webb Sound* was first broadcast on Radio 4 and went on to win a Sony Radio Award for 'Best Comedy Programme'. There were nearly two years between the first and second series, the second being aired in 2005. A third series came another two years later in 2007. It was this sketch show which was adapted to become BBC2's *That Mitchell and Webb Look* in 2006.

As well as Mitchell and Webb there were other writers and performers involved with the show. These included regular collaborators James Bachman and Olivia Colman. Not performing but writing for the show were both Jesse Armstrong and Sam Bain, the writers of *Peep Show*.

Unlike a number of other sketch shows commissioned for the radio in recent years, such as *Little Britain*, *That Mitchell and Webb Sound* does not use exaggerated characters. Instead it employs a skewed view of the world centralised in the characters played by David and Robert.

These characters include a pair of world-weary snooker commentators called Ted and Pete who are more interested in the seedy underbelly of the sport and their private lives than they are in commentating on the matches taking place. This regular sketch is likely to have arisen due to Mitchell and Webb's enjoyment of snooker, as we have already commented, their work tends to suffer when the snooker is on TV. There are also sketches based on two party planners who find one of their guests is bringing someone seen as a party wrecker – and these wreckers are always famous, if not infamous, people. One example is Ghandi, who is seen as being a bad party guest because of his inappropriate clothing and the fact that he will fast if he does not like the music.

Another series of sketches revolves around a parody of an intelligent quiz show and is called 'Imagine That'. In it, intellectuals are asked to conceive of bizarre ideas, such as 'the biggest jacket potato they can think of'.

Then there's 'Big Talk,' a panel show where the host, Raymond Terrific (Webb), shouts at boffins to solve the world's problems. There's Adrian Locket, played by Mitchell, who is a late-night radio DJ who is sad and lonely. Finally there is 'The Lazy Film Writers', which is a sketch parodying Hollywood films and film genres. In it the lazy writers can't be bothered to arrive at original ideas so they bolt together ideas from already released movies to form incredibly improbable plots, such as a mix of the tennis film *Wimbledon* (2004) and the working class drama *Brassed Off* (1996). There are also smaller sketches in the show, such as birdsong being translated into English.

> **Peep Show Quote**
> 'God, I only asked her to be a hooker, it's not like I asked her to be in telesales.' Jeremy

From the above it is clear that the show's writers take the familiar and spin it in a different way. So instead of *The Sopranos* they bring us the '*Castrati*' and instead of call centres staffed by people from Scotland or India we are presented with ones staffed by children because people find it easier to shout at them (though they do feel guilty afterwards).

When *That Mitchell and Webb Sound* expanded to become *That Mitchell and Webb Look* in 2006 the programme director was David Kerr, who had also directed their Play UK show, *That Mitchell and Webb Situation*. Olivia Colman was again involved, as was James Bachman and Mark Evans, all of whom worked on '*Sound*'. When asked about the involvement of these regular contributors, including Armstrong and Bain, Webb responded, 'It was just because we know them and we love working with them, especially in the case of Olivia and Paterson... And James Bachman has always been on our radio show.'[15]

When referring to his pitch proposing to transfer *That Mitchell and Webb Sound* to television, Webb says '...[it] was the shortest pitch I've ever written.' In the pitch he said that the show '...has worked on radio, just like *Little Britain* worked on radio and *Dead Ringers* worked on the radio, and they transferred successfully to TV, so why don't you transfer this one to TV as well?'[16]

The BBC did as suggested and the show went on to win a BAFTA for 'Best Comedy Programme or Series' in 2007 and its viewing figures soon reached nearly double that of *Peep Show*.

The show featured many of the same sketches as '*Sound*', simply transferring them to the visual format. Ted and Pete, the snooker commentators could be seen and not just heard for the first time as they got drunk and talked about the player's private lives. Also making the move between programmes were 'The Party Planners' and 'Big Talk'.

New to the show was a parody of quiz shows such as Channel 4's *Countdown*. Two contestants shout out what appear to be random numbers until one of them manages to reach 'Numberwang,' which seems to be random and is the title of the sketch. The presenter of this show was played by Robert Webb until they created a German version in Episode 5 featuring David Mitchell at the helm. Then, in the following episode, a new version called 'Wordwang' was shown with the use of numbers being replaced by words and letters.

Also new to *That Mitchell and Webb Look* were 'The Angel Summoner and BMX Bandit', which is a parody of crime-fighting duos like Batman and Robin. There was also 'The Surprising Adventures of Sir Digby Chicken-Caesar,' which had already appeared on '*Sound*', but as Sir Digby Caesar-Salad. These sketches comprised of Sir Digby and his sidekick, Ginger, believing they were detectives of the same ilk as Sherlock Holmes and Doctor Watson when in fact they are drunken tramps.

There was also a sketch about the Nazis which refers to the semiotics of their uniforms with two Nazi soldiers noticing such things as the skulls on their helmets and realising they're supposed to be the bad guys. There is also reference to Nazis in *Peep Show* when Mark is winning the war for them while playing a computer game. Such elements are present partly because of Mitchell's love of history, but he has said of the Second World War, 'I'm always a little bit worried making light of it because of the millions of people who died.'[17]

> ### *Peep Show* Quote
>
> 'What this department needs as a kick up the arse so hard my foot will go right up your digestive tract and wiggle out your mouth like a little leather tongue.' Johnson

What set '*Look*' apart from '*Sound*' was the inclusion of 'behind the scenes' sketches. These featured Mitchell and Webb as themselves on the set of the show. In a way these acted similarly to the Millman parts in *Extras* in that the rest of the show can be seen as fake in comparison to this supposed reality. Therefore you have a divide between the 'staged' and the 'real'. In this case the 'staged' is the character-driven sketches, whereas in *Extras* it was the catchphrase driven sitcom '*When the Whistle Blows*'. The 'real' is Mitchell and Webb behind the scenes and in *Extras* it was Andy Millman's life beyond creating and acting in his sitcom.

This creates an interesting contrast in that, in the case of *That Mitchell and Webb Look*, we see apparent 'real' life presented as comical sketches. In this light real life can be seen as comic and ridiculous. The show is saying that life is both funny and stupid, ridiculous and hilarious, and that we should not take it too seriously.

Unlike other recent comic creations, there are no catchphrases in Mitchell and Webb's shows. The phrase 'Numberwang' is the only phrase from the show to have stuck in the viewing public's mind, though it should be pointed out that the show was never intended to spawn catchphrases. The use of this word in fact came about by chance – both Mitchell and Webb had the phrase shouted at them in the street.[18]

The sketches are filmed in front of a live audience. The tickets for these filmings are in high demand as soon as they are made available, which is indicative of the kind of following the pair

> **Webb Quote**
>
> 'If you had told me five years ago that any of this would have happened, I really wouldn't have believed you'
> Robert Webb speaking in April 2007 [19]

have now got. As the shows' producer, Gareth Edwards, points out: 'The minute you put the tickets on the website people bite your hand off.'[20]

Late in 2006 Mitchell and Webb took '*Look*' on a live tour around the UK, calling it *The Two Faces of Mitchell and Webb*. Effectively they took both *'Sound'* and '*Look*' on tour because it was the live extension of both shows.

This stage show received criticism because the sketches being performed were exact copies from the programme. Brian Logan of the *Guardian* was amongst those who were not impressed, feeling that something else should have been added for the live show to be considered a success: 'Certain TV sequences are recreated verbatim, and little effort has been made to re-imagine the format'.[21]

In *The Times* Dominic Maxwell commented: '(The show)... doesn't just recycle characters and formats, it reproduces whole routines. Hooray, you think, when the show opens with the Blofeld-style villain and his pathetic henchman. "Oh is that it?" you think, when you realise that it IS the TV sketch.'

However, Maxwell does concede that because the show is a TV spin-off there needs to be familiarity with characters, and that the audience have attended in order to see the characters in the flesh. He also goes on, at least, to say that 'Mitchell and Webb's show is witty and well performed.'[22]

Included in these repeated sketches is the one about the anxious Nazi soldier realising that he is one of the bad guys through the semiotics of his uniform. 'Numberwang' also made it into the live act and was used to start the second half, something which immediately got the audience on-side thanks to their recognition and love of the 'Numberwang' sketches in the television show.

'*Big Talk*', the strange show featuring host Raymond Terrific, is said to have had the audience in 'hysterics,' thanks largely to the answers the boffin called Leonard, played by Mitchell, gives to Terrific's questions.[23]

Despite the criticism there was an additional element which did not appear in the TV show, though it could be equated with the 'behind the scenes' sections. This was the theme that the supporting cast of James Bachman and Abigail Burgess were frustrated with their status in the show. This aspect was created through a number of interludes between the other sketches and provided both continuity and originality to the live show.

One thing which is certain about *The Two Faces of Mitchell and Webb'* is that it drew much larger audiences than most, if not all, of their performances in the ten years prior to getting cast in *Peep Show*. In fact, Webb recalls a time when he played at the Brighton Dome with the 1994 Footlights show and in the 2,000 seat arena there were just fifteen people.[24]

Mitchell and Webb's sketch show, in all three of its formats, has less in common with *Little Britain* than it does with *The Catherine Tate Show*. *Little Britain* is more exaggerated and flamboyant than both of the other shows. Like Tate's world, that of Mitchell and Webb is slightly twisted, but still immediately recognisable. We can easily identify elements which reflect our everyday experiences, just from different and often bizarre angles.

Mitchell and Webb displays a element of darkness of the kind discussed in relation to *Peep Show*. In sketches like the ones featuring Nazis or the lonely radio DJ we find a clash between the often bleak or extreme outlook and the humour, which heightens our experience of the latter. This is firstly because it can be rather unexpected to find such things in a comedy show and secondly because the contrast simply makes the humour stand out.

The humour of *That Mitchell and Webb Sound, That Mitchell and Web Look* and *The Two Faces of Mitchell and Webb* is quite different from that displayed in *Peep Show*. The slightly askew view of things is still present and the humour is predominantly based on this rather than any awkwardness or the horrid. The laughs arise from the clever take on various familiar characters and situations, such as the snooker commentators and the panel quiz shows.

In 2007 Mitchell and Webb had a pilot for a science-fiction comedy broadcast on Radio 4. This show, called *Daydream Believers*, starred Mitchell as a tetchy sci-fi writer with Webb's character constantly interrupting him to such a degree that their tedious conversations find their way into the stories the writer is creating, which are the adventures of an alien called

'Baron Amstrad' and his interrupting android companion called 'Info'.[25]

Though much of their work is produced as a team, Mitchell and Webb do work independently from time to time. In April 2007 Webb did a play for Radio 4 called *Portia*, which was about a man waking up in a woman's body. Webb has also gone solo in the BBC Three sitcom *The Smoking Room* and in the improvised wedding comedy flick called *Confetti* (2006).

Confetti was a British film written and directed by Debbie Isitt. It had a mockumentary style and was about three couples trying to win 'Most Original Wedding of the Year.' Also starring in the film were Martin Freeman, who played Tim in *The Office*, quiz show host and stand-up comedian Jimmy Carr, as well as regular Mitchell and Webb collaborator Olivia Colman. The wedding that Webb's character was involved in was a naturist one and Webb took his kit off for the role, though, much to his chagrin, one reviewer later made reference to the 'saggy, flabby Robert Webb'.[26]

Mitchell has become a familiar face on the panels of quiz shows such as *QI* and *Have I Got News For You*. He's also been involved in two shows about lying called *Would I Lie To You?* and *The Unbelievable Truth*. The first is a production for BBC television and the other is for Radio 4. The idea behind the first is a kind of modern take on *Call My Bluff*, only utilising such things as celebrities and television shows rather than words. It's hosted by Angus Deayton and Mitchell is one of the team captains, the other being Lee Mack, the man who noticed Catherine Tate's talent whilst she was doing stand-up at the Edinburgh Festival.

Mitchell is also to be seen in the Michelle Pfeiffer romantic comedy called *I Could Never Be Your Woman*

Sacha Baron-Cohen in the guise of Borat

A typical Ali G pose

Ali G 'Gangster Stylee'

The humour in *Borat* is often visual

Emily Howard and Florence from *Little Britain*

Daffyd 'the only gay in the village' from *Little Britain*

Vicky Pollard, *Little Britain*'s famously obnoxious teenager

Best of friends: Lou and Andy from *Little Britain*

David Brent and the infamous dance scene in *The Office*

Keith dresses up as Ali G in *The Office*

David Bowie sings the 'little fat man' song in *Extras*

Darren Lamb, 'Barry Evans' and Andy Millman from *Extras*

Catherine Tate as the abusive and 'up-front' Nan Taylor

Catherine Tate as stroppy teenager Lauren

Robert Webb and David Mitchell

A distorted 'point of view' shot from *Peep Show*

Peter Kay during his stand-up routine

Peter Kay in *Phoenix Nights* as Brian Potter

Edward and Tubbs in *The League of Gentlemen*

Pauline the jobstart officer from *The League of Gentlemen*

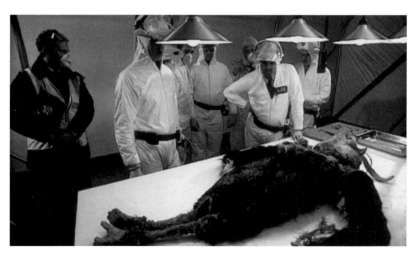

The autopsy of the beast in *The League of Gentlemen*

The 'Local Shop' in Royston Vasey; home of *The League of Gentlemen*

Chris Morris in the *Brass Eye* episode on 'Cake'

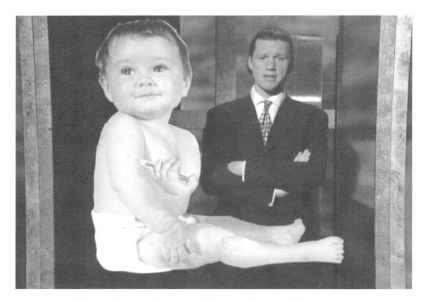

Brass Eye makes good use of surreal humour

Phil Collins duped in the *Brass Eye* episode: 'Paedogeddon'

Alan Partridge, aka Steve Coogan, a pioneer
of horribly awkward comedy

Alan Partridge on *Knowing Me, Knowing You*

Alan Partridge 'live on air' for the fictional 'Radio Norwich'

(2007). However, the biggest film role he has had to date is alongside Webb in the movie called *Magicians* (2007). This was their first film outing together and was directed by Andrew O'Connor. It was written by Jesse Armstrong and Sam Bain, the brains behind *Peep Show* and also co-writers of Mitchell and Webb's sketch show.

The film is about a magic double-act which splits after Webb is found to be having an affair with Mitchell's wife. The night the act splits the woman at the centre of the problems is accidentally sawn in half during the show. After such a public cock-up and the commercial failure that follows, the two magicians are forced back together, though not happily, to try and win a competition.

The effect of entering and taking part in this magic competition is not only an improvement for the duo in terms of finances and status, but also an improvement in their relationship. This shows one of the biggest differences between film comedy and sitcoms. In a film the main characters must undergo change which leads to a new status-quo different from the old. In a sitcom they can attempt to change, or someone can try and change them, but 'they have to revert to type by the end of the episode'.[27]

Webb's character is more of a media flirt than his partner, more of a Darren Brown type, whereas Mitchell's is more of a traditionalist. This reflects their characters in *Peep Show*, though as with the Apple Mac adverts, they have been toned down in the film. This may have been a mistake as the extreme nature of some activities and thoughts in the sitcom are part of its successful cult appeal. By removing this you lose a strong element of humour and are likely to disappoint fans hoping to see more of the same.

Another element in the film which reflects *Peep Show* is

the fact that it is a black comedy. However, such similarities are bound to arise considering it was written by and stars the same people as the sitcom.

In summary, we can see that Mitchell and Webb are by no means responsible for the scripts for *Peep Show* or *Magicians,* which were created by the writing partnership of Armstrong and Bain, who also contributed to the BBC sketch shows, writing such things as the 'Numberwang' sketches. Others also had a hand in writing the sketches for *That Mitchell and Webb Sound, That Mitchell and Webb Look,* and *The Two Faces of Mitchell and Webb* and the acting was also a shared affair. Though Mitchell and Webb fronted all the programmes and were at the centre of the on-screen action, people like Olivia Colman, James Bachman and Mark Evans have also been regulars.

'The Mitchell and Webb effect' is actually a group achievement rather than a partnership, the duo themselves are simply the front men of this group. The shows discussed have all been products of a talented collective, quite a few of whom knew each other from their days at Cambridge Footlights, echoing the foundations of *Monty Python.* Without this collective comedy the UK would be much the poorer. The Mitchell and Webb group have brought us memorable characters, scenarios and shows. They have brought us laughter, both the horribly awkward kind and that of the parodic and slightly surreal nature. All we can hope for is that they continue to deliver their brand of humour to their fans, who have benefited greatly from a peep at the 'sound', 'look' and faces of David Mitchell, Robert Webb and co.

ENDNOTES

1. Ross, D, '*Peep Show*'s David Mitchell and Robert Webb,' p3 (http://news.independent.co.uk/people/profiles/article1988496.ece)

2. Oatts, J, 'Mitchell & Webb,' p.6 (www.digitalspy.co.uk/tv/a43909/mitchell--webb)

3. Mitchell, B, 'Masters of comedy,' (27th August 2006, *The Observer*)

4. Oatts, J, 'Mitchell & Webb,' p.4 (www.digitalspy.co.uk/tv/a43909/mitchell--webb)

5. Ross, D, '*Peep Show*'s David Mitchell and Robert Webb,' p3 (http://news.independent.co.uk/people/profiles/article1988496.ece)

6. Mitchell, B, 'Masters of comedy,' (27th August 2006, *The Observer*)

7. Mitchell, B. 'Masters of comedy,' (27th August 2006, *The Observer*)

8. Mitchell, B, 'Masters of comedy,' (27th August 2006, *The Observer*)

9. Oatts, J. 'Mitchell & Webb,' p.2 (www.digitalspy.co.uk/tv/a43909/mitchell--webb)

10. Oatts, J. 'Mitchell & Webb,' p.2 (www.digitalspy.co.uk/tv/a43909/mitchell--webb)

11. Mitchell, B, 'Masters of comedy,' (27th August 2006, *The Observer*)

12. Oatts, J, 'Mitchell & Webb,' p.3 (www.digitalspy.co.uk/tv/a43909/mitchell--webb)

13. Armstrong, S, 'How the tide turned for Mitchell and Webb,' (29th April 2007, *The Sunday Times*)

14. Oatts, J, 'Mitchell & Webb,' p.2 (www.digitalspy.co.uk/tv/a43909/mitchell--webb)

15. Oatts, J, 'Mitchell & Webb,' p.1 (www.digitalspy.co.uk/tv/a43909/mitchell--webb)

16. Mitchell, B, 'Masters of comedy,' (27th August 2006, *The Observer*)

17. Oatts, J, 'Mitchell & Webb,' p.4 (www.digitalspy.co.uk/tv/a43909/mitchell--webb)

18. Oatts, J, 'Mitchell & Webb,' p.1 (www.digitalspy.co.uk/tv/a43909/mitchell--webb)

19. Mitchell, B, 'Masters of comedy,' (27th August 2006, *The Observer*)

20. Logan, B, 'The Two Faces of Mitchell and Webb,' (http://arts.guardian.co.uk/reviews/story/0,,1929726,00.html)

21. Maxwell, D, 'Mitchell & Webb,' (23rd October 2006, *The Times*)

22. Lowe, B, 'The Two Faces of Mitchell & Webb,' (www.bbc.co.uk/birmingham/content/articles/2006/11/09/mitchell_and_webb_feature)

23. Mitchell, B, 'Masters of comedy,' (27th August 2006, *The Observer*)

24. Armstrong, S, 'How the tide turned for Mitchell and Webb (29th April 2007, *The Sunday Times*)

25. Armstrong, S, 'How the tide turned for Mitchell and Webb,' (29th April 2007, *The Sunday Times*)

26. Mitchell, B, 'Masters of comedy,' (27th August 2006, *The Observer*)

27. Oatts, J, 'Mitchell & Webb,' p.4 (www.digitalspy.co.uk/tv/a43909/mitchell--webb)

6. THE SOUND OF UNSTOPPABLE LAUGHTER: Peter Kay's Road to Somewhere

Peter Kay was born in 1973 in Bolton, where he still lives with his wife, Susan. This you may already know. Something you may not know is that on his second date with Susan he broke his arm while taking her ice-skating. Actually, judging from the phenomenal sales of his autobiography, *The Sound of Laughter,* you may well be aware of this also.

Kay's relatively quick rise to the status of national treasure echoes those of all the other comedians already discussed, but with one difference. His success was built on his reputation in the north of England, though his observational humour translates just as well to a southern audience, as proved by the success of his various stand-up shows.

Kay discovered he had comic talent at an early age. As with Lucas, Walliams, Tate and Robert Webb, he was a classroom entertainer – for the simple reason that he liked getting laughs from fellow pupils at his Catholic primary and secondary schools (his mother being an Irish Catholic). One of his school reports from a teacher who many might consider lucky to have played audience to this emerging talent reads, 'Peter seems unable to resist trying to amuse the children around him.'[1] This trait has continued, only it is adults as well as children that he is targeting these days.

Of his school days Kay says: 'Even then I kind of knew my talent for comedy was more of a vocation, a calling.' A statement which seems very apt considering the nuns who taught him would have seen their lives as a 'calling' too. The nuns at his primary school did not often organise school plays, but did stage a nativity every year. Peter got to play the Innkeeper at one such performance and rather than telling Mary and Joseph there was no room for them to stay he offered them an en-suite room with full English. Though the nuns weren't impressed, the audience loved it and Kay says of that experience: 'What a wonderful feeling it was to stand on stage and listen to that sound, the sound of laughter. I felt happy, I felt safe.'[2]

In secondary school he played the lion in *The Wizard of Oz* and proceeded to cock his leg up to relieve himself on stage, something which drew the same kind of response from the audience as his 'Innkeeper' antics. Kay was clearly shaping up to be something of an audience favourite. And it was not only in live audiences that he was able to charm. Despite leaving school with only one GCSE in Art, Kay managed to lie his way into Liverpool University, pretending not only that he had more GCSEs, but A-levels as well.

Finding the more academically orientated work hard going, he transferred to Salford in 1994, where there was much more hands-on experience and less essay work. Finding that he really thrived in this atmosphere, Kay decided to take a comedy option which happened to be offered at the time.

Unfortunately, his comic career did not exactly take off when he graduated. Instead he spent six years doing various low-pay, low-status jobs. Not a pleasant introduction to working life, you might think, but these were surprisingly fruitful years. Apart from giving him the impetus to pursue his comedy career at a later stage, this period provided him with some invaluable material for the shows which he would end up writing, acting in, and often directing. Amongst other things, he worked at a bingo hall, in the Franny Lee toilet roll factory in Bolton and as an usher in a cinema.

It was not until his family started to encourage him to make the most of his talent, and after he'd been given the heave-ho from yet another job, that Kay decided it was time to try and build a career in comedy. When he first began doing stand-up, Kay found that a number of other comedians on the circuit accused him of pilfering their material. As a result he started to devote his act to the observational humour we have come to know and love, the logic being that if he was telling stories from his own life he could not possibly be accused of theft.

Kay soon noticed that any success he enjoyed on the stand-up circuit was due to the simplest of narrative techniques when relaying his anecdotes. He realised that they were best told in first person. As soon as he told jokes in the third person, such as 'You know when you're walking down the street...' rather than, 'I was walking down the street...' the audience did not laugh as much.[3]

On starting out, and at a time when he was trying to get gigs at clubs near to his home in order to avoid the expenditure of travel, Kay rang Manchester's Buzz Club and they suggested he put himself in for the North-West Comedian of the Year

Competition. Kay took the advice and won the coveted title in 1997, beating Johnny Vegas into second place.[4] This was the first of a number of awards for Kay. He went on to win Channel 4's 'So You Think You're Funny' and came in as runner-up in the BBC's 'New Comedy' award. In 1998 he was also nominated for a Perrier Award at the Edinburgh Festival, which Catherine Tate was later nominated for in 2000 whilst appearing in the Lee Mack show called 'New Bits'.

> ### Kay Quote
>
> 'When I was a kid I used to pray every night for a new bike. Then I realised that the Lord doesn't work in that way, so I stole one and asked him to forgive me.'

The first time Kay ventured from the stage and onto our television screens was in 1997. This was in a programme intended to showcase new talent called *New Voices* and the episode in which he appeared was entitled 'Two Minutes'. Though he did not write the script (this credit going to Johanne McAndrew), he starred as a getaway driver for two friends who were attempting to rob a pub.

Kay's next break involved him replacing Dennis Pennis on *The Sunday Show,* where his segment was named 'Peter Kay's World of Entertainment'. Now familiar with his work, and seeing how effectively he had handled his slot on *The Sunday Show,* in 1998 Channel 4 offered him the chance to make an episode for their programme *The Comedy Lab.* Called 'The Services', it had a similar 'spoof documentary' feel to it as would later prove so popular in *That Peter Kay Thing* – and in fact served as a pilot for that series. 'The Services' showcased Kay's writing ability, along with his talent for playing multiple characters, something also seen in *Phoenix Nights.*

That Peter Kay Thing was co-written by Peter Kay, Dave

Spikey and Neil Fitzmaurice, all of whom are comedians. Kay and Spikey had met at the North-West Comedian of the Year Competition the year Kay had won. Spikey had been the winner in the previous year and was compering at the 1997 event. In *That Peter Kay Thing* there are actually twenty-two other comedians and many of the extras are friends from Bolton. Kay even managed to get a production job for a friend who was an ex-cinema usher like him.[5]

It was this programme which finally introduced a wide audience to Peter Kay's comic talent and in which we first saw him playing multiple characters. It was based almost entirely on Kay's experiences during his six years moving from one job to another. The first episode was called 'In The Club', and featured characters who would later go on to appear in a spin-off we all know, *Phoenix Nights*, which actually had 'In The Club' as its working title. However, in this opening episode of *That Peter Kay Thing* the club was called 'The Neptune'. At the end of the episode it burns down and this paved the way for its rebuilding and renaming as 'The Phoenix'.

Kay's previous jobs were the direct inspiration for episodes entitled 'Eyes Down,' 'The Arena,' and the pilot episode made for Channel 4's *Comedy Lab*, 'The Services' (in which Kay makes a rare appearance as a woman called 'Pearl Harbour'). The first of these episodes draws on his time working in a bingo hall and the second on his time at Manchester Arena. These allow us to see that Kay not only draws on his life for stand-up, but can also successfully do so when creating a comedy series. The depth of experiences he encountered in the work place before becoming a professional comedian stands him in good stead, as do his great observational skills.

In 2000 the heavy promotional campaign for his new

stand-up show entitled 'Live at the Top of the Tower' ensured that fame came knocking on Kay's door with some vigour.

> ## Kay Quote
>
> 'I might be collecting wheely bins in twelve months time, but at least they'll be wheely bins outside back gates that I know, in a part of the country that I love. There's no place like home'.[6]

The first series of *Phoenix Nights* followed in 2001, its main characters having already appeared in the first episode of *That Peter Kay Thing*. The downbeat and lacklustre sense of northern club land is palpable in the show. However, it has a nostalgic feel to it rather than a patronising one, just as his stand-up does. At times the show even feels like it could have been filmed in the 70s thanks to the authentically styled club, harking back to the golden age of variety shows and weekends when the surrounding community came together to watch the acts. Kay's portrayal is obviously affectionate, recalling a time much different from the present day.

Though the environment portrayed in *Phoenix Nights* is looked upon with evident fondness, the characters themselves are not all likeable. With his downbeat attitude and almost complete lack of admirable traits, Brian Potter, the licensee of the Phoenix Club is not a person we can empathise with. As a perfect example of his not-so-likeable but very funny character, take the incident in which an employee of the club, the Captain, is accidentally killed. Rather than showing any distress at the Captain's demise Potter is more worried about who is going to do the door duty at the club, putting his own petty concerns first. The man is clearly selfish and business-obsessed, but there is a lot of humour created through his character's somewhat surprising reaction to the death. In our everyday experience this isn't how we'd expect people to act.

Though some people might think such things as 'Who's going to do the door duty?', most would be far too embarrassed to say such things out loud in such circumstances.

This lack of likeable qualities is evident in many of Kay's lead characters and is essential to his style of humour. If we were to like Potter *et al* then the events conspiring against them, as they so often do, wouldn't be as funny. Instead we would simply empathise with and feel sorry for these characters. Part of Kay's cleverness is in creating personalities that we recognise from our own life experience, people that we don't necessarily dislike while at the same time we don't particularly like either. This ambivalence enables us to laugh when things go wrong for these people.

As with *That Peter Kay Thing*, the cast of *Phoenix Nights* consisted largely of comedians the writers had met on the comedy circuit. In a particularly unusual set-up, Kay's mother was also a member of the cast and any jokes she didn't find funny were cut from the show. Kay's wife, Susan, also found herself involved when she stepped in after an actress did not make it to the auditions. Commenting on the fact that people like his mother, his wife and his best friend have taken roles in *Phoenix Nights* Kay said: 'Like me, they hadn't done any acting before this. But acting is bollocks, it's just confidence'.[7]

A second series of *Phoenix Nights* aired in 2002 and won the 'People's Choice Award' at the British Comedy Awards that year. Unlike the first series, this featured not only the writing and acting talents of Kay, but also his directing skills. The first series of the show had been partially filmed at the St Gregory's Social Club in the Farnworth area of Bolton, but this time around it was decided that the entire series should be filmed on location.

The year 2002 was a good one for Kay. His tour entitled *My Mum Wants a Bungalow* sold out and broke box office records. He even managed to turn the high demand for tickets into a joke used in the act, stating that the empty seats of late arrivals could have fetched £600 on eBay. Forty extra dates had to be added in order to cope with the show's popularity, proving that the comedian already had a huge following despite his avoidance of performances in London, preferring to stay nearer to home in the north of the country.

When asked about his preference for performing in the north Kay stated, 'I'm not particularly patriotic towards the north. It's just that's where my home is and I love being at home.' This said, he is conscious of alienating those who live in the south. When Channel 4 suggested naming *That Peter Kay Thing* 'Our Friends in the North' Kay strongly objected.[8]

In 2003 the DVD of Peter Kay live at the Bolton Albert Hall was the fastest selling stand-up comedy DVD of all time, shifting nearly 300,000 copies within two weeks of its release. In 2004 Channel 4 showed an abridged version of the performance and it brought in a massive 6.7 million viewers. This is truly an impressive audience share, especially when you consider that *Peep Show*, starring Mitchell and Webb, only managed about 1.3 million viewers for its first four seasons and Gervais and Merchant's *The Office* pulled in 4 million.

Max and Paddy's Road to Nowhere also aired in 2004. It was a spin-off from *Phoenix Nights* written by Peter Kay and Patrick McGuinness – who plays Paddy and is a good friend of Kay's, to the extent that he was the best man at his wedding. The series also starred the writers in the lead roles and Kay directed. Despite the fact it came two years after *Phoenix Nights* it is set immediately afterwards.

In April 2006 and repeated in March 2007, Channel 4 aired a night of programmes dedicated to Peter Kay. During this festival of fun Max and Paddy were seen discussing the tribute, with 'Max' joking that he didn't like Kay and thought the channel was going downhill for devoting a whole night's programming to him.

> ### Kay Quote
>
> 'I was doing some decorating, so I got out my stepladder. I don't get on with my real ladder'.

The reason Channel 4 could dedicate an entire evening to Kay and still achieve decent ratings is due to his immensely broad appeal. Kay's humour crosses any north/south divide and contains much material that resonates with the working and lower middle classes. The attraction is in part due to his use of material from his experiences doing the kinds of jobs many of us have had at some point during our own lives. We recognise the kinds of situations he is talking about and the people in them. This recognition means the comedy is inclusive – we, the audience, are party to the jokes because they relate to everyday life – and this is very evident in his next venture.

In 2006, Kay's autobiography, *The Sound of Laughter,* was published, beating all records for the genre by selling nearly 600,000 copies in the first two months. It easily outsold other biographies of the time, including those of giant global names like Sharon Osbourne and David Beckham. Part of its success is no doubt due to the fact that it acts as an extension to his comedy. Rather than writing it from a serious angle, Kay has written his life's story filled with humour, nostalgia and references to pop culture. What you end up with is a comedy book which almost reads like fiction, so prolific are the humorous incidents in Kay's life that it seems like they cannot possibly all be true.

Like Catherine Tate, in 2006 Peter Kay, also appeared in *Doctor Who*. In an episode called 'Love & Monsters', Kay played the sinister Victor Kennedy, an unsavoury character who turns out to be an alien called 'the Abzorbaloff' in disguise. Though this episode of the popular series was a lot funnier than most of *Doctor Who*, Kay's role was still more serious than the majority of other characters he has played. The part was given to him thanks to a fan letter he wrote praising the lead writer of the show, Russell T. Davies.[9]

Another link with Catherine Tate is Peter Kay's appearance on her show. He played an old man called Tommy who was a friend of Nan Taylor, the swearing and highly critical 'old biddy' played to great effect by Tate. Catherine Tate also appeared in *That Peter Kay Thing*, playing community leader Valerie in the episode about the oldest paperboy in Britain.

Like any good comedian, Kay does his utmost to ensure his vision is retained during the filming of his shows. He will fight his corner so that we get to see what he intended – though with his mum acting as his 'humour barometer' there are sometimes modifications.

There are other notable connections within the comedy scene that involve Peter Kay. Along with Catherine Tate's appearance on *That Peter Kay Thing*, a number of well known faces have appeared in Kay's programmes, all with a certain cult status. In the first episode of *Phoenix Nights* Series One, Roy Walker, one time host of the game show Catchphrase, took a cameo role. Then, in the first episode of Series Two, Jim Bowen, who used to host Channel 4's game show *Bullseye,* appeared. In the second episode of *Max and Paddy's Road to Nowhere* old rocker and Slade lead singer

Noddy Holder even made an appearance. By including this type of 'guest star' – whom many would consider as being past their prime – Kay feeds his habit of referencing popular culture whilst also adding to the nostalgia evident in his shows.

Peter Kay has made appearances in both the 2003 and 2005 Comic Relief programmes on the BBC. In the first of these he shared the stage with Steve Coogan's creation Alan Partridge (we will be taking a closer look at the work of Coogan in Chapter Nine). For the 2005 event Tony Christie re-released his 1971 hit '(Is This the Way to) Amarillo?' and Kay was featured in the song's video, the tune having been used in *Phoenix Nights*. The single reached Number 1 in the UK and stayed there for an incredible seven weeks, raising a considerable amount of money for charity in the process. Also raising funds for Comic Relief in 2007 was a re-recording of The Proclaimer's hit 'I'm Gonna Be (500 Miles)', which Kay performed alongside *Little Britain*'s Matt Lucas.

Away from the small screen, Peter Kay can be found making appearances in a number of movies. He can be seen in Steve Coogan's *24 Hour Party People* (2002), as well as in *Roddy Smythe Investigates* (2003) and *The League of Gentleman's Apocalypse* (2005). The voice of PC McIntosh in *Wallace & Gromit: The Curse of the Were-Rabbit* (2005) was also provided by Kay.

Despite the fact Kay rarely drinks alcohol, he featured in the highly popular ad campaign by John Smiths. He has also appeared in *Coronation Street* and on *Parkinson, Friday Night with Jonathan Ross* and *The Paul O'Grady Show*. In fact, he was once the warm-up act for Michael Parkinson. This man is certainly not shy of public appearances.

In terms of influences, Kay's greatest comic hero is probably Ronnie Barker. When he was young he sent a fan letter to the late star of British comedy and received a reply. Barker wrote his response as the central character from the prison-based sitcom *Porridge*, called Norman Fletcher, even writing it on Her Majesty's Prison notepaper.[10] A tribute was made to Barker at the British Academy of Film and Television in 2004, and as a speaker at the event, Kay paid his dues to Barker, whom he cited as an inspiration to his work.

> ### Kay Quote
> 'Knowledge is knowing a tomato is a fruit. Wisdom is not putting it in a fruit salad.'

Though he is not a particular fan of the Bolton Wanderers Football Club, Kay has performed at their home ground: the Reebok Stadium. The club's fans have also adopted 'Amarillo' as their theme song and you can hear it being played whenever the team score at the ground.

Unlike Lucas, Walliams and Tate, Pete Kay's comedic tendencies have not been formed by any childhood trauma. His humour is largely derived from his observational nature, as he has always entertained himself by writing down funny events that took place at his various jobs and even amusing things managers or co-workers would say.

That his reliance on nostalgia and references to popular culture makes Kay immediately and easily accessible to a very wide audience is aided by the fact he rarely swears. There is also no cruelty or malice evident in his stand-up, though there is evidence of the former in his television shows.

He talks about things that people are familiar with and enjoy hearing about. Jokes from his stand-up shows that reference popular culture include musings like: 'Do illiterate people get the full effect of Alphabet Soup?' and 'Old women with mobile phones look wrong!' He also mentions such things as Cup-A-Soup, Frisbees and Hobnob biscuits. The familiar and the everyday get a look in every time. Products like these have been around for decades and people will relate to them through childhood memories as they are not commonly used or eaten in adulthood. Therefore they evoke the past and make people feel nostalgic.

> **Kay Quote**
>
> 'My nana belongs to the generation that is totally oblivious to the ever-changing world of political correctness. I could have died the other week when we were in Primark and she asked the young shop assistant if the blouse that she'd seen in the sale was available in nigger brown.'

To play up the nostalgic appeal of his shows, Kay also mentions old sayings like 'Sticks and stones may break my bones, but names will never hurt me!' and 'Fight fire with fire', to the great amusement of his audience who are aware that these doctrines they were brought-up to believe in were often quite ridiculous. But sayings like these evoke strong memories of childhood, and are powerful tools in adding warmth to the comedy here.

'So, where does Peter Kay fit into a book about horribly awkward humour?' you may ask. Well, it's evident both in his stand-up and his TV shows. In Kay's stand-up there is plenty of the horrible, but none of the awkward: 'I saw six men kicking and punching the mother-in-law. My neighbour said "Are you going to help?" I said "No, six should be enough."'

Though it is funny, the actual events described are not. What makes us laugh is the fact this joke follows a great tradition of mother-in-law gags whilst also twisting what we would expect to be his reaction when witnessing such an attack.

Kay Quote

'He's not in the tradition of the modern comedian at all...his comedy is observational in the best sense, sweet and honest. When we first saw him, I remember thinking he was a great talent who would be around for a long time.' Kevin Lygo, Channel 4's director of television who first brought Peter Kay to our screens.[11]

Further examples of the horrid from his stand-up include, 'My mum was a ventriloquist and she was always throwing her voice. For ten years I thought the dog was telling me to kill my father,' or 'I've often wanted to drown my troubles, but I can't get my wife to go swimming.'

These create humour because, coupled with the horrid, they are unexpected and produce highly amusing images in our minds.

Like the previous example, they also fall into strong traditions in humour and are therefore instantly identifiable as belonging to the plethora of jokes about marriage and relationships that centre on dissatisfaction and discord. We can see that Peter Kay is adhering to comic traditions and in so doing he creates 'safe' humour for the audience which may not be challenging, but is comfortingly recognisable.

That Peter Kay Thing was a six-part series with a spoof documentary format which also contained elements of this humour, but took the elements of the awkward and/ or horrible further still. Broadcast in 1999, the first episode features the Neptune club, the licensee being the now well known, wheelchair-bound Brian Potter. Played by Kay, Potter is a stingy and rather drab man who lost the use of his legs after getting trapped behind a fruit machine when his previous club got flooded. This in itself is a good example of horrible humour; the events themselves being funny, but the result not so.

Another good example of horribly awkward humour in *That Peter Kay Thing* arises in the episode entitled 'The Ice Cream Man Cometh': The man referenced in the title, the ridiculously named Mr Softytop, tries selling his wares at the site of road accidents. He also tries to increase profits by renting pornographic films, two of the titles in stock being *Shaving Private Ryan* and *Look Who's Porkin'*.

These elements are part of the pantheon of horrid humour. Mr Softytop's business sales method is ruthless and makes viewers feel awkward while also providing humour because it is so shocking and opposed to normality. It is a desperate measure that no ice cream man would really lower himself to.

In the first episode of Series One of *Phoenix Nights* we find evidence of horrible humour in the form of a Nazi fruit machine and a racist folk band. The latter provides some awkward moments for the club's licensee, Brain Potter. We witness his discomfort as he realises the nature of the band's songs and desperately wants them off the stage. We feel the awkwardness of the situation as the audience take in the lyrics and Potter realises that things have gone badly wrong.

In Episode Two Ray Von accidentally kills the Captain and there's a violent confrontation in an echo of the War of the Roses as a bucking bronco tournament turns nasty and those from Lancashire fight people from Yorkshire. There is also an unforgettable piece of horrible humour when a drunk horse attempts to have sex with the bronco.

Brian Lard, the fire safety inspector who is rumoured to interfere with dogs, appears in Episode Three. A picture is altered on a computer to make it look like a virtually naked man with a dog is actually Lard acting out his warped fetish. This is funny in a shocking and unusual way, while also being quite a gross image to implant in audience members' minds. In the same episode there is also a psychic who tells people the kind of news they do not want to hear. We feel awkward when witnessing the reactions of those who fall victim to her predictions, and also as we watch Potter try to cope with the problem. It also gives rise to humour because we all know about psychics and it is a funny take on what they do, like the slightly warped view of things that Mitchell and Webb have in their comedy.

Kay Quote

Paddy: 'Prostitutes in Amsterdam are dead filthy, this one I went to, she made me wash my old man in the sink.'

Max: 'What, you took your dad?'

The same elements of humour are evident in the second series of *Phoenix Nights*. In Episode Two there is a memorable inflatable which bears more than a passing resemblance to a penis and causes Potter more headaches. In Episode Four we see Jerry (Dave Spikey) urinating in front of some of the club's clientele after his medication makes him lose the plot. The amusement arises as a result of his actions and also the reaction of the crowd as we watch and cringe.

In the fifth episode of Series Two, Brain is stuck for a whole night on his stair lift thanks to a power cut. In the same episode, Max the doorman (Peter Kay) is hired to kill a woman's husband, though he cannot go through with it, despite taking Paddy along.

This latter plot line is part of the build-up to Max and Paddy leaving in order to star in their own spin-off show. In the final episode of this series of *Phoenix Nights* the duo meet the man that Max was paid £8,000 to kill, and his wife confronts them about their failure to do so. She goes on to inform them that she has in turn paid someone to kill them.

At the end of the final episode Max and Paddy leave in a motor home Max bought with his 'hit' money at the end of episode five. This sets the stage for *Max and Paddy's Road to Nowhere*, which, incidentally, never explains or even mentions the reason for the pair of hapless doormen being on the road together.

The elements discussed above show that *Phoenix Nights* contains both the horrible and the awkward. Without them Brian Potter's character would be lessened because it is him who has to deal with things when they go horribly wrong. He is as inept as most of the other characters, and this adds a great deal to the comedy. We watch as each episode pleasingly builds to what we know will be a catastrophe, and we wait in anticipation to see how the chaos will unfold and be dealt with.

Returning briefly to the fire safety officer called Keith Lard who appeared both in *That Peter Kay Thing* and *Phoenix Nights*, it is of note that the show's makers paid an undisclosed sum to 'a Mr Keith Laird'. Laird was a real fire safety officer in Bolton who claimed the character had caused him distress. It had been publicly affirmed that the character was not based on the real safety officer, however as this was contradicted by early interviews with Kay when he was doing promotional work, the man clearly felt he had a case against the programme makers.[12] *Max and Paddy's Road to Nowhere* displays some horribly awkward humour too, not least when Paddy takes part in a shoot for a porn movie only to discover it's not for the heterosexual market. Like Kay's stand-up, the series also contains some pop culture references. These include an *A-Team* parody when the pair modify their van in order to escape from a garage, an homage to the Dustin Hoffman and Jon Voight film *Midnight Cowboy* (1969), and a reference to Kay's John Smiths advertising campaign.

This last element is self-referential and there is more of this type of material in the series when several characters from Phoenix Nights are seen in Episode Two. We also see Brain Potter in Episode Four when he visits the pair in prison and tries to secure their release.

There had been a second series of *Road to Nowhere* announced and it was supposed to be broadcast in 2006. However, it seems that instead of continuing with this idea Kay is going create a programme with Channel 4 called '*I'm Peter Kay*', though no progress has been made with this project.

Peter Kay says that he has already penned Series Three of *Phoenix Nights*, though without Spikey or Fitzmaurice, who apparently no longer even speak to him (allegedly due to the fact that the full title of the first series was Peter Kay's *Phoenix Nights*, though the decision to name it thus was reportedly taken by Channel 4 executives and not Peter Kay himself).

Some people have been very pleased at the prospect of a third series of the show. Others have expressed concern that two of the writers of both previous series are not involved and also will not be playing their on-screen characters – Jerry St Clair and Roy Von. Adding to this concern is the fact that Max and Paddy are unlikely to return after hitting the road at the end of the second series and going on to star in their own spin-off, which even gave rise to a spoof fitness DVD called *Max & Paddy's: The Power of Two*.

In 2007 Kay revealed that he and Craig Cash from *The Royle Family* were going to write a new sitcom together. In it Peter is set to play a binman. At the time of writing they are still in talks with broadcasters. It is also the case that two specials of *Max and Paddy's Road to Nowhere* have apparently been written, though there is no news on when they may be produced.

Writing for *The Times* in 2006, Jane Wheatley notes that, 'According to his fans, the secret of Kay's success lies partly in his kindness – he doesn't do cruel humour – and partly in his small-town, small-time material.'

You could also add to this statement that his comedy is somewhat old fashioned, lacking the swearing of many contemporary comedians and also lacking the shock value of a show like *Little Britain* or the challenging nature to be found in such programmes as *Have I Got News For You*.

Another clear reason why Peter Kay is so popular with the public is because he has stayed true to his roots. In this way he has followed in the footsteps of other comedians who have used their backgrounds to shape their humour, the most notable being Victoria Wood. Kay has managed to utilise his background not only for his stand-up, but also in his TV shows. This means Peter Kay's popularity is underpinned by his common touch, the basis of Kay's comedy.

ENDNOTES

1. Kay, P, *The Sound of Laughter*, p.33 (2007, Century)

2. Kay, P, *The Sound of Laughter*, p.35 (2007, Century)

3. 'Profile: Peter Kay: There's Nowt as Funny as him Sticking to his Roots,' (www.timesonline.co.uk/tol/comment/article495220.ece?token=null&offset=12)

4. 'The Pride of Bolton,' p.1 (www.prideofmanchester.com/comedy/peterkay)

5. Wilson, O, 'Bolton Wanderer,' p.4 (www.wilco.dircon.co.uk/peterkay)

6. 'Profile: Peter Kay: There's Nowt as Funny as him Sticking to his Roots,' (www.timesonline.

co.uk/tol/comment/article495220.ece?token=null&offset=12)

7. Wilson, O. 'Bolton Wanderer,' p.4 (www.wilco.dircon.co.uk/peterkay)

8. 'The Pride of Bolton,' p.1 (www.prideofmanchester.com/comedy/peterkay)

9. Wheatley, J, 'The Face: Peter Kay - Bolton Wonder,' (*The Times*, 10th March 2006)

10. Wheatley, J. 'The Face: Peter Kay - Bolton Wonder,' (*The Times*, 10th March 2006)

11. McLean, G, 'The *Guardian* profile: Peter Kay (*The Guardian*, 15th October 2004)

12. 'The Pride of Bolton,' p.3 (www.prideofmanchester.com/comedy/peterkay)

7. THE LEAGUE OF GENTLEMEN: You'll Never Leave Royston Vasey

'The League of Gentlemen' is not just the name of a macabre comedy, it is also the name of the group of four men who work together to create the blackly comic creations that inhabit the infamous village of Royston Vasey. This group is made up of Mark Gatiss, Steve Pemberton, Reece Shearsmith and Jeremy Dyson.

The first three met at Bretton Hall drama college early in the 90s. Dyson had studied at Leeds University and was introduced to the group by Gatiss. All four write the comedy series, though only Gatiss, Pemberton and Shearsmith are actors and they play all the main characters.

The 'League' was formed in 1995, taking the name 'The League of Gentlemen' from the 1960 crime comedy movie starring Jack Hawkins and based on a novel by John Boland. The group had in fact been performing together since 1994, though without their familiar collective name and before making their alliance official.

They first began to get noticed when they took their sketch

show to the Edinburgh Fringe Festival in 1996. Wearing tuxedos and devoid of costumes or make-up, they wanted to avoid the 'northern comedian' tag. This image, along with their name, was intended to give the impression of a 1950s revue.[1] They went back to Edinburgh in 1997 and won the Perrier Award which, as mentioned, both Catherine Tate and Peter Kay had been nominated for in 2000 and 1998 respectively, and which Steve Coogan won in 1992.

This led to a series on BBC Radio 4 called *On the Town with The League of Gentlemen*, which aired late in 1997. This won a Sony Award and went on to transfer onto the small screen, becoming *The League of Gentlemen*. In the radio series the town where the characters lived was called 'Spent'. The change to 'Royston Vasey' occurred in the transition to TV and is the real name of stand-up comedian Roy Chubby Brown. He was not offended by the use of his name and even made appearances in the show as the foul-mouthed mayor of the village.

The League... went on to have three television series on BBC2 in 1999, 2000 and 2002, as well as a Christmas Special in 2000. A movie called *The League of Gentlemen's Apocalypse* was released in 2005 and featured appearances by Victoria Wood, Simon Pegg, Peter Kay and Bernard Hill. The series has won not only with a BAFTA, but also a Royal Television Society award and the Golden Rose of Montreux.

BBC Choice aired a half-hour special in 2000 which was a behind-the-scenes look at the show. In 2002 another programme was broadcast on the same channel, this one looking at the making of the third series and entitled *The Making of The League of Gentlemen*. The show has also been aired in the US both on Comedy Central and BBC America, and has got quite a following in Australia.

As part of the Comic Aid charity benefit for the tsunami disaster, which was held in 2005, a one-off sketch was shown in which the characters of Tubbs and Papa Lazarou kidnap the actress Miranda Richardson.

The League of Gentlemen is best described as a gothic comedy with touches of the sketch show, the sitcom and the soap opera, though these are all dark touches. It gives numerous nods to horror films. Its horror-based tones meant the programme gained immediate cult status. The show is also credited by some people with having helped revive the sketch show format, along with *Little Britain* and *The Catherine Tate Show*.

The show's acutely awkward nature is immediately apparent. Its influences include the portmanteau[2] horror films of the 1970s, such as *Tales from the Crypt* (1962) and *Vault of Horror* (1973). There are also references to various horror flicks dotted throughout the episodes. These references include a policeman visiting local shop owners Edward and Tubbs in the first episode of the first series, a nod to the 1973 cult favourite *The Wicker Man*, in which Edward Woodward plays a policeman whose investigations take him to a strange and sinister community. This *Wicker Man* connection is underlined when Tubbs calls out 'we didn't burn him' in reference to the hiker the policeman is trying to track down. This joke involves a knowing nod to the fact that Edward Woodward's character is burnt to death in the movie.

Another reference to classic horror films can be seen in the second episode of Series One and again involves the local shop. When two building surveyors go into the shop and one taps a glass container with pink and red material in it, the material suddenly moves and he jumps back. This is a reference to the *Alien* films. In the second film of the quartet a character taps a container with an alien egg-impregnator inside and the creature suddenly moves. The pink and red material within the local shop container is also reminiscent of the alien eggs seen in the films.

Along with the horror references there is also a reference to Quentin Tarantino's *Reservoir Dogs* (1992) in Series One. The relevant scene is set in a warehouse and *The League of Gentlemen* team use camera angles and motion which is similar to that seen in Tarantino's film. The use of a camera circling characters, for example, is used at the start of *Reservoir Dogs* and during the three-way stand-off in the warehouse, and the scene in *The League of Gentlemen* we mention echoes this as we see Pop, the Greek immigrant and his two sons, Al and Rich.

One reference which has been mentioned is the Stanley Kubrick film *A Clockwork Orange* (1971). In the relevant 'Solutions' sketch, the characters can be seen drinking glasses of milk, like the violent gang in the movie who are repeatedly seen visiting the Milk Bar under the watchful eye of their leader, Alex. However, in an interview Mark Gatiss has denied that this scene is influenced by Kubrick's film, so the parallels may simply be coincidental.[3]

The village of Royston Vasey, which is really a town called Hadfield in Derbyshire, is a character in itself. The name has become synonymous with the *League* and with 'dark goings on'. It creates a sinister and brooding backdrop for the characters and the situations they find themselves in. It's always present, and its presence is palpable. It is located in the Peak District in the north of England and the sign when you enter the parish reads 'Welcome to Royston Vasey. You'll Never Leave.' This sets the tone of the village populated with often strange, sinister, monstrous and murderous individuals played by Gatiss, Pemberton and Shearsmith.

Royston Vasey is used to unite the sketches and the characters, which gain depth through being inhabitants of the same village and having a shared location with a strong character in itself. This echoes *Little Britain*'s use of Tom Baker's narration to create a sense of unity in the show.

Due to there being a lot of location work the majority of *The League of Gentlemen* was not shot in front of a live audience. Instead a studio audience was played the film footage and their laughter track was added to Series One and Two, the third lacking any laughter whatsoever, as is the case with *The Office*, *Extras* and *Phoenix Nights*. The Christmas Special also eschewed a laughter track.

> **The League... Quote**
>
> Tubbs: 'Look Edward, a freak show. Shall we take David?'
> Edward: 'No Tubs, we don't want to frighten them.'

The first television series of *The League of Gentlemen* had two main narratives running throughout the six episodes. The first of these is the arrival of Benjamin Denton in Royston Vasey. He was supposed to be meeting a friend in order to go hiking and briefly staying with his aunt and uncle, Val and Harvey, before heading off. However, his brief stay is repeatedly prolonged despite his wish to leave and his friend is nowhere to be found, having met with a grizzly end at the hands of local shopkeepers Edward and Tubbs Tattsyrup.

The second continuous plot line mainly concerns Edward and Tubbs and the former's fear of outsiders. A road is planned for Royston Vasey which will guarantee an increase of non-locals coming into the area, something Edward certainly does not want, and neither does Tubbs – or so it first appears. However, it becomes increasingly apparent that she is in fact both excited and intrigued by strangers and by the world beyond Vasey.

This latter point is underlined when their son David returns from London in the final episode of Series One. He has studied at university and is now head of the construction company building the new road. When he suggests to his mother that she and Edward should go with him to spend a weekend in London, Tubbs gets very excited and clearly wants to go, though her excitement is quickly brought to a bitter end by a slap from Edward. Tubbs even goes so far as to pack a bag, preparing to leave Edward in favour of the big, wide world. This hope is soon dashed after Edward turns David into a pig-nosed local-lover like himself.

> ### The League... **Quote**
>
> 'Perhaps you are a naturally slothful person, sluggish and indolent, a dawdling flaneur, content to waste his life spread-eagled on pillows forever indulging himself in the pleasures of the palm?' Harvey Denton

The way into Vasey is shown to be no more than a muddy, waterlogged farm track, which is part of the reason for building a new road. This adds to the village's out-of-the-way feel and to the idea that it is removed from usual reality. It is also the case that episodes often begin on this path and so the opening sketches are commonly centred around the local shop, set as it is beside this track and outside the main village.

In the second TV series, the writers decided to go for something even more peculiar, repugnant and horrific than the material chosen for inclusion on the first series. This time around, the plot was centred on a nosebleed epidemic and its cause – which is a pretty dark but also amusing element, even before you have the visual imagery and character interaction to accompany it.

There was also a lot of footage focusing on the increasingly awkward position of Benjamin, who is desperate to leave, which Mark Gatiss describes as, 'a very real domestic situation about an enforced stay with relatives when you are not sure what you should do, taken to the extreme'[4]

The nosebleed epidemic actually claims the lives of a number of villagers and it emerges that it has arisen through an addiction to the 'special stuff' sold by freaky butcher Hilary Briss.

In their Christmas Special *The League of Gentlemen* team tried to give us yet another slant to life in Royston Vasey, as it was intended specifically as a horror spoof. This one-off concentrated on three stories about characters who were all hoping to get the help of Bernice Woodall, the Reverend of Vasey. In one segment the action reverts back to Victorian times, in order for us to understand the curse placed on the ancestor of Henry Chinnery, the unfortunate village veterinarian. Rather than administering successful cures, Chinnery kills every animal he tries to treat, usually in horribly funny ways, and provides a nod to Peter Davidson's TV vet from *All Creatures Great and Small*, both in appearance and mannerisms. One example of Chinnery's often fatal 'aid' to animals is provided in the scene where he has an audience of school children at a farm and is helping a cow give birth. Reaching inside the cow to tie a rope around the calf's hooves in order to pull it out, he accidentally ties the rope around the cow's intestines instead and pulls out its internal organs, killing the poor beast. The results are obviously not pretty, but this programme is not one to shy away from the grotesque, or the gory.

The use of the Victorian era in the Christmas Special is a reference to films like *The Draughtsman's Contract* (1982) and

Blood on Satan's Claw (1971), which the team behind *The League of Gentlemen* are huge fans of. The League also chose that particular period in history because of the costumes they would get to wear, including the impressive wigs and frocks.[5]

The third series also departed from the format of the first two. This presented a different story in each episode, all of which were occurring at the same time and ended with a white van crashing into a garden wall. The resolution of all the stories comes at the end of the final episode.

In making the full length film, The League took another completely new format. The plot involves Royston Vasey facing an apocalypse. The only way to avoid this is for the characters to find a way to transport themselves from fiction to reality in order to confront their creators. In a sense Royston Vasey bleeds through into the real location of Hadfield.

The League wanted the film to be a self-contained story so that to understand it you needn't necessarily be a fan of the TV series, as no prior knowledge of the characters or setting is assumed. They also made the film with a slightly lighter touch, in terms of content, and a blood-filled vein of strong comedy.

The majority of the film involves the characters Geoff Tipps, the gay German called Herr Lipp and butcher Hilary Briss, played by Shearsmith, Pemberton and Gatiss respectively. The actors also play themselves as well as characters from *The King's Evil*, which is a 17th century gothic horror which they are working on. The fourth creator of *The League of Gentlemen* series, Jeremy Dyson, is played by actor Michael Sheen, though Dyson does make appearances in the background.

Because only three of the League are actors the maximum number of main characters usually seen on screen at any one time is limited to three, each played by a different member. However, there have been occasions when two characters played by the same actor have met. In Series Two we can see two Gatiss characters coming face to face when Alvin Steele is at the supermarket checkout being operated by Iris. In the Christmas Special Papa Lazarou meets Reverend Bernice, both of whom are played by Shearsmith. This is taken a step further in the movie when the characters actually get to meet their creators, especially in the case of Herr Lipp and Steve Pemberton.

> ### The League... Quote
>
> 'I'll welcome this new road and every blast of carbon monoxide it brings. If god meant us to walk everywhere he wouldn't have given us Little Chefs.' Reverend Bernice Woodall

An example of the on screen balance created by the use of three main actors is offered by the characters of Harvey and Val Denton and their visiting nephew, Benjamin. Each is played by a different actor from The League, these being Pemberton, Gatiss and Shearsmith. Harvey and Val are obsessed by the possibility of Benjamin masturbating at any given opportunity and can be heard saying such things as, 'If you spent a little less time cavorting with Madam Palm and her five daughters you'd be a little more alert.'

One significant element in regards to Harvey and Val are their twin daughters, Chloe and Radcliffe. They are a reference to Stephen King's *The Shining*, in which the ghosts of twin girls appear. The reference is further strengthened by the fact that the girls sometimes speak in unison and seem to appear and disappear at will.

Chloe and Radcliffe first appear in Episode Four of the first series in a sketch which displays some fairly horrible humour when it comes to Harvey's much prized toads, Sonny and Cher. Benjamin is playing with the girls and the toads are burnt and crushed to death to the sounds of laughter and groans of disgust from the audience.

At the end of Series Two these two girls lock their parents in a room intended to be a prison for Benjamin, who manages to get away. Harvey, Val and their nephew do not go on to appear in the third series of the show.

Benjamin's position is unusual, in that he is the only non-local character who is a permanent fixture of Royston Vasey in the first two series, despite his various attempts to leave (one of which leads to advances from the eager Barbara in her steamed-up cab). In the opening episode he acts as a representative of the audience in a peculiar fashion, in that we enter the weird world of Royston Vasey with him and also find it hard to leave once we have been caught up in the intriguingly odd behaviour and activities of some of its inhabitants.

> **The League... Quote**
> 'There's a lot of fun English games; hop cock, British bull dykes, and stick your tail in a donkey.' Herr Lipp

Like *Little Britain*, which was to follow *The League of Gentlemen*, many of the characters are exaggerated versions of real people. These include Edward and Tubbs, the proprietors of the local shop which is situated on a hill beyond the main village and is the first place visitors come across, often with fatal consequences. Edward and Tubbs are the logical extension of the kind of local shopkeeper who is dubious of strangers, telling visitors to their shop: 'Don't touch the things. This is a local shop for local people, there is nothing for you here.'

The couple were inspired by real people encountered when The League were visiting a local shop in the village of Rottingdean near Brighton. Shearsmith remembers the episode: 'The owner was absolutely terrified that we might be trying to steal or beat her up just because we were four men walking in and picking up her shells.'[6]

The list of characters in *The League of Gentlemen* also includes a Restart Officer for the unemployed called Pauline Campbell-Jones. She is contemptuous of her charges, as well as rude, vindictive and condescending, saying things like 'Do you see how easy it is? It's as simple as Mickey,' (Mickey being a rather stupid member of the Restart club). Pauline is an exaggerated stereotype of the type of person found in job centres all over the country (and experienced by the writer of this book). She is based on Shearsmith's own experience of signing-on. The Restart Officer assigned to him during a period of unemployment was the seed for what would become the contemptuous Pauline with her precious pens.[7]

> **The League... Quote**
>
> Chloe Denton: 'If you don't play a game with us we'll tell daddy.'
> Benjamin Denton: 'Tell?'
> Radcliffe Denton: 'We'll say we came down here and saw you doing something naughty.'
> Benjamin Denton: 'Like what?'
> Both twins: 'Shaking hands with the governor of love.'

Some characters, such as Bernice and Henry Chinnery, have very simple beginnings when compared with the inspiration behind others, such as Edward and Tubbs. As Jeremy Dyson has said, 'Some characters, like Bernice or Mr Chinnery, begin as single jokes, although we do tend to flesh out the details of their lives for our own amusement.'[8]

For the characters of Edward and Tubbs, Shearsmith and Pemberton had their noses held up with tape, giving them an unusual, pig-like appearance. This links into the idea that they indulge in bestiality, something more than hinted at by the shocking sight of Tubbs breast feeding a piglet in Series One. They apparently also indulge in incest as they appear to be brother and sister as well as husband and wife.

This couple are serial killers, Tubbs having killed four people (at the time of writing) and Edward having notched up an impressive 501 victims. Their shop is burnt down at the end of Series Two by villagers who mistakenly believe they are responsible for the nosebleed epidemic. They then appear briefly at the start of Series Three, but are dispatched by a speeding train. Following on from this is their appearance as angels in the live show.

The use of material involving incest and bestiality does show a somewhat stereotypical comic approach to isolated, rural communities, as does the aversion to strangers. However, the use of such elements is entirely suited to what is a rural nightmare rather than a idyll.

Another character who highlights the oddities of Royston Vasey inhabitants and who also acts as a link between scenes placed in different locations is Barbara Dixon, owner of Bab's Cabs. When driving characters in her brightly coloured cab she likes to go into graphic detail when describing her forthcoming sex change operation and other aspects of her transexuality, stating such things as, 'One little prick and it'll be over. Then they cut my cock off.' She has a deep voice and a generous amount of chest hair with a necklace bearing her name nestled on top. We never get to see her face apart from in rear-view mirror flashes.

Despite only appearing in two episodes of the entire three seasons of *The League of Gentlemen*, Papa Lazarou is one of the most popular and widely remembered characters, possibly because he is arguably the most detached from reality. Papa

Lazarou is the owner of The Pandemonium Carnival and has a black face crudely painted on with big white circles outlining his eyes and his mouth in a clown-like fashion – albeit a twisted, morbid and quite disturbing clown. Lazarou collects pegs and wives, one of which he memorably acquires by getting into a woman's home while constantly asking for someone called 'Dave'. The woman is so frightened by this invasion of her home and his insistence concerning 'Dave' that she ends up giving him her wedding ring and Lazarou then pronounces the now infamous sentence, 'You're my wife now.' This sketch is seen as one of the most genuinely frightening and disturbing in *The League of Gentlemen*, but as a result it has also proved one of the most popular. Audiences love it. There is something repulsive about the wheedling, rasping tones of Lazarou, his gestures and appearance that strikes a chord – unpleasant, but certainly memorable.

Larazou is based on an old landlord of the League's who was called Peter Papalazarou. Whenever he rung he would always insist on talking to Steve Pemberton rather than any of the others, asking for him by his first name and leading to the inspiration for the character's persistent questioning: 'Is Dave there?' It just goes to show that the most innocent of habits can be warped quite extensively in the hands of a team with such dark imaginations as *The League of Gentlemen* team.

Some of the more sitcom-esque sketches in the show are those involving Harvey, Val and Benjamin Denton. They tend to be some of the most humorous sketches in each episode, and this may have something to do with the normality of Benjamin being contrasted with his odd, urine drinking uncle and aunt.

It is the strange appearance and behaviour of characters such as Edward, Tubbs, Barbara and Lazarou which makes the programme almost like the kind of freak show you would find in Victorian England. In the case of Barbara this is most obvious because of the hairy arms and legs, along with the hairy chest, coupled with a bright red dress and heels.

Benjamin is not the only example of normality. Other characters who behave normally and have relatively normal personalities are the majority of the Restart job club which feature in the show, and two businessmen from the local plastics injection and moulding company, called Brian and Mike. They contrast with Pauline and Mickey in the case of Restart and with the psychotic, gun-wielding Geoff in the case of the businessmen. This is a clever juxtaposition of normal and abnormal.

There is another quite different factor which adds to the dark and brooding atmosphere of the show: the surrounding countryside and the wonderful cinematography which captures it to full effect. The series was filmed on high-definition video tape and post-processed, which is a process that creates high-quality film resolution. High production standards in all areas are maintained throughout each series, including incredible attention to the detail of props, costume and sets, as well as to atmospherics, such as lighting and sound. In fact, the production standards rival that of major motion pictures.

An example of particularly effective lighting can be seen in the aforementioned warehouse scene that echoes Tarantino's *Reservoir Dogs*. Lighting is always carefully considered in the show, but in this scene it is more prominent than most because of the stark contrast between light and shadow which is employed, along with the use of back lighting when Pop enters the warehouse (a bit like Mr Blonde entering in Tarantino's cult classic).

The lighting is even used as part of a joke in relation to the goat-pig-chimp monster that Edward creates in Series One and which is discovered while the new road is being built. Under cover of a specially erected tent, with low lighting and wearing protective suits, the monster is examined by someone who declares it must be some kind of new creature never before seen. Then they hear a report on the radio about a missing goat, pig and chimp. The lights are turned up to full brightness, revealing the monster to be an obvious hoax made from the remnants of the decapitated missing animals. This is gory, blood-stained horrible humour – which is all the more effective because of the utterly horrific visual element.

> **The League... Quote**
>
> Barbara Dixon: 'As a woman I could have you under the sex discrimination act'.
>
> Geoff Tipps: 'As a woman, we could have you under the trade descriptions act'.

One of the most memorable horribly awkward scenes in *The League of Gentlemen* takes place in the third series. In it Pauline and Ross have had sex and in the aftermath an atmosphere of extreme awkwardness overtakes them both. They've had sex in the heat of the moment and the realisation of 'What have we done?' has dawned on them simultaneously. This is a situation many audience members will be able to identify with; the embarrassment of an awkward situation with a member of the opposite sex.

The cinematography and lighting in *The League of Gentlemen* are primarily the work of director Steve Bendeback, who directed both the series and the film. It is also of note that the theme tune was composed by Joby Talbot of the UK indie-pop band The Divine Comedy.

As with many of the other shows discussed in this book,

there is an element of the audience being 'in on the joke'. The character's specific personalities mean we know what to expect from them week-by-week. We know what sort of reaction Edward and Tubbs will have to any strangers entering their shop. We know that Barbara will mention something to do with her sex change. We know that Chinnery will kill animals in unusual ways. This means the audience not only has certain expectations which can create a degree of excitement, but that we become even more involved in the action, through this feeling of being in on the jokes that are being made.

> ### *The League...* **Quote**
>
> Pauline: 'Now, we were thinking yesterday, weren't we, about jobs. Do you remember? And what did we conclude?
>
> Ross: 'There aren't any.'

However, the way in which these characters' traits make themselves apparent in the different episodes varies, partly due to character development. The narrative also moves on week-by-week, especially in relation to Edward, Tubbs and the Dentons who provide its consistency. The action which involves these main characters forms the backbone of the over-arching stories contained within the show, whereas many of the other characters are removed and isolated from them.

These characters are all worked on through a process of initial rehearsals, viewed only by the four creators of the show. This early review process is deemed extremely important because of the fact that three of the group are actors, and during the private rehearsing they have found themselves arriving at new jokes which they wouldn't have thought of purely through the writing process. Therefore, this two-fold process of bringing a character to life and to the screen improves the characterisation, the sketches, and the comedy, giving their performances the polish we have come to appreciate.

It is worth noting here that this chapter has only concentrated on the main characters. There are many others which have not been discussed, and all are brought to life with care and attention.

The League of Gentlemen has had its fair share of critical praise – partly due to the quality of the show's polished content and its high production values – but this has not translated into a broad audience base. This is no doubt down to the darkness and strangeness of the show, attributable to its horror influences. In fact, the viewing figures for Series Three saw quite a rapid decline even though critical reviews remained positive. This has been linked to the aforementioned change in format compared with the preceding seasons.

Another possible reason for the decline in ratings is a corresponding decline in the humour content of the show. In each progressive series there have been less jokes and The League have concentrated ever more on the horror and the dramatic. It was in Series Three that this trend became the most obvious and at one point they even forgot to include a joke in a scene involving Pauline and Ross, a lack that was soon rectified.

One element which has remained constant is Royston Vasey. At first glance the world of Royston Vasey, which is a few steps and a large leap into the shadows at the edge of reality, can seem quite frightening, and the appearance of the show has put some people off watching it. However, once you have entered into the lives of the characters, this sinister initial impression is undermined by the comedy. The show becomes more strange than scary, more twisted than terrifying. As Reece Shearsmith puts it: 'We do look at life a certain way, you have to have kind of murky-tinged specs on.'

To this we can also add the words of Mark Gatiss, who states that, 'We write what makes us laugh, it's our sense of humour. We have no mission to shock.'[9]

> **The League... Quote**
>
> 'To be honest, I think I favour internal protection over towels. I mean, who wants to walk around with a great big mattress between their legs all day?' Barbara Dixon

It is the overriding sense of horror in the programme that can make us a little uneasy as we watch. There are many unsettling scenes and particular incidents when we are made to squirm, such as Tubbs breast feeding the piglet, as mentioned already. This is a trait common to much horribly awkward humour, and the success of such humour largely arises from the fact that human situations and interaction in real life can be more than a little horribly awkward itself. The action in *The League of Gentlemen* is based on a twisted view of reality and the characters which inhabit the real world, which can make us feel uncomfortable in parts, just as with the comedy and characters of programmes mentioned earlier.

When asked about the trend towards uncomfortable, horribly awkward humour and its present popularity Reece Shearsmith replied, 'It's strange, it's happened all in one era, because it kind of has and you do feel that. We've gone from *Harry Enfield* and *The Fast Show*, which were much broader and cosy.'[10] This 'broader and cosy' comedy was intended simply to make people laugh and of the work discussed in this book, *The Catherine Tate Show* and Peter Kay's stand-up have the most in common with this type of comedy.

Now the 'broad and cosy' has been replaced by shows

with more bite and a greater range of emotional influence on audiences. We are no longer simply made to laugh, we are made to feel other sensations; to squirm in disgust, gasp in surprise or horror, to feel the awkwardness of the characters (or interviewees in the case of Baron-Cohen and Chris Morris) and to feel awkward ourselves, partly through empathy with the people interacting on the screen and connecting with the humanity of such interactions.

> **The League... Quote**
>
> 'If you think I'm sticking digestives down my knickers and calling next door's dog in you can forget it.' Stella Hull

All of these horribly awkward factors meant that the sketch-based show which the League took on the road was a massive success. For the first half of the show they wore tuxedos as they did early in their career at the Edinburgh Fringe Festival. It was not until the second half that they got into full character both visually and verbally. This tour was hugely popular with all age groups, something underlined by the fact that after only booking a week at Drury Lane in London they had to expand their stay to six weeks, each night playing to 3,500 people.

In 1998 Gatiss, Pemberton and Shearsmith all appeared in a BBC adaptation of Mark Tevener's darkly comic murder mystery *In the Red*. They could also be seen at the Whitehall Theatre in London in 2001 as part of the comedy play called *Art* and were billed as 'The League of Gentlemen.'

The League also provided voices for the Vogons in *The Hitchhiker's Guide to the Galaxy* (2005), which starred Martin Freeman as Arthur Dent, who many will know as Tim from *The Office*. Later that year Gatiss, Pemberton and Shearsmith toured with a show entitled *The League of Gentlemen is Behind You* which, as can be gleaned from the title, was a pantomime-based show.

The League are friends with Simon Pegg's stable-mate writer/director Edgar Wright (who worked with Pegg to produce *Spaced, Shaun of the Dead* and *Hot Fuzz*), and as a result of this friendship members of the group featured in the pop-culture-riffing Channel 4 sitcom *Spaced*, starring Pegg alongside Jessica Stevenson and Nick Frost, amongst others. They also had roles in *Shaun of the Dead* (2004) and Pegg was in *The League of Gentlemen's Apocalypse*.

> ## *The League...* **Quote**
>
> Dr Matthew Chinnery: 'Reverend, do you believe a man can be cursed?'
>
> Reverend Bernice Woodall: 'Have you met Barbara?'

All of the members of The League have enjoyed success with their individual projects. Mark Gatiss is the busiest of them all. He has written for Charlie '*The Fast Show*' Higson's remake of *Randall and Hopkirk (Deceased)*, starring Vic Reeves and Bob Mortimer, appeared as a parody of *The Matrix*'s Agent Smith in *Spaced*, and been in BBC Three's 2003 comedy *Nighty Night*. He has also both written for and appeared in *Doctor Who*. He wrote two episodes entitled 'The Unquiet Dead' and 'The Idiot's Lantern' and appeared as Professor Lazarus in the episode called 'The Lazarus Experiment' (Catherine Tate and Peter Kay also having made appearances in the series).

In fact, the majority of Gatiss' writing beyond work with The League has been connected with *Doctor Who*, having penned four novels and two audio plays about the cult series. He also narrated *Doctor Who Confidential* in 2006, filling the boots of Simon Pegg who had previously narrated the programme. For the BBC's '*Doctor Who* Night' he wrote and performed the comedy sketches entitled 'The Web of Caves,' 'The Kidnappers' and 'The Pitch of Fear.' Appearing alongside

Gatiss was *Little Britain*'s David Walliams.

Gatiss has even written a column for the *Doctor Who Magazine* under the name Sam Kisgart. This is an anagram of 'Mark Gatiss,' something which itself is a tribute to the *Doctor Who* character The Master, who used anagrams of his name for false identities.

Considering the amount of *Doctor Who*-related work it is hardly surprising that we find the programme referenced in the first series of *The League of Gentlemen*. *The Stump Hole Caverns*' guide mentions both the Cybermen and Tom Baker, the fourth Doctor in the BBC Series, which he says were both in the main cavern when filming for the programme supposedly took place there.

Gatiss is not entirely obsessed by the BBC's favourite Time Lord however, and has produced other work that is in no way related to *Doctor Who*. He has written a biography of film director James Whale (1995) as well as two novels called *The Vesuvius Club* (2004) and *The Devil in Amber* (2006). In fact, the former was so well-received that it was nominated for the 'Best Newcomer' Award at the 2006 British Book Awards.

Steve Pemberton has also appeared in *Randall and Hopkirk (Deceased)*, as well as the TV series *Hotel Babylon* and *Shameless*. Further to this he has had parts in Agatha Christie's *Poirot: Death on the Nile* and the 2005 film, *Lassie*.

Reece Shearsmith appeared in Peter Kay's *Max and Paddy's Road to Nowhere* and in 2007 had a role in *Miss Marple: Ordeal by Innocence*. He has also been in the Reeves and Mortimer comedy called *Catterick* and appeared twice in *Spaced* as Dexter, the Territorial Army soldier who's obsessed with *Robot Wars* and whose robot creation battles against the ultimately superior one made by Simon Pegg and Nick Frost's characters.

Though Jeremy Dyson hasn't made appearances in other shows because he isn't an actor, he has written a novel called *What Happens Now,* which was published in 2006 and met with positive reviews. He's also written a book of short stories called *Never Trust a Rabbit* and a guide to horror movies entitled *Bright Darkness: The Lost Art of the Supernatural Horror Film,* a work which underlines the horror influences evident in the style and content of *The League of Gentlemen.*

Dyson has also adapted the work of Robert Aickman for the silver screen, an author who wrote supernatural fiction. Further to this, he's a keyboard player for a band called Rudolf Rocker who are signed to Mook Records.

The BBC has already secured the rights to a fourth series of *The League of Gentlemen* should The League decide to pen one. Shearsmith has said that it probably would not be set in Royston Vasey due to the fact they all believe the comedic possibilities of the warped village have been worn out by the previous series, the special and the film. They have explored every darkened crevice of Vasey and would have to find a new setting in which the characters can exist.

Whether or not they go on to bring the series back to life, The League have left their darkly humorous mark upon us. We'll never forget the highly atmospheric Royston Vasey and it's collection of weird, twisted inhabitants. Thanks to the sense of brooding darkness and general strangeness of the show, *The League of Gentlemen* are truly in a league of their own.

Ten Questions & Answers with

Steve Pemberton and Mark Gatiss

Question 1: Where's the strangest place you've found inspiration for a character?
Steve Pemberton: A Landlord called Mr. Papalazarou.
Mark Gatiss: They tend to be more from mundane sources, but I suppose the mental hospital opposite which I grew up.

Question 2: Which is your favourite character to play and why?
SP: Pauline – most unlike me.
MG: Mickey probably. I like disappearing behind the teeth and spots.

Question 3: Which medium have you most enjoyed working in, radio, television, or film?
SP: TV, though I do enjoy live shows too.
MG: I love TV and still feel it's somewhat looked down on. I hate it when actors say they've only done TV between stage jobs etc. I'm devoted to the history of TV and think it's a wonderful medium.

Question 4: Has any particular comedy programme or comedian been an influence on your work?
SP: Alan Bennett, Victoria Wood.
MG: Clement & La Frenais (especially *Porridge* & *Whatever Happened to the Likely Lads*) & Galton & Simpson's writing. Leonard Rossiter, Alistair Sim, Ronnie Barker

Question 5: What have you most enjoyed working on beyond *The League of Gentlemen*?
SP: *Benidorm* and *Death on the Nile* – nice to work in the sun.
MG: *Doctor Who* obviously, plus my various collaborations with Julia Davis.

Question 6: Were you the type of child who liked to entertain your class mates and make them laugh?

SP: Not particularly, but I always did drama.

MG: Yes, although not in the clichéd way in order to avoid bullying. I also used to write horror stories in which various hated teachers died a horrible death. They were very popular!

Question 7: If not a writer and actor, what career path do you think you may have followed?

SP: Languages – I speak French and German.

MG: I can't do anything else so I'd probably have turned to crime. I also wanted to be a palaeontologist, but I didn't have the Latin or the chemistry or the biology

Question 8: Which other comic writers or actors do you most admire from past or present?

SP: See above.

MG: See above. Plus Reeves and Mortimer, Jon Pertwee, Larry David, Garry Shandling. Too many to list.

Question 9: What's your favourite horror film?

SP: *Wicker Man.*

MG: *Theatre of Blood*

Question 10: What's the best piece of advice you could give to someone wishing to pursue a career in comedy?

SP: Work hard and build up a pile of good material because TV eats it up fast.

MG: Stick at it. It's easy to be distracted by real life. Real life doesn't help.

ENDNOTES

1. The League of Gentlemen Interview (www.leagueofgentlemen.co.uk)

2. Portmanteau films are, loosely defined, films that knit together a series of connecting plotlines with some unifying theme.

3. Kenny, J, 'Interview...A Mass Murderer, a Sadistic Gay German and Me...' p.3 (www.leagueofgentlemen.co.uk/myinterview.shtml)

4. The League of Gentlemen Interview (www.leagueofgentlemen.co.uk)

5. Kenny, J, 'Interview... A Mass Murderer, a Sadistic Gay German and Me...' p.3 (www.leagueofgentlemen.co.uk/myinterview.shtml)

6. The League of Gentlemen Interview (www.leagueofgentlemen.co.uk)

7. The League of Gentlemen Interview (www.leagueofgentlemen.co.uk)

8. The League of Gentlemen Interview! (www.leagueofgentlemen.co.uk)

9. The League of Gentlemen Interview (www.leagueofgentlemen.co.uk)

10. 'Jan –You're my wife now, Dave!' (www.leagueofgentlemen.co.uk/newinterview.shtml)

8. *BRASS EYE:*

The Controversial

Chris Morris

Just the mention of Chris Morris or his most renowned programme *Brass Eye* is enough to cause a variety of strong reactions; open-mouthed shock, steely-faced disgust, wide-eyed horror or laughter and a knowing smile. He is the heavyweight champion when it comes to unsettling comedy, and one who wears knuckle dusters beneath his gloves. His humour displays the horribly awkward in the extreme.

He's a satirical subversive, hiding in the shadows, avoiding the 'celebrity' tag that so many seem desperate for. He keeps himself to himself so much that the real Chris Morris is almost an unknown quantity. Then, when we are least expecting it, he strikes. Those who enjoy his cutting humour will laugh. Those that do not will either tune in and complain, or just complain anyway because that is what the rest of the flock is doing. This was the case with a *Brass Eye* special when some members of parliament voiced concern and later admitted they had not even seen the programme.

To achieve this status as both a revered and yet loathed humorist, Chris Morris's career has taken a number of turns. Born in Bristol in 1965, Morris returned there to attend university, attaining a degree in zoology. He took a traineeship with BBC Radio Cambridgeshire upon graduating and then went on to work at Radio Bristol and Greater London Radio.

There are a number of stories relating to these latter jobs. One is that Morris was fired from Radio Bristol after releasing helium into a news studio. This he did, but it was a prepared sketch and not the reason for his dismissal. People have also suggested he was fired from Greater London Radio, but this is an entirely false allegation, as Morris continued to work for the station until his career in television took off.

His DJ days were left behind him when, in 1991, he concentrated on his comedy and the creation of the Radio 4 show *On the Hour*. A spoof news programme, Morris worked on this alongside the likes of Steve Coogan, Patrick Marber and Armando Iannucci (who would later work with him on Alan Partridge's show). In 1994 this programme transferred to television under the name of *The Day Today*. .

Some say *On the Hour* and *The Day Today* marked a renaissance in British comedy, and this may be especially true in terms of horribly awkward humour. These programmes not only launched the career of Chris Morris, the creator of the most extreme type of comedy within this genre, but also resulted in the creation of Alan Partridge, who was the first of a number of horribly awkward characters who were to emerge in the following years (Steve Coogan's creations will be discussed in the next chapter, including Alan Partridge himself).

Also in 1994, Morris made some recordings of conversations

with comedy legend Peter Cook. These were broadcast on Radio 3 and entitled *Why Bother?* In them Morris acted as an interviewer and Cook adopted the character of Sir Arthur Streeb-Greebling, a bee-keeper who had found the remains of the infant Christ. The conversations between the two men were precursors of the interviews that Morris would go on to have with celebrities on *Brass Eye*, only Peter Cook obviously knew they were a set-up and had donned his own fictional persona.

> **Morris Quote**
>
> 'If a terrorist group wanted to hit Britain, all they'd have to do is kill 100 random celebrities. The country would have a nervous breakdown,' Chris Morris

There was one occasion when Peter Cook, a heavy drinker at the time of the recordings, had badly bruised one of his arms at home and it had swelled considerably. After arriving at the studio, Morris began the recorded interview by saying, 'Sir Arthur, you're very shortly going to be dead, and the idea of this amuses me.' So, as with much of Morris' work, he was not afraid to tackle taboo subjects such as death, and could do so with one carefully considered sentence which also contained humour. The humour in this particular case arises through the surprising reaction to someone else's injury and through the idea that the interviewee's death would be found amusing by the interviewer. The approach is harsh, admittedly, but contemporary audiences appreciate this. Our taste for the extreme is so far developed that we enjoy being shocked, we enjoy finding a comic's behaviour outrageous.

Morris also created a sketch concerning gangster rap in 1994. In it he played a rapper called 'Fur-Q', who was promoting his new song called 'Uzi Lover', which was a take on the Phil Collins hit 'Easy Lover.' The lyrics of the piece include, 'Uzi like a metal dick in my hand, magazine like a big testicle gland.' This may not have been subtle, but it was effective in satirising the glamorisation of gun crime and use of sexual lyrics in rap music. We can see that with Morris' heavyweight style the point hits home with considerable force and audiences can be left more than a little dazed at the affront.

Morris followed Fur-Q with 'JLB-8', another rapper who appeared on *Brass Eye*. This rapper, as his name suggests, had paedophilic lyrics in his songs which had attracted a preteen fan-base

As well as creating shows for Radio 4 and Radio 3, Morris worked on Radio 1. The programme he created for this station was called *Blue Jam* and featured sketches mixed with ambient music. This would go on to be reworked for Channel 4, and was broadcast under the name *Jam*. Both were aired late at night, something Morris specifically wanted because of the dreamlike and often nightmarish quality to the programmes.

Blue Jam and *Jam* set the tone for the work that would follow from Chris Morris and first defined his signature style. These programmes tackled taboo subjects like incest, rape and suicide with often unsettling sketches. These had a dark quality to them, something made all the more powerful by the use of ambient music in juxtaposition. They were like strange dreams rising through the listener's or viewer's subconscious, at once disturbing, amusing and strangely gripping.

Actions which underline Morris' subversive status in the media include announcing the deaths of Jimmy Savile and Tory MP Michael Heseltine on the radio and then asking other celebrities to comment, even though both men were still very much alive. He also had a broadcast on Radio 1 faded out when playing a tampered version of the Archbishop of Canterbury's speech at the funeral service for Princess Diana. The station had actually cleared this particular piece to air, but must have had second thoughts while it was being broadcast.

Morris was beginning to attract attention. However, it was the infamous spoof current affair/news programme *Brass Eye* which catapulted him to fame through its controversial treatment of difficult subjects and routine humiliation of well-known celebrities and politicians.

The series was first broadcast in 1997 and then again in 2001 with the addition of the special entitled 'Paedogeddon', which had paedophilia as its theme and was perhaps the most objectionable episode of all.

The initial broadcast of the first series had been delayed because it contained a piece that made reference to Moors murderer Myra Hindley. This included a song in the style of Brit-pop band Pulp. At the time Hindley was back in the news so the 'powers that be' at Channel 4 decided it was unwise to show the series on the originally scheduled dates. However, the special almost failed to make it to our TV screens at all.

Michael Grade was the chief executive of Channel 4 at the time and such were his concerns that he threatened to pull the programme entirely. If it had not been for pressure from Chris Morris himself, this may well have happened, but thankfully for his increasing fan base, the show was ultimately allowed to air.

Grade also repeatedly intervened when it came to editing the show. His constant interfering angered Morris to such a degree that in the final episode a single frame was inserted stating, 'Grade is a cunt'. Though it was not evident in the second broadcast of the series in 2001 or on the DVD release, its message was clear.

In fact, Morris' negative feelings towards Grade ran so deep that he went so far as to write to Nelson Mandela in order to tell him that Grade had wanted him kept in prison. He also wrote to Paul Simon to inform him that Grade thought Art Garfunkle was the talented one of the pop/folk duo.

Watching Morris as spoof host and reporter of the programme is like watching the combative Jeremy Paxman on *Newsnight* on a bad acid trip (or should that be 'cake trip'?). The viewer is presented with something like a nightmare version of a news and current affairs programme, something which reflects the nightmarish qualities of *Jam*. It is a darker place than the reality we're used to, and much more warped. In this sense it reflects *Little Britain*, but only to the extent that we are being given a twisted view of reality, one that makes a comment on certain issues and aspects of society through its juxtaposition with reality.

It is the darkness and warped nature which is part of the glory of this programme, as with others mentioned in this book. It makes us cringe, it makes us recoil and it makes us laugh all the more because of the contrast between these feelings. We feel somewhat awkward as Morris tackles quite horrific topics with an effective blade of satire, slicing straight to the bone to reveal the more sensitive issues which he wants us to think about, such as media hype surrounding paedophilia and the celebrity culture that has developed to a point of utter farce in recent years.

The horribly awkward humour of *Brass Eye* is visceral. Morris goes for the knockout with blow-after-blow of surprising, jaw-dropping and shocking content, much of it supplied by celebrities who have been duped despite the obvious ridiculousness of what they've been asked to say or are reading from an auto-cue.

Some of the surprising and somewhat bizarre conversations which took place between Morris and his celebrity 'victims' include one with former Conservative MP Rhodes Boyson, the very same MP who we saw duped by Ali G in the first chapter. They discussed Bruce Wayne's style of Gotham City crime fighting initiatives and whether they could be adopted in Britain. Morris has also enjoyed an absurd conversation with Eve Pollard about keeping a genetically modified giant testicle alive in an incubator. The reason such discussions and debates are so amusing is partly due to their bizarre content, partly a result of seeing celebrities making fools of themselves, and partly because of their take on current affairs issues, such as inner-city crime and advances in genetic science. The three components mixed together create a heady mix of humour.

One of the most memorable of these mixes was in the second episode about the fictional yellow drug called 'cake' (though the celebrities appearing didn't know it was fictional). Politicians denounced it, along with TV personalities like Noel Edmonds and Bernard Manning. Tory MP David Amess even talked about the evils of cake and went so far as to ask a question in Parliament in relation to the terrible drug, so convinced was he of its reality – this despite the fact that the acronyms for the organisations against the drug were 'F.U.K.D.' and 'B.O.M.B.D.'

In this episode the drug was regularly referred to as a 'made-up drug'. This was supposedly a reference to the fact it was made from chemicals rather than natural substances. However, the audience are in on the joke as we fully realise the term refers to the fact that cake is fictional. This use of terminology, along with the clever use of acronyms, highlights Morris' use of linguistics as part of the show's humour.

In the *Brass Eye* episode that focuses on sex, Morris took
on the role of a chat show host with a highly dubious attitude
to AIDS. In his opinion there were two types of this disease,
'good AIDS' and 'bad AIDS'. The former was caught through
blood transfusion whilst the latter was caught through
indulgence in gay sex or drugs. This was clearly a satirical
approach to right-wing views on the subject and resulted in
some highly-amusing reactions from members of the studio
audience. Many might disapprove of his provocative approach
but in adopting these kind of opinions, Morris makes it clear
how ridiculous they truly are. His humour can be a valuable
political tool.

It is pertinent to note that part of the social commentary in
Brass Eye is concerned with the media portrayal of such things
as drugs and paedophilia. Morris is
part of this media and has managed
to criticise it from within its own
confines – not an easy thing to do.

> **Brass Eye Quote**
>
> 'One little kiddie on cake
> cried all the water out of
> his body. Just imagine
> how his mother felt. It's a
> fucking disgrace.' Bernard
> Manning on *Brass Eye*

One strange phenomenon of
note in regards to the media storm
created by the airing of *Brass Eye*,
or, rather, the reactions of the
tabloid press to the show, is that the
anger and outrage was aimed at Morris himself. An interesting
question arises from this fact; why weren't the celebrities who
let themselves be taken for such a wild ride also targeted?
It seemed their desire to have their faces on television, to
be seen backing apparently important causes and speaking
about important issues in order to raise their standing with
the general public, far outweighed their common sense.

How could DJ Dr Fox genuinely believe paedophiles have
more in common genetically with a crab than with other

human beings? How could presenter Richard Blackwood really think that paedophiles using the internet to lure children were able to make the keyboards of their targets give off fumes which made them more suggestible, even to the extent of claiming he could smell the fumes and felt more suggestible when sniffing a keyboard himself?

TV presenter Philippa Forrester even appeared on the programme to explain how paedophiles could reach through computer screens and grope children simply by donning a special pair of gloves. This piece of absolute nonsense was something she was duped into doing, and it is not implausible that her appearance on *Brass Eye* caused her resignation from the technology programme; *Tomorrow's World*.

Brass Eye Quote

'Paedophiles have more in common with crabs than they do with you or me. Now that is scientific fact. There's no actual evidence for it, but it is a fact.'

Dr Fox on *Brass Eye*

One of the most unforgettable images from the show was pop icon Phil Collins talking about the dangers of paedophiles while wearing a T-shirt bearing the words 'Nonce Sense'. It is hard to believe that he could go ahead with this piece without realising he was being duped. This wonderment is made all the stronger because the first line Collins says is 'I'm talking nonce sense.'

Other celebrities to have appeared in various episodes of the programme were Rolf Harris, Carla Lane, Paul Daniels, Richard Briers, Peter Stringfellow, Lord Coe, Vanessa Feltz and film director Michael Winner. As can be seen from this list and those already mentioned, *Brass Eye* included quite a line-up of red faces.

Of the above celebrities it has to be said that Dr Fox did take his duping well, at least in public. On his Capital Radio show he had the grace to mention *Brass Eye*, stating, 'I'm a fan and Chris Morris is very clever.'[1] But no avowals of appreciation of *Brass Eye*'s format could change the fact that what Fox, and the others, were seen to have declared in all sincerity on public television was simply nonsense. Unbelievably, these public slip-ups barely received a mention in the tabloids. Actually, the tabloids managed to shoot themselves in the foot

> ### *Brass Eye* Quote
> 'Kids burst shops by filling them with rice and pouring in water, then standing back laughing while the bricks are ripped apart by the swelling food.' Morris' character, Ted Maul on *Brass Eye*

when it came to their rants against Morris and *Brass Eye*. For example, one *Daily Mail* headline on the *Brass Eye* special read 'Unspeakably Sick', which was a quote from an MP who had not even seen the programme. This story was preceded by pictures of Princess Beatrice and Princess Eugenie, at the time only thirteen and eleven years old respectively. These were not your average shots of the princesses in party dresses on the palace balcony, they were pictures of the young girls wearing only bikinis. Did the *Mail* expect people to take them seriously when displaying semi-naked children whilst attacking someone for highlighting the media's hysteria-fuelled coverage of paedophilia?

A similarly mistaken editorial decision was seen in *The Daily Star*. This newspaper unbelievably printed an article attacking the paedophile episode next to a report about singer Charlotte Church's breasts, the headline reading, 'She's a big girl now.' At the time Church was only fifteen.

In response to the tabloid coverage and the programme itself, *The Guardian* pointed out that Morris was in no way condoning paedophilia. *The Times* and *The Telegraph* talked about the dangers of censorship and praised the impact that satire can have.

It is also important to note that the tabloid press are forever changing their opinions in order to glean the highest possible readership, so are happy to jump on any passing bandwagon, such as supposed public outrage at *Brass Eye*. Further to this point is the fact that the tabloid reaction matched the show's purpose to a degree. It caused an intense debate, not just about Morris and the rights or wrongs of making a programme about paedophilia. It also caused debate over media hype and scare-mongering in general and particularly in relation to the subject of children and paedophilia. If it was the intention of the programme's creators to bring these subjects to the fore, they certainly succeeded. People were forced to think about issues they might otherwise have swept under the carpet.

As Morris explains: 'The very specific nature of *Brass Eye* is in identifying a thoughtless, knee-jerk reaction to an issue… if you tackle drugs or paedophilia, then you're dealing with something where people's brains are nowhere near the point of debate.'[2]

When considering the show on paedophilia, it is important to remember that Morris has two children of his own. This means he has had first-hand experience from the standpoint of a parent when it came to the scare-mongering conducted by sections of the mass media. The media coverage at the time that *Brass Eye* was being aired made it seem like paedophiles were lurking in every shadow, that it could be your child next, suggesting that at every turn most children were being hunted and preyed upon by these individuals

Another element of note in relation to the *Brass Eye* special is that it features an appearance by Simon Pegg, though not as one of the gullible celebrities as this was in the early days of his career, before *Spaced* and his films had shot him to fame. He played Gerard Chote, the spokesman for a pro-paedophile group who staged an invasion of the *Brass Eye* studio. He was placed in stocks and asked if he wanted to have sex with Morris' son. When he replied that he did not fancy the boy Morris went on to take offence.

There were reportedly an astounding 2000 complaints about the special. However, this was outweighed by 3000 calls supporting it. The episode even went on to win an award in 2002 from *Broadcast* magazine. In the same year the series was released on DVD and included the special. It was a bestseller.

Brass Eye is rife with horribly awkward humour. In a sense it is the extreme pinnacle of this kind of humour and involves all the elements previously discussed in this book in relation to other shows and comedians. We have visual awkwardness in the form of Morris' clever play on words, such as 'nonce sense', and his use of acronyms such as F.U.K.D. We, the audience understand the real meaning of these visual props while the T-shirt wearing celebrity is blissfully unaware – it can be almost excruciating to watch.

Another level of almost painful-to-witness humour is created by the verbal idiocies the celebrities spout concerning the topics they are presented with. Further to this is Morris' presenting style, which lampoons newsreaders in a humorous way, something underlined with the use of phrases such as 'Find out exactly what to think next,' and 'So much for recorded crime, but crimes we know nothing about are going up as well.' Then there are the news stories, which present the extremities of media hype, as well as a warped view of reality. For example, there is one story about a man dressing as a school in Sheffield, in order to entrap children; an absurd but also very amusing idea.

Political correctness is thrown out of the window in order for the programme to make its various observations about social issues and the way they are portrayed by the mass media. Morris is clearly unafraid of the PC brigade and the way this correctness governs much of what people say and do. He is fearless in terms of broaching subjects which he believes deserve scrutiny, and does not shy away from the exposure of unrealistic or ill informed views on subjects like drugs and crime.

> **Brass Eye Quote**
>
> Chris Morris: 'What I want to know is how you feel about other people who are feeding off the same...carcass. People who make computer games like 'The Last Chase' where you play a paparazzo chasing a car through a tunnel, subtitle of the game 'Snap the Dying Bitch'.
>
> Andrew Morton, biographer of Princess Diana: 'Well, I find them very abhorrent because all you're doing is exploiting someone's death.'

As mentioned in Chapter One, Sacha Baron-Cohen's work has a lot in common with that of Chris Morris. Both have used a mock interview format to fool interviewees into saying and doing ridiculous things. Both have also conducted these interviews as someone other than themselves, characters which the interviewees believed were real people (Paul Kaye's celebrity-hounding Dennis Pennis is another example of this).

This interview and fake persona technique has brought both Sacha Baron-Cohen and Chris Morris more than their fair share of controversy. In regards to Sacha Baron-Cohen, this was especially the case with Borat, who caused a minor international incident when the government of Kazakhstan complained about his allegedly insulting portrayal of their country (they were of course missing the point entirely, since

Borat was meant to highlight prejudice not perpetuate it). Morris, on the other hand, did not just flirt with controversy, he made it the cornerstone of the *Brass Eye* series. As we have seen, it was the final special of this programme which whipped up the biggest storm, though such episodes as the one about the drug called 'cake' had already paved the way and given us a glimpse of what he was capable of when it came to satirising sensitive and taboo topics.

Another link between these two humorists is their notoriety when it comes to avoiding press attention. Both of them like to keep their private lives private and avoid the media spotlight like the

> **Nathan Barley Quote**
>
> Toby: 'Listen, I've been thinking about Claire...'
>
> Nathan: 'Did you clean up afterwards?'

plague. Morris even goes to the extent of not allowing any pictures to be taken of himself out of character. This shunning of the limelight is also apparent to a certain extent with Steve Coogan, as we shall see in the following chapter, though Coogan cannot always prevent stories of his well publicised hedonism becoming tabloid fodder. Unlike Baron-Cohen and Coogan, Morris doesn't have any interest in making his name in Hollywood, so his complete lack of a public profile allows his work to speak for itself.

Following the success of *Brass Eye*, Morris' next project was a sitcom. This was entitled *Nathan Barley*, and was written by Chris Morris and Charlie Brooker. Morris directed the series and described the title character as a 'meaningless, strutting cadaver-in-waiting.' Barley originated from Brooker's website which parodied television listings and was called 'TVGoHome'. The character was the centre of a fly-on-the-wall documentary with the rather blunt title 'Cunt'.

In the Channel 4 sitcom Barley is a pretty dislikeable character. He's a twenty-something living in London and is convinced of his own talent. He sees himself as a webmaster, guerrilla filmmaker, screenwriter and DJ, though most people wouldn't see him in the same light. These supposed talents derive from the fact he's got some web space and a camcorder (the webpage having been created as the official site for the show). Barley is a member of the brigades of hapless people living in the capital who try too hard to be 'cool' and are desperate to be perceived as such.

> **IT Crowd Quote**
>
> 'She's quite an oddball. Did you notice how she didn't even get excited when she saw this original ZX-81?'
>
> Maurice Moss

The comedy of the show arises partly through the interaction of Nathan Barley with the two other main characters from the show, Claire and Dan Ashcroft. Claire is a documentary maker and her brother is a writer, though much jaded after having written an article called 'The Rise of the Idiots', only to find himself adopted as the figurehead/guru of the idiots he was writing about (these idiots being Barley and his ilk).

The programme highlights how the idiots have accessed the media by using the internet as a launch pad. The established media has then taken them to their bosom, thinking Barley and similar people have something worth saying, though this is far from being the case, at least in the sitcom.

Barley's internet output consists of posting films of idiotic pranks on his website. He has also posted pictures of himself with beautiful women posing on the streets of various major cities around the world. Despite this very minimal display of talent, their internet presence ensures that Barley and the rest of the idiots are often hired or published by the media, getting precedence over established and talented writers.

One of these neglected writers is Dan, and some people believe he is representative of Morris, reflecting his struggle to be seen and heard amidst a clamour of mediocre talent desperate for celebrity status. In the face of the clamour Dan attempts to retain his standards and focus. (Dan is played by Julian Ashcroft, who created the marvelously wacky hit *The Mighty Boosh* along with Noel Fielding, who in *Nathan Barley* takes the role of Barley's flat mate, a DJ called Jones.)

Nathan Barley first aired in 2005. Prior to its broadcast an advertising campaign was used which underlined the tone of the show and its dig at the hordes of 'cool' wannabes. Billboard adverts centred around a mobile phone called the Wasp T12 Speechtool. The phone was said to be very loud, only played annoying ring tones, had an oversized key for the number five because it is apparently the most used key, and featured a projector, business card printer, miniature turntable for mixing and scratching MP3s, and was even said to be shark proof. It parodies the mobile phone junkies looking for the next phone featuring all the latest gadgets and then using it as a statement of cool.

Nathan Barley is an attack on mediocre talents that emerge on the internet and move into mainstream media. It mocks their often inane material and takes a giant stab at the entirely superficial culture of 'being cool' which pervades London's hippest hangouts. It also seems that Nathan Barley will be stepping into the ring for a second time as Morris recently told students at Bournemouth University that he was working on new material for the show.[3]

In 2006 the first series of *The IT Crowd* was broadcast on Channel 4 and was followed by a second series in 2007. It featured Chris Morris as the eccentric Denholm Reynholm, the managing director of a company called Reynholm Industries. This BAFTA nominated sitcom was written and directed by Graham Lineham, who was one of the creators of *Father Ted* and who has worked repeatedly with Steve Coogan. Lineham appears as a Mexican singer in Episode Three (Chris Tarrant appearing as himself in the same episode).

> **The IT Crowd Quote**
>
> Roy: (singing) 'We don't need no education.'
> Moss: 'Yes you do. You've just used a double negative.'

The title of this programme is a play on the phrase 'the In crowd' and in so being highlights the fact that the main characters are most definitely not part of this group. The IT support team consists of three people. Moss and Roy are the two technicians and Jen is their superior. She managed to lie her way into the managerial post despite not knowing much about information technology. All three inhabit the basement of the office building where they work. The basement is dingy, messy, and has no natural light. This stands in stark contrast to the rest of the building, which is light and open with a modern feel.

Moss is the most prominent character because his nerdy nature is captured so well by Richard Ayoade, who is perfect for the part. He is a computer geek who uses computer dating and lives with his mum at the age of thirty-two. The humour connected with his character arises predominantly from nerd jokes centred around his technical knowledge. This knowledge of computer systems is extensive and he can deal with any IT-related problem. When it comes to dealing with practical things, such as putting out fires, he is completely inept. The same can also be said for his social skills, which are limited to say the least.

This is the first project that Morris has appeared in which

wasn't his own creation. Morris's character, Reynholm, is a parody of upper management and he creates initiatives within the work place which are usually ridiculous. These include introducing unisex lavatories and a policy of only employing attractive people.

The techno-babble used, predominantly by Moss, is genuine and the set is filled with nerdy references to such things as *The Hitchhiker's Guide to the Galaxy* author Douglas Adams and classic computer games. The theme tune is also purposefully reminiscent of Gary Numan's 1979 hit 'Are Friends Electric?' All of this was much appreciated by the multitude of IT people who tuned in to watch the show along with other members of the general public. Having this kind of technologically-minded fan-base meant that the copy protection on the DVD release of the sitcom was soon cracked and the programme was shared amongst the IT community.

Noel Fielding appears for the second time in this chapter after having been mentioned in relation to *Nathan Barley*. In *The IT Crowd* he plays Richmond Avenal, a goth who fell from grace. He was once Reynholm's right-hand man, but thanks to an obsession with the band Cradle of Filth he was shunned by the 'beautiful people' and ends up working alone in the server room, which is accessed from the basement through a red door. This morose, darkly dressed individual notably thinks of himself as 'cheerful', and Jen's discovery of him behind the red door has echoes of Tim Burton's film *Edward Scissorhands* (1990).

One thing of special note in relation to the DVD release of the first season of the show is that David Walliams features in a Graham Lineham short film called *Hello Friend*, which is included as an extra. Also, like *The Office*, *The IT Crowd* is being remade in the US. NBC are creating the stateside version of the show and have retained Richard Ayoade in the role of Moss because of his brilliant portrayal of a computer nerd. There are those, however, who would object that this is a pretty average sitcom and the fact that Morris was not involved in the writing really shows.

As well as his radio and television work, Morris also created a column for *The Observer*. This ran in 1999 and was supposedly written by a man named Richard Geefe. In the column, named 'Second Class Male/Time to Go,' Geefe documented his progression towards a planned suicide. After pressure from readers the paper revealed that it was a spoof column written by Morris.

In 2001 the British band Stereolab released an album called *Sound Dust*. One of the songs featured was entitled 'Nothing To Do With Me' and contained lyrics lifted from Chris Morris sketches. Strangely enough, Stereolab are only one of a number of bands who have used Morris' work within their music, though they are the best known.

My Wrongs 8245-8249 and 117 is the only film Chris Morris has created to date. It was made in 2002 and was a short about a man being guided by a rather sinister talking dog. The story was adapted from one of the monologues in *Blue Jam* and the film was made by Warp Films. This company was a new branch of Warp Records and this was their first film venture, one that led to a BAFTA award in 2003.

Chris Morris wrote and directed the piece whilst also providing the voice for the dog. This dog claims to be the lead character's lawyer. The lead is played by Paddy Considine (from the film the *Last Resort*). Considine said that Morris was 'a brilliant, hands-on director,' and that he was as good as any other he'd worked with.[4] The tone of the piece is similar to the feel of *Brass Eye*, but has more in common with *Blue Jam* and *Jam*. In 2004 Chris Morris was ranked at Number 11 in Channel

4's programme *The Comedian's Comedian*. In this programme comedians had been asked to list their favourite peers and a Top 50 listing had been created from the responses. Morris' position was higher than such greats as the surreal Eddie Izzard, cult US stand-up Bill Hicks, and even British comic legend Peter Sellers, which just goes to show how highly regarded his satirical work is amongst those in his profession.

Love him or hate him, Chris Morris has made an important and memorable contribution to a new era of British comedy and to the emergence of a new wave of horribly awkward humour. He has made both the celebrities taking part and we, the audience, squirm as we watch or listen to his shows tackling serious issues with a satirical uppercut. The conclusion is obvious; Chris Morris is a comedy KO.

ENDNOTES

1. Flett, K, 'Stupidity Scuttled Survivor,' (*The Observer*, 29th July 2001)

2. Brooks, X, 'Chris Morris: The Movie,' (*The Guardian*, 21st February 2003)

3. Homwood, L. (http://www.guardian.co.uk/media/2007/mar/19/broadcasting.channel4)

4. Brooks, X, 'Chris Morris: The Movie,' (*The Guardian*, 21st February 2003)

9. *I'M ALAN PARTRIDGE!*: Steve Coogan Blazes a Comedy Trail

Steve Coogan paved the way for the new wave of horribly awkward humour through the immense popularity of his alter ego, Alan Partridge. With his social ineptitude, cringe-worthy ability to say the wrong thing at the wrong time and extreme physical awkwardness, the nylon-suited and slippery-haired Alan Partridge was arguably the first of the now numerous characters displaying this brand of humour. Partridge hit our screens before David Brent of *The Office*, before Brain Potter of *Phoenix Nights* and before Jeremy Osborne of *Peep Show*. Coogan, it seems, was the trendsetter. In fact, Alan Partridge also introduced us to the format of the mock chat show and interviews later popularised by Ali G and Borat. Though Alan Partridge's guests were fictional and were not being duped into thinking their host was genuine, there are still recognisable glimpses of Coogan's most memorable creation in Sacha Baron-Cohen's approach. The foundations had been laid.

This is not to suggest that Coogan was a direct influence on comedians such as those mentioned above, but it is fair to say that he was a trail blazer, bringing us a new blend of humour for the 90s and beyond. He helped create a particular atmosphere and instigated the demand for acts of a similar bent which would follow.

Coogan grew up in a suburb of Manchester as part of a lower-middle/upper-working-class Irish Catholic family and has said that he had an unremarkable, but happy childhood. He recalls the family sitting around the TV to watch shows like *Fawlty Towers, The Two Ronnies, Morecambe and Wise* and *Porridge*. He also remembers how he loved his father's Tony Hancock albums and his brother's Monty Python records.[1] Though he recalls having friends over and enjoying watching their reactions to the *Monty Python* albums, he has said that he was never an entertainer at school, unlike many of those discussed in this book.

Although he had always been interested in comedy it was only at the age of eighteen that Coogan realised he wanted to pursue a career in it. He describes this revelation as 'a sort of moment of clarity', an epiphany that occurred the moment he realised that his heroes, the comedy greats of that time, could not keep on performing forever and would have to be replaced by a new generation of comedic talent. That's when he thought, 'Why can't I be one of the new generation?'[2]

It was during the time he spent at Manchester Polytechnic School of Theatre (where he became friends with Caroline Aherne) that Coogan discovered how much he enjoyed making people laugh – and more to the point he found that he had a real talent for it. Like Peter Kay, he discovered his talent from the stage itself.

Coogan had always been good at voices and impersonations, and one night as a student when he went to a comedy revue, the acts were going down so badly that a friend got him up on stage hoping that he would rescue the situation. This he did, though, with modesty, Coogan says the audience were not necessarily laughing because of the strength of his material, but because what had gone before was so bad in comparison. However, this spontaneous performance during his student years gave Coogan his first real audience and he recalls thinking, 'This is an incredible feeling,' as the crowd laughed at his impressions. He also realised how much funnier he would be if he wasn't ad-libbing, but had material prepared beforehand.[3]

At Manchester Polytechnic Coogan also became friends with John Thomson, who went on to star in the hit TV comedy/drama Cold Feet, and the two of them have since worked on a number of projects together. They first met when he was in his first year and Coogan was in his third. Both had heard that the other did impressions and when they met there was an 'impersonation stand-off' where each took the opportunity to display their talents.

During his time as a student, Coogan drew inspiration from the Parr's Wood pub across from the polytechnic to create the character Paul Calf, the student hater. Though students did frequent the establishment it also had its fair share of hard-drinking, tough locals and anti-student types, and it was these which stirred Coogan and Thomson's creativity.

Coogan continued performing and working on his impressionist skills in order to get an Equity card and even while he was still at the poly his talent was sufficiently obvious for him to be offered work on a variety of TV shows. He says of that time, 'I thought, "I'll go for this comic thing, pursue it to the *nth* degree and try and get back into acting."'[4] This is very similar to Catherine Tate, who saw comedy as a way to perhaps eventually build a career in serious acting, as discussed in Chapter Three.

According to Coogan, when he was starting out there wasn't really an alternative comedy circuit beyond the bounds of London, so he

> **Alan Partridge Quote**
> 'The Day Today – slamming the wasps from the pure apple of truth.' Voiceover

ended up supporting bands at various student venues. By the age of twenty-two he had put together a routine which managed to get him a gig alongside Jimmy Tarbuck at The London Palladium. This, however, was not the type of career he had hoped for, and thanks to the popularity of the character Paul Calf, Coogan managed to escape this kind of gig and change the course of his career. Paul Calf was a yob who hated students and his sister, Pauline, gave us a chance to see Steve Coogan in short skirts and push-up bras.

Paul Calf was brought to the public's attention by a show Coogan and Thomson put together, entitled 'Steve Coogan in Character with John Thomson'. They performed this at the Edinburgh Festival in 1992, winning the coveted Perrier Award, which Catherine Tate and Peter Kay have also been nominated for, but haven't won. This show helped steer Coogan away from his earlier focus on impressions and live shows.

He later went on to work for *Spitting Image* for a while, providing character voices, then created a TV pilot called *The Dead Good Show*. When it became clear that this was not going to get taken by any of the independent broadcasters, Coogan decided to work for the BBC on a radio show called *On the Hour,* which was a spoof news programme. The character he played on this show was a sports reporter called Alan Partridge. A legend was born.

Alan Partridge's fictional career saw him progress from his role as a sports broadcaster to a chat show host and then a Radio Norwich DJ. All three career changes were charted in and by the BBC programmes he appeared in, starting with the Radio 4 show *On the Hour*, which aired in the early 90s and also featured the talent of *Brass Eye*'s Chris Morris (discussed in the previous chapter), who went on to appear in *I'm Alan Partridge* as the leader of a farmer's union.

On the Hour transferred from radio and onto the small screen in 1994, changing its name to *The Day Today*, and with Alan Partridge continuing to work as a sports reporter. (This kind of transfer from radio to TV has also been seen with *Little Britain*, as well as other comedy shows.)

Partridge's career only really took off when he made the move from being a sports-caster to a chat show host on the BBC's *Knowing Me, Knowing You... with Alan Partridge*. The title was taken from the title of a song by Alan's favourite group, *Abba,* and his infamous catchphrase, 'A-ha!' was taken from that song. On this spoof chat show Partridge insulted his weird and wonderful selection of guests and there were a number of complaints from viewers tuning in and believing that the dialogue was genuine.

The success of Alan Partridge at this point in his career was in part due to the originality of the mock-chat show format and in part because of his horribly awkward persona. People had not seen a programme like this before and enjoyed the send-up of what was an extremely popular format at the time. The contrast between *Knowing Me, Knowing You* and such shows as *Parkinson* created part of the humour for the audience, who were also enthralled by the way in which

Partridge behaved. His role as host was part of the contrast between this show and genuine chat shows. No one in their right mind would actually employ someone like Partridge to take the reins. Seeing him bumble through interviews helped create laughter throughout the country as we watched his ineptness.

Knowing Me, Knowing You first aired on Radio 4 in 1992 and transferred to television in 1994. The TV version won 'Best New Television Comedy' at the British Comedy Awards, where Coogan/Partridge also won a brace of other awards, including 'Top Male Comedy Performer' and 'Top Comedy Personality'. The show was actually co-written with other writers, including Armando Iannucci, who had been the producer of *On the Hour*.

In the Christmas special of the programme, aired in 1995 and called *Knowing Me, Knowing Yule*, Partridge hit the Chief Commissioning Editor of the BBC, Tony Hayers, with a stuffed partridge. He was promptly fired from the BBC due to this and two other factors. The first was decreasing audience viewing figures and the second was the general lack of quality that the programme displayed. Of course, Partridge is only a character and these events were part of the plot of his fictional life which Coogan had created.

The character then went on to appear in two series of *I'm Alan Partridge,* which is shot in the style of a mock fly-on-the-wall documentary. When asked about ending *Knowing Me, Knowing You* and moving to *I'm Alan Partridge* Coogan said, 'There wasn't much more we could do with a chat show, but we knew there was a lot more we could do with Alan.'[5]

In the first series, which aired in 1997, Alan finds himself separated from his wife and living in a hotel. At this juncture he is working as a DJ on a local station, Radio Norwich, with a programme called *Up with the Partridge*. This show is aired during the very early hours of the morning, and he has an ongoing rivalry with the DJ whose show is broadcast after this graveyard shift, the two of them indulging in on-air banter during the changeover and the other DJ usually coming out on top.

The second series of *I'm Alan Partridge* did not air until five years after the first and was broadcast in 2002. In this series we discover that Partridge has suffered from a mental breakdown since the previous series and is now living in a static caravan beside the site where his dream house is being built. His radio show has an evening slot rather than the graveyard one it previously occupied, which is now filled by the rival DJ at the station. Partridge has also managed to secure a military-themed quiz show on a digital TV station and has published his autobiography, titled *Bouncing Back*, though its sales are nothing to write home about.

The long-suffering Lynn, played by Felicity Montagu, is a major character in both series of the show. She is Alan's PA and he treats her with contempt most of the time. However, it is apparent that he would not be able to cope without her constant help and her ability to put up with his inane chatter.

In *I'm Alan Partridge* we see the title character's life is quite empty. His main sources of human interaction in Series One are Lynn and the employees at the hotel where he is living. Because of this he tends to speak almost constantly about the most inane and inappropriate topics. The man has absolutely no social graces, a tendency to say exactly the wrong thing whenever he opens his mouth, and is one of the most offensive and self-centred comic creations of our time.

Every episode of *I'm Alan Partridge* had a title which was

a play on movie names, such as 'Watership Alan,' 'To Kill a Mocking Alan,' 'The Talented Mr Alan,' and 'I Know What Alan Did Last Summer.' The show gleaned two BAFTAs for 'Best Comedy Series' and 'Best Comedy Programme'.

The winning of these awards was partly due to two original tropes used in the series, which have proved to be a memorable hit with audiences. The first is a fantasy that Alan has of himself as a table dancer in a night club. This fantasy occurs at very inopportune moments and he's always dancing for various television representatives in order to be noticed but with the overriding aim of simply pleasing them, the most usual of his spectators being the commissioning editor who he hit in the face, Tony Hayers.

Even in his private fantasies Partridge retains the same personality, he is essentially a dull, middle-aged man who is extremely socially inept. Part of the humour created

> **Alan Partridge Quote**
>
> Yvonne Boyd (guest):
> 'Underneath our clothes we are, all of us, naked. Even you, Alan.'
> Alan Partridge: 'No, I'm not!'

by these segments is produced by Alan's ensemble; he wears his usual dated-looking pullovers with shirt and tie beneath, but couples this with an outrageous rubber thong, creating quite a memorable – and not exactly pleasant – clash. These scenes are really quite hideous to witness, a perfect example of horrible awkwardness of the type at issue here. Coogan does not hold back.

The second trope used in the programme is evident in the first series and concerns a drawer in Alan's hotel room. We never get to see what is kept in the drawer, though other characters do catch glimpses and this causes various reactions. For example, Lynn is left speechless and Sophie, the receptionist at the hotel, can't stop giggling. This is reminiscent of the '666' briefcase in Quentin Tarantino's *Pulp Fiction* (1994). Its contents remain a mystery to the audience while creating noteworthy reactions when any of the characters look inside.

Interesting tropes were also used in *Little Britain* and *Peep Show*. In the former, the use of Tom Baker's narration effectively brings a sense of cohesion to the programme as a whole and his deep baritone voice adds a degree of authenticity to the mockumentary style. In the latter, as mentioned, point-of-view shots are used so that everything is seen from the viewpoints of the characters. The result of this is quite close to Alan Partridge's night club fantasy in that both let us into the minds of the characters involved, something cemented by voiceover thoughts in *Peep Show*.

Alan Partridge's character has an inflated ego, but his perception of himself is clearly self-deluding considering his social awkwardness, both physically and in terms of his interaction with others. In many ways this is akin to Basil Fawlty in that they both see themselves as invaluable and other people as the source of all problems, never acknowledging that it is they who are causing the problems. Both characters clearly share a physical awkwardness, something aided by their height and rather gangly appearance. Alan also dresses in dull clothes, which reflects his personality, though he thinks he's a fascinating man and entertaining speaker. Of course, parallels can be drawn with characters that followed him, not just predecessors like Fawlty. His complete inability to empathise with those around him is not unlike that of David Brent and Darren Lamb from *The Office* and *Extras* respectively.

He says and does the wrong things continually, and is often completely politically incorrect, a trait common to quite a number of characters discussed in this book. This lack of political correctness adds to the horrible humour, and makes itself apparent in the racism, homophobia, sexism and general bigotry that Partridge displays.

That Alan Partridge often has no idea of the right thing to say – though he thinks he does – and always manages to put his foot in his mouth is well demonstrated during the episode where he attends the funeral of the commissioning editor at the BBC – an editor who had previously given him the sack. At the wake he cannot hide his pleasure that the man has passed on, rubbing his hands together at the opportunity to get back into the BBC's fold.

Coogan is gallant enough not to try and take sole credit for the character of Alan Partridge, but says the creation is a collaboration, stating, 'I'm just the one that dresses up as Alan.'[6] This is just one more example of a successful team effort, along the lines of that discussed in Chapter Five on Mitchell and Webb, whose *Peep Show* is very much a collaboration, with the actors simply fronting the show.

Unlike *The Office*'s David Brent, the character of Alan Partridge did not make much of mark in the US. However, Coogan found this to be to his advantage as the character had not defined him or created the same expectations as in the UK. Coogan says, 'If you do something very successful, you will then be defined by it and you'll be competing against yourself.'[7]

Essentially, in the UK Coogan now has to live up to both the public and critical acclaim that Alan Partridge received. Partridge created a benchmark by which his other work has been judged, just as *The Office* created a benchmark by which *Extras* was judged.

Since 2000 Roger Daltry, lead singer of The Who, has been holding fund-raising events at London's Royal Albert Hall for the Teenage Cancer Trust. In 2004 this event was hosted by Alan Partridge, who introduced acts like The Stereophonics and Tom Jones. Also included in the show was a Milky Bar kid sketch featuring Simon Pegg and some sketches from Ricky Gervais and Welsh comedian Rob Brydon.

> ### *Alan Partridge* Quote
>
> 'That was "Big Yellow Taxi" by Joni Mitchell, a song in which Joni complains they "Paved paradise to put up a parking lot," a measure which actually would have alleviated traffic congestion on the outskirts of paradise, something which Joni singularly fails to point out... Nevertheless, nice song.' Alan Partridge

There has been much discussion about the possibility of taking Alan Partridge to the big screen, though no definite plans have been laid yet. Coogan is pretty confident that the project will take off at some point, commenting in 2005 that, 'It will happen. It's not "if" it's sort of "when". At the moment it's proposed – an idea and a script outline.'[8]

However, the film was billed for release in 2007 and at the time of writing production is on hold so fans will have to wait and see.

Steve Coogan became so popular in 1994 that *The Sun* newspaper did a feature called '20 Things Worth Knowing About *Alan Partridge* Star.' However, a number of the so-called facts presented were complete fabrications. These included the idea that Paul Calf, Coogan's anti-student character, had been banned from drinking Heineken because the company didn't want any association with the drunken, yobbish character. Another falsehood which had been told to the media was that the police had stopped Coogan to give him a breath test on the way home from the studio, as they were completely convinced by the drunken performance of Calf (and therefore Coogan).[9]

Steve Coogan managed to use the tabloid press, but not to the extent they have used him, selling papers with sensationalist reports about his notorious private life over the years. His wild nights of drink, drugs and rampant womanising have often made the headlines, including, most notoriously, a highly publicized affair with Courtney Love. Love was quoted as stating that he was a 'sex addict... and has a major substance problem.'[10] She also claims that she has had his love child, an allegation that Coogan describes as 'inaccurate from the start'.

In response to the tabloid titillation about his life Coogan says, 'There's more to me than what's in the tabloids – that's disproportionately representative of who I am,' though he does admit that the reports are not wholly unfounded.[11] However, he has not taken the route so many before him have chosen to take in order to offset the negative press by revealing the truth about himself in a 'tell all' kind of press story: 'Some people need to have approval from the media and people, and to do that they open themselves up... but you have nothing left which is private. I'd rather have the media misinterpret me and have part of myself private and not play the game.'[12]

So Coogan stays silent and lets the other people go to the newspapers with their tales of wild times. By doing this he remains to an extent an unknown quantity, thus retaining at least some degree of privacy from the prying eyes of tabloid reporters.

Not only is he known for flamboyance in his sexual activities, even his cars seem to highlight this extravagant side of his personality. Coogan has been the proud owner of a number of brand new Ferraris and has also owned quite a few other sports cars.

In 2003 Steve Coogan could be seen in an hour-long BBC drama called *The Private Life of Samuel Pepys* (who was a 17th Century diarist). Coogan plays the title character, who can be seen having sex through the bars of a cell and bringing a colleague's wife to a climax with his fingers. By all accounts the sexual appetite of Pepys seems to have rivalled Coogan's, if all that has been written in the tabloids is to be believed.

> ### *Alan Partridge* Quote
> 'If you see a lovely field with a family having a picnic and there's a nice pond in it, you fill in the pond with concrete, you plough the family into the field, you blow up the trees and use the leaves to make a dress for your wife who is also your brother.' Alan Partridge talking to the Farmer's Union Representataive on the radio

In fact, Coogan agreed to do the drama for no fee after reading the script, partly because he feels suited to playing flawed characters and partly because he hoped appearing in the drama would enable him to move away from the character of Alan Partridge and further his career as a serious actor. As Coogan appeared for no fee and thanks to a relatively quick shoot of just twelve days, the drama cost a mere £650,000, which may seem a lot at first glance, but not when you consider the fact that it costs half a million to make a single episode of the ITV drama *Casualty*.

In the year following *Knowing Me, Knowing You*, 1995, Steve helped create the show entitled *Coogan's Run*. The series was about a number of strange characters all inhabiting the fictional town of Ottle. Coogan was just one of the writers, working alongside his common collaborators Henry Normal and Patrick Marber, who had co-written and acted in *The*

Day Today and *Knowing Me, Knowing You.* Also working on this show were writers Graham Lineham and Arthur Mathews, who were the creators of *Father Ted*, a role Coogan turned down after his agent said the idea was no good – a decision he still regrets today.[13] Lineham and Mathews had also appeared in *I'm Alan Partridge* as two executives interested in giving Alan a show on Irish television and then as Alan's audience in one of his table-dancing fantasies.

The first episode of *Coogan's Run* notably featured Paul and Pauline Calf, both played by Coogan. In it Paul had to identify three bank robbing criminals in court and then went to join a cult, only to find himself in a porn movie. In the second episode Coogan's penchant for playing horribly awkward characters is exploited to the utmost. He plays Gareth Cheeseman, a microchip salesman with an expansive ego and complete lack of sensitivity. Cheeseman is also self-obsessed, something which is common to the characters Steve tends to play. Cheeseman was created by Lineham and Mathews, as was another character from the show, pub singer Mike Crystal.

Another series which Coogan created, and one which did not meet with a particularly good response, was *Dr Terrible's House of Horrible*. Broadcast in 2001 (the year prior to the long-awaited second season of I'm Alan Partridge), this was a series of six parts with high production standards which sent up popular horror subjects, such as vampires, witchcraft and mad scientists. Coogan played Dr Terrible and introduced each theme, much like Criswell at the start of notorious horror filmmaker Ed Wood's film *Plan 9 From Outer Space*.

However, as Coogan himself admits, the amount of time that was spent concentrating on the style of the show meant that he and the other creators took their eye off the ball when it came to comic content. The material was relatively weak in comparison to his other shows, and didn't live up to the promise of a new Coogan venture. However, it did contain various fond homages to horror movies, notably the British *Hammer Horror* films. Unfortunately, though the idea behind the show was a good one, it was not well-received, which is a pity as the show would undoubtedly have met with success had the material been stronger.

> **Saxondale Quote**
>
> Vicky: 'Wow! That's beautiful on the back of your jacket.'
> Tommy: 'Designed by a native American.'
> Vicky: 'What does it mean?.'
> Tommy: 'Born to kill.'
> Vicky: 'Kill what? Moths?'

Dr Terrible's House of Horrible was backed by Coogan's own production company, Baby Cow, which he co-founded with Henry Normal. The company brought a number of other shows to the small screen, including *Marion and Geoff,* a new series of which aired in 2007. Further projects on the company's resumé include *Up In Town* with Joanna Lumley and the TV film called *Cruise of the Gods* which was shown on BBC2 in 2002 and co-starred Rob Brydon, apparently a regular with Baby Cow productions. Commenting on his work with Baby Cow, Coogan proves he is not the self-obsessed hedonist the tabloids paint him to be: '…just helping other comic talent get their stuff up and running is great.'[14]

Altruism is not entirely unfamiliar to him, and the company is clearly close to his heart. For one thing, you might notice that the name 'baby cow' is another way of saying 'calf' – and it was of course the characters of Paul and Pauline Calf which gave Coogan his first taste of success. We might wonder if he is superstitious.

Whatever the reason for the moniker, Baby Cow proved

popular and gained more work for Coogan. In 2004 Coogan appeared in and produced (as part of Baby Cow Productions) *The All Star Comedy Show.* This was an ITV programme which was the brainchild of comedians Vic Reeves and Bob Mortimer. It featured characters played by a large assortment of comedic talent, including Vic and Bob, impressionist Alistair McGowan, Neil Morrissey of *Men Behaving Badly, The Fast Show's* Charlie Higson along with Coogan himself. Added to these were appearances by *Little Britain's* Matt Lucas and David Walliams, Ronnie Corbett, Jane *'Little Voice'* Horrocks, and Ricky *'The Royle Family'* Tomlinson. So the show had an extremely impressive line-up. However, its reviews weren't as impressive, many critics saw it as quite hit and miss, with some of the characters working and others missing the mark.

One of these characters was a lonely, sinister and obsessive owner of a toy shop played by Coogan. The toys he was peddling were bizarrely realistic. This fitted in well with the general feel of the show, which displayed Reeves and Mortimer's brand of twisted and mad-cap humour. This kind of humour relies on the surreal and bizarre. Though a skewed view of reality is often utilised, it is not one that we necessarily recognise, unlike the exaggerated reality of the horribly awkward. This is part of the reason why the horribly awkward brand of humour works; we recognise the reality being portrayed as a slightly removed version of the one which we inhabit. This allows for identification with characters and situations, even when they are taken to the limit of the horrible, as with the personality of Alan Partridge. With surreal and bizarre humour there is often little room for identification and the laughter arises simply due to the bizarreness of what is presented.

A second series of Vic and Bob's strange show aired in 2005, but changed its name to *Monkey Trousers.* This title was taken from the nonsense phrases spoken by a Vic Reeves character called 'gibberish man'.

In the same year that Coogan both appeared in and produced *The All Star Comedy Show* he also provided the voice for a character called 'Mark the Bird' in the animation series called *I Am Not an Animal*. This was about a group of animals who had been subjected to scientific experimentation and the programme followed them as they tried to find a place to live while at the same time avoiding a creature the scientists had sent after them. Simon Pegg also provided various voices for the programme.

Saxondale was Coogan's next television outing and once again this was produced by Baby Cow Productions. The sitcom is about a man called Tommy Saxondale who, after a nasty split from his wife, lives with his anarchic girlfriend Magz, who ran a T-shirt business called 'Smash the System'. Tommy was an ex-roadie who had moved into a career in pest control. He has a problem with excessive anger, drives a mustang, and lives in Stevenage. He is the type of guy who, despite being middle-aged, likes to still appear to have a rebellious, wild side. Though Tommy takes anger management courses he feels continually frustrated at not getting the respect he feels he deserves. This is akin to Partridge and many other horribly awkward characters. They have a tendency not to be able to see their own, obvious shortcomings. David Brent could not see that he was not funny or politically correct, Jeremy in *Peep Show* could not see how offensive some of his comments were to women, and Partridge could not see how extremely tedious he was. They all suffer from a kind of blindness and are unable to see their own flaws, Tommy shares these limits.

Tommy has an assistant called Raymond who has to endure his boss's self-obsessed chatter whilst being trained in the art of pest control. He lives with Tommy and Magz in their spare room and on a daily basis has to bear witness to their often incendiary relationship.

Tommy Saxondale is another of Coogan's flawed characters. He is fixated with himself and continually feels that people take him for granted and do not understand the difficulties and technicalities of his pest control job. His life is by no means a happy one, as he rarely experiences fulfilment and is involved in a number of unhappy relationships. Like Alan Partridge he is tedious to the point of being an absolute bore, as his conversation revolves virtually exclusively around himself and his job – and there are not that many people who are interested in the minutiae of life as a pest controller.

> **Coogan Quote**
> 'And what have they accused me of? Spying for the French and taking bribes. I never spied for the French.' Samuel Pepys

The first series of *Saxondale* was released in 2006 and Coogan apparently began work on a second series in 2007, also appearing as a psychiatrist in an episode of the US hit comedy *Curb Your Enthusiasm* in the same year. NBC, the US TV company, announced their intention to make an American version of *Saxondale* after signing a two-year deal with Baby Cow Productions. The vice president of NBC said he wanted to be able to utilise the creative sensibilities of Coogan and co.

Of all the comedic talent we have so far discussed, Coogan is arguably the best suited to utilising the horrible and the awkward within comedy – and was one of the first people to really play these elements up. One of Coogan's general rules when it comes to portraying characters is that he is best suited to those who are 'essentially unsympathetic'. He even says, 'I don't think I'm actually that good at playing characters who are generally likeable.'[15]

There are exceptions to this rule. For example, his portrayal of Simon Garden in a film entitled *The Parole Officer* saw Coogan playing a likeable character successfully, creating an empathic bond between Garden and the audience. *The Parole Officer* was Steve Coogan's first venture onto cinema screens. Released in 2001 the film was co-written by Coogan and Henry Normal and starred Steve alongside Steven Waddington from *Last of the Mohicans* (1992) and Om Puri from *East is East* (1999), as well as the Hollywood great Omar Sherif, who, amongst many other films, was in *Lawrence of Arabia* (1962) with Peter O'Toole.

The critics did not like the film, but it still went on to be one of the highest grossing British films of the year. Coogan says, 'That film turned out not quite the way I wrote it, but loads of kids come up to me and say they love it, and I realise that I've accidentally made a children's film.'[16]

This film is a harmless piece of light-hearted entertainment that I'd personally recommend. Supporting this view of how the film works best, as light entertainment, Coogan said, 'I was trying to do something more like an Ealing comedy, which gives you a gentle kind of tempo but with a character you cared enough about to want to know what happens next.'[17]

In the film Coogan plays Simon Garden, a mild-mannered parole officer framed for murder. Getting together a group of ex-cons he knows from his work, he sets out to prove his innocence. When asked about the similarities between himself and the character Coogan said, '…all my characters have similar traits because they're all me, so that's sort of inevitable. But Simon Garden is probably closer to me than a lot of my TV characters.'[18]

The Parole Officer is a warm-hearted film, but without much of the horribly awkward humour we had come to expect from Coogan's characters at the time of its release. There are traces of it in the overly polite and genteel character of Garden, but not enough to satisfy critics who were probably expecting a little more bite, something more extreme and perhaps akin to the style of comedy they had come to know and love from the small screen appearances of Alan Partridge.

In Chapter Five we heard how writing comedy for a television series differs from writing for a film. In a TV show the main characters cannot change, but have to return to the status quo by the end of each episode as a general rule. When it comes to film the lead character must undergo some kind of change and a new *status quo* must be established by the end of the movie. This is something Steve Coogan concurs with, stating, '…writing for TV is simpler because your central character has to end up the same person at the end of each episode, whereas this film [*The Parole Officer*] is about someone who learns about himself, and becomes a slightly different person.'[19]

24 Hour Party People was the second film in which Steve Coogan starred and came close on the heels of *The Parole Officer* with its release in April 2002. It is possibly his best known role both in the film industry and with the British public. In it he plays the lead character, Tony Wilson, co-founder of the renowned Factory Records and Manchester's Hacienda club (Rob Gretton being the other founder). Factory Records brought us the bands Joy Division, New Order and the Happy Mondays. The company was at the forefront of the music scene for a long time and the film concentrates on its 'glory years' between 1976 and 1992. The film tells the story of those years with affection and the Hacienda is recreated with an attention to detail, the club having opened in 1982 and helped the emergence of acid house music and early rave culture.

At one point, Coogan had actually worked with Tony Wilson on a local television programme. The show, broadcast in the early 90s, was called *Up Front* and featured debates about issues such as leukaemia and Sellafield, debates which would often become quite heated. Wilson would then introduce Coogan, who had to follow-on with a light-hearted and pun-ridden look at the week's news, something which was not easy to do. Though he may not have enjoyed his role on *Up Front*, at least he came away with first-hand experience of Wilson which would prove invaluable for his later role. Coogan would also have been aware of the man's background and reputation, which was hard to avoid in the Greater Manchester area. Wilson was a man not known for his charm or subtlety when dealing with other people and so Coogan was a natural choice for the role considering the characters he had previously played on television.

24 Hour Party People was directed by Michael Winterbottom. He's known for not giving much direction to the actors, instead providing mere pointers as to what he wants and allowing scenes to unfold in front of the camera in an organic and natural way. He also refrains from using the type of large film crew used in productions with big budgets. This lack of personnel has the effect of reducing the pressure on the actors to perform, as noted by Coogan himself who reports that: 'Whenever I've worked with Michael I always felt that it was just real life, it never felt like it was acting.'[20]

One especially noteworthy big screen appearance by Coogan takes place in the movie called *Coffee and Cigarettes* by indie film director Jim Jarmusch. It was thanks to *24 Hour*

Party People that Coogan got to be in the film, Jarmusch having seen it and liked Steve's acting.

Coffee and Cigarettes consists of eleven vignettes which Jarmusch had been filming since 1986, the year of the film's release being 2003. Despite the fact that it took so many years to film the various different segments, when they come together make a cohesive whole.

> **Coogan Quote**
>
> Rob Brydon:'The thing is, I can't act...'
> Steve Coogan:'I know that.'
> Rob Brydon: '...with Gillian Anderson. I have a sexual thing for Gillian Anderson.'

Some of the other stars to appear in different segments of the film to Coogan are US comic icon Bill Murray, old punk rocker Iggy Pop and Cate Blanchett. Starring opposite Coogan in the vignette in which he appears is English actor Alfred Molina and the two of them mock their celebrity status. In fact, they did their job so well that Steven Jenkins of the San Francisco Film Festival described their segment as 'the film's most memorable episode'.[21]

Steve Coogan's next cinematic role was in *Around the World in 80 Days,* and this was his first appearance in a Hollywood-backed movie. Again, it was thanks to *24 Hour Party People* that he got the part. The director, Frank Coraci, had seen the film, which is said to have 'registered very significantly with the industry in Hollywood.'[22]

Produced by Walt Disney Pictures, amongst others, and released in 2004, *80 Days* was a critical and commercial flop. Based on the Jules Verne novel, there had already been a 1956 version starring David Niven in the lead role. The story is well known and follows the exploits of Phileas Fogg as he tries to circumnavigate the globe in just eighty days. Coogan plays the lead role and co-stars with martial arts expert Jackie Chan. Also featured in the film are Jim Broadbent and John Cleese. Even Arnold Schwarzenegger appears in a cameo as a Turkish prince with a severe case of vanity.

Coogan plays the character of Phileas Fogg, who suffers extreme levels of awkwardness when it comes to human interaction. The character is more comfortable with machines than with people, showing a social inadequacy which places him firmly in the catalogue of flawed characters that Coogan likes to play.

Also appearing in the film is Owen Wilson, who is one of the contemporary humorists for whom Coogan has expressed admiration, along with Ben Stiller, whom Coogan appeared alongside in *Night at the Museum*. He has also cited Tony Hancock, Peter Sellers and *Monty Python* as influences.

Coogan also has connections with a variety of UK contemporaries. He appeared in the 2006 *Little Britain* Christmas special as a pilot taking the characters of Lou and Andy to Disneyland. In 2007 he made an uncredited appearance in Simon Pegg and Edgar Wright's film *Hot Fuzz* (see the final chapter for more on Pegg and Wright). This cameo is said to be a show of

> ## Coogan Quote
>
> 'I love Manchester. The crumbling warehouses, the railway arches, the cheap, abundant drugs. That's what did it in the end. Not the money, not the music, not even the guns. That is my heroic flaw: my excess of civic pride.'
>
> Tony Wilson

gratitude on the part of Pegg, who was part of Coogan's live tour called '*Steve Coogan: The Man Who Thinks He's It*' and had parts in *The Parole Officer* and *24 Hour Party People*.

Coogan also starred in *A Cock and Bull Story*, which was released in 2005 and is based on Laurence Sterne's rambling mock autobiography called *The Life and Opinions of Tristram Shandy, Gentleman*, a book which many people said could not be translated onto the big screen. Director Michael Winterbottom, who also directed Coogan in his second film role in *24 Hour Party People*, is known to like a challenge and was ambitious enough to take the project on.

To circumnavigate the problem of making a movie of the book, Winterbottom introduced the clever mechanism of making the film about trying to make a movie of the book. Because of this we have Steve Coogan playing three roles, firstly as a version of himself, secondly as the subject of the story, Tristram's father Walter, and finally as Tristram, the narrator.

Echoing the classic Jean-Luc Godard French New Wave film called *Le Mepris* (meaning 'contempt'), we see the behind-the-scenes production of Tristram Shandy's story. We see the film crew as the actors don period costumes in order to bring the book to the big screen, and as an audience get to enjoy both a contemporary story and a period drama. The narrative structure is reminiscent of Gervais and Merchant's *Extras*, which is presented as a sitcom within a sitcom, *A Cock and Bull Story* giving us a film within a film. Because of this set-up, complete with fake film crew, Coogan apparently found

> ### *The Parole Officer* **Quote**
>
> Simon Garden: 'You can't intimidate me.'
>
> Inspector Burton: 'Let me give it a shot. If you open your mouth I won't lay a finger on you, but you'll go to prison. And when those nonces and those perverts get hold of a clever boy like you – and I'll make sure they do – they'll be queuing up round the block. You're going to end up with an arsehole like a clown's pocket.'
>
> Simon Garden: 'That was pretty good.'

it a little confusing working out which camera he should be taking note of when filming was due to take place, no doubt resulting in some humorous out takes.

Because of the 'film within a film' format in *A Cock and Bull Story* we see Steve Coogan playing a slightly fictionalised 'Steve Coogen' as well as the characters from the mock autobiography. The Steve Coogan portrayed in *A Cock and Bull Story* is arrogant and insecure whilst also displaying a severe lack of self-awareness. Thus, like Coogan's other characters, he remains seriously flawed. The flawed personality is one of the main stays of British comedy. It can clearly be seen in the likes of Basil Fawlty, as mentioned, along with Reginald Perrin from hit sitcom *Rising Damp*, and more recently in *The Young Ones* and the characters of Gary and Tony in *Men Behaving Badly*. All are flawed and often in more ways than one.

This film also brought Steve Coogan and Rob Brydon back together on screen and their friendship had some bearing on how the two of them interacted, including their competitiveness. When asked who he thought was naturally funnier than him Coogan gave two names; Peter Kay and Rob Brydon.[23] Steve feels comfortable working with Brydon and this created a less pressurised atmosphere. Also adding to the relaxed working environment was the fact that it was an independent film. This meant there wasn't as much money riding on the production as there would be with a Hollywood film so everyone involved could be more flexible when filming. Winterbottom's style of directing also encourages this type of flexible and spontaneous approach.

When Coogan agreed to take on the role of Samuel Pepys, this was mostly due to the quality of the script, but when it came to *A Cock and Bull Story* he had such faith in the project that he agreed to take the part even without a completed script. The bottom line was that he wanted to work with Winterbottom again. Another reason why he agreed to work on the film was a result of its unconventional structure – it appears that Coogan is also a man who likes a challenge.

Other films that Steve Coogan has appeared in include the 2006 Ben Stiller film *Night at the Museum*, which was mentioned previously. This film also featured Robin Williams and, in his first foray into the world of Hollywood, Ricky Gervais. He also starred alongside Lisa Kudrow and Laura Dern in *Happy Endings* (2005).

It is evident that Coogan has been incredibly busy of late. As well as the productions mentioned above, he appeared with Kirsten Dunst in the period drama *Marie Antoinette* (2006). This was directed by Francis Ford Coppola's daughter Sofia, and it was her direction which was one of the draws for Coogan when it came to taking the part. He says, '…the reason I did that movie was because of her. I put her in the same category as Michael Winterbottom,'[24] which is high praise indeed considering his admiration for the latter.

Due to all these movie roles and the fact that Alan Partridge never took off in the States, Coogan is seen more as a serious actor across the Atlantic than he is a comic actor. Considering Coogan did not want to get typecast by the horribly awkward creation of Alan Partridge, this view of him as a more serious actor is beneficial and allows him to continue pursuing a career in Hollywood without carrying the baggage of his past roles, something which is considerably harder for Ricky Gervais after the success of *The Office* in the US.

Steve Coogan has made the transition from television to the cinema screens with a reasonable amount of success and his film career shows no sign of coming to an end. He plays the lead role in the film *For the Love of God*, released in 2007, starring alongside the critic's favourite Sir Ian McKellen. But does this mean Coogan is being taken as a successful persona? Is he beginning to play characters that are able to integrate with society, form friendships, be happy even? Not necessarily. This film is about a man called Graham who still lives with his mother and a pet jackdaw. They run a Christian bookshop and both love God, though in very different ways. His forthcoming roles may see him play stronger characters however.

In 2008 there are three further film appearances on the cards for Coogan. He will be in his second Ben Stiller film, *Tropic Thunder*, with Hollywood stars Owen Wilson, Jack Black and Robert Downey Jr. In this movie a group of actors find themselves becoming the soldiers they are portraying in a big-budget war film after a number of freak occurrences. Coogan will also play Craig Murray, the lead character in his third Michael Winterbottom film, *Murder in Samarkand,* based on the memoirs of a former UK ambassador to Uzbekistan who brought human rights violations to light. Finally, taking the lead role yet again, he will play Campbell Babbit in *Safety Glass*, also starring Hilary Duff. In this film he is a reporter who gets involved in the lives of some high school kids after having been sent to cover the launch of the Challenger space shuttle.

Does all this flirtation with Hollywood and independent film making mean the end of his television based comedy in the UK? When asked this question he replied, 'No, because I have a reputation I've established here in comedy and that's very valuable to me.'[25] So it seems that whether his Hollywood career is lasting or otherwise, Steve Coogan intends to continue entertaining us with his TV antics.

We can look forward to much more from the man who

created Alan Partridge and began the new wave of horribly awkward humour. And thanks to his enjoyment of playing awkward and flawed characters, we can expect this trend to continue. I for one am rubbing my hands together in anticipation of more social ineptness, more cringe-worthy situations, more political correctness being thrown out the window, and many more laughs.

ENDNOTES

1. 'Sex, drugs, cardigans, Courtney Love...and Coogan,' p.3 (www.coogans-run.co.uk/h/steve-coogan-newsitem.php?id=635)

2. 'Sex, drugs, cardigans, Courtney Love...and Coogan, p.3 (www.coogans-run.co.uk/h/steve-coogan-newsitem.php?id=635)

3 'Sex, drugs, cardigans, Courtney Love...and Coogan, p.3 (www.coogans-run.co.uk/h/steve-coogan-newsitem.php?id=635)

4.Interview from *GQ Magazine*, p.3 (www.coogans-run.co.uk/h/steve-coogan-newsitem.php?id=9)

5.Alan Partridge (www.coogans-run.co.uk/alanpartridge)

6.Lyall, S, 'Steve Coogan's Hollywood Ending,' (*The New York Times*, 13th June 2004)

7.Wollaston, S, 'The Life and Opinions of Steve Coogan,' (*The Guardian*, 21st October 2005)

8.Murray, R, 'Interview with *Tristram Shandy* Star Steve Coogan,' p.3 (http://movies.about.com/od/interviewswithactors/a/tristram011506.htm)

9.Interview from *GQ Magazine*, p.2 (www.coogans-run.co.uk/h/steve-coogan-newsitem.php?id=9)

10.Wollaston, S, 'The Life and Opinions of Steve Coogan (*The Guardian*, 21st October 2005)

11.Wollaston, S, The Life and Opinions of Steve Coogan (*The Guardian*, 21st October 2005)

12. 'Sex, drugs, cardigans, Courtney Love...and Coogan,' p.1 (www.coogans-run.co.uk/h/steve-coogan-newsitem.php?id=635)

13.Whiley, J, 'From the BBC with Jo Whiley,' p.2 (www.coogans-run.co.uk/h/steve-coogan-newsitem.php?id=6)

14. 'Coogan Calms Down,' p.2 (www.tiscali.co.uk/entertainment/film/interviews/steve_coogan)

15. 'Sex, drugs, cardigans, Courtney Love… and Coogan,' p.2 (www.coogans-run.co.uk/h/steve-coogan-newsitem.php?id=635)

16. Wollaston, S. 'The Life and Opinions of Steve Coogan,' (*The Guardian*, 21st October 2005)

17. 'Coogan Calms Down,' p.2 (www.tiscali.co.uk/entertainment/film/interviews/steve_coogan)

18. Applebaum, S, 'Knowing Steve, Knowing You,' (*The Guardian*, 11th August 2001)

19. Applebaum, S. 'Knowing Steve, Knowing You (*The Guardian*, 11th August 2001)

20. Utichi, J, 'Exclusive Interview with Steve Coogan, Rob Brydon and Shirley Henderson – *A Cock And Bull Story*,' p.1 (www.filmfocus.co.uk/lookat.asp?FilmbaseID=358&FeatureID=43)

21. 'Coffee And Cigarettes,' (www.coogans-run.co.uk/coffeeandcigarettes)

22. Papamichael, S, 'Steve Coogan: Around The World in 80 Days,' p.1 (www.bbc.co.uk/films/2004/06/22/steve_coogan_80_days_interview)

23. 'Sex, drugs, cardigans, Courtney Love…and Coogan,' p.2 (www.coogans-run.co.uk/h/steve-coogan-newsitem.php?id=635)

24. Murray, R, 'Interview with "Tristram Shandy" Star Steve Coogan, p.2 (http://movies.about.com/od/interviewswithactors/a/tristram011506.htm)

25. Papamichael, S, 'Steve Coogan: Around The World in 80 Days,' p.2 (www.bbc.co.uk/films/2004/06/22/steve_coogan_80_days_interview)

10. ANIMATED ANTICS: The Simpsons, South Park, Family Guy and more...

In this chapter the focus will shift across the Atlantic to another important trend in contemporary comedy: animation. The shows to be discussed in particular are *The Simpsons*, *Futurama*, *The Ren and Stimpy Show*, *South Park* and *Family Guy*.

One of the largest differences between the comedy programmes discussed so far and the comedy in this chapter, apart from the fact that they are animated of course, concerns the number of artists involved. As was previously mentioned in Chapter Three when discussing the American version of *The Office*, American programmes are usually written by a team of writers whereas in Britain the writing is generally done by a much smaller group, if not the on-screen talent itself. This means that American programmes are often the result of a collaborative effort – the creators of a show are only one part of a larger team.

The Simpsons
The Simpsons is, of course, the most successful show discussed

in this book, being the longest running cartoon sitcom of all time. Created originally by Matt Groening and produced by James L. Brooks, this now ubiquitous cartoon family began life as animated shorts on *The Tracey Ullman Show* in 1987.

> ## *The Simpsons* Quote
>
> Homer: (To Bart) Stealing? How could you?! Haven't you learned anything from that guy who gives those sermons at church? Captain Whatshisname? We live in a society of laws! Why do you think I took you to all those Police Academy movies? For fun? Well, I didn't hear anybody laughing, did you? Except at that guy who made sound effects. (Makes sound effects and laughs). Where was I? Oh yeah! Stay out of my booze.

The rough animations that appeared then are almost unrecognisable in comparison to the polished versions that we see today, (indeed, Matt Groening has admitted that he wouldn't be allowed to do the drawings for the animation for the current series[1]). However, *The Simpsons'* core characters – Homer, Marge, Bart, Lisa, Maggie and Grandpa – were all there right from the beginning.

The shorts, forty eight in all, each lasted about a minute and ran from 1987-89. They included the kind of family-based satire that would be developed later in the stand alone series, showing everyday situations such as Homer and Marge trying to put Bart and Lisa to bed or Bart and Lisa fighting over what TV channel to watch.

The full length *Simpsons* sitcom debuted towards the end of 1989 having been commissioned by the FOX Broadcasting Company. It was developed for a prime-time slot and its viewing figures have remained constantly impressive down the years. The first season drew an average audience of a massive 13.4 million viewers in the US. Even by the eighteenth season this figure had only dropped to 9.2 million, which is still larger than any audience previously mentioned in this book.

This success paved the way for a number of new animated shows, some aimed at both children

The Simpsons Quote

Homer: Donuts. Is there anything they can't do?

and adults, such as *Futurama*, and others for adults only, such as *South Park* and *Family Guy*. It is fair to suggest that these later animated programmes owe their existence to *The Simpsons* to some degree, not only due to its popularity, but because it proved that an animated series could be produced relatively economically by outsourcing much of the animation work to studios in Korea.[2] The show has won twenty three Emmy Awards, as well as numerous other accolades.

The commercial success of *The Simpsons* has also been astonishing: Not only has it become a staple of television schedules in the USA and across the world, it has also generated billions of dollars in merchandising.

In 2007 the show celebrated its 20th year of broadcasting, as well as making its 400th episode. 2007 also saw the first feature length *Simpsons Movie*, which was a world wide success.

This popularity has attracted a long list of celebrities eager to make guest appearances. The impressive line-up includes James Woods, Danny DeVito, Jeff Goldblum, Kirk Douglas, The Red Hot Chilli Peppers, Paul and Linda McCartney, Professor Stephen Hawking, Bette Midler and many more.

Dustin Hoffman and Michael Jackson have also added their voices to the show, though neither was openly credited: Hoffman's voice can be heard in the Season Two episode entitled 'Lisa's Substitute' and Jackson's in the Season Three episode called 'Stark Raving Dad'. The use of such a wide range of famous people underscores the fact that this show has cross-generational appeal and also creates immediate audience identification with familiar personalities.

One of the most prominent guest voices is that of Kelsey Grammer, AKA Dr. Frasier Crane of *Cheers* and its spin-off *Frasier*. He provides the voice for the character of Sideshow Bob. In the episode called 'Brother from Another Series' we also see Bob Terwilliger alongside his cartoon brother Cecil, the voice being provided by David Hyde Pierce, who plays Frasier's brother, Niles.

> ### *The Simpsons* Quote
>
> Bart: 'Yo, Dad, can I have a sip of your beer?'
>
> Homer: 'Now, son, you don't wanna drink beer. That's for daddies and kids with fake IDs. Besides, it's such a beautiful night. How about a ghost story?' (later, Bart has a flashlight underneath his chin as he concludes his horror story)
>
> Bart (in a spooky voice): 'And that is how much college will cost for Maggie.'
>
> Homer: 'No, no, NO!!'

The theme tune for the series was written by regular Tim Burton collaborator Danny Elfman. The title sequence itself contains three elements which regularly change and this has become one of the signatures of the show. These three elements are what Bart writes on the classroom chalk board, the tune Lisa plays as she leaves the music room, and what will happen when the family enter their house and rush for the couch in front of the television.

Although the animated format has traditionally been used for children's entertainment, the humour of *The Simpsons* is complex and obviously meant for an adult audience as well as children. The range of the show, covering everything from

Homer and Marge's sex life to the workings of the American political system and the heavy use of cultural and historical references make it impossible for *The Simpsons* to be taken as merely a children's programme although they are also included. The humour for children stems mainly from Bart, Lisa, and Maggie, and the general interactions of the family unit with which younger audience members can identify. They, like adults, can also enjoy the visual humour of the show due to its numerous sight gags and elements of slapstick.

The Simpsons is littered with catchphrases, a kind of humour we have already seen utilised in the work of Catherine Tate and *Little Britain*. This humour was particularly strong in early seasons of *The Simpsons* with specific attention being drawn to it in the episodes 'Summer of 4ft.2' and 'Bart Gets Famous'. In the first of these, the writers' make a point of drawing attention to the character's catchphrases, even to the extent of showing that Barney Gumble's burp and Marge Simpsons' disapproving grunts are in fact their catchphrases.

In the second the plot mocks the popularity of catchphrases when Bart accidentally finds fame on Krusty the Clown's show with the phrase 'I didn't do it.'

Bart's catchphrases include 'Don't have a cow, man,' and 'Eat my shorts!' Kwik-E-Mart store manager Apu says 'Thank you, come again,' school boy Nelson Munce ridicules people's blunders or misfortunes with 'ha ha,' and Mr Burns hails the success of one of his evil schemes with a drawn out 'Excellent'.

There are many more catchphrases within the show, but the one which deserves special mention is Homer's infamous exclamation: 'd'oh!', which was given an entry into the Oxford English Dictionary in 2001.[3] However, 'd'oh!' doesn't actually originate from the show. Its first known use was in a BBC radio script in 1945. Dan Castellaneta, who creates Homer's voice, amongst others, copied James Finlayson, an actor who used to appear in old Laurel and Hardy films and would say 'd'oh' in a long and more drawn out manner.[4]

As already mentioned, some of the humour in *The Simpsons* is created through references to popular culture, something we've already seen in Peter Kay's comedy. There are references to movies including *Naked Lunch*, *Halloween*, *Deliverance*, *Beetlejuice*, *Star Wars*, *Chocolat* and *Charlie and the Chocolate Factory*, and television programmes such as *Dr Who*, *Star Trek*, *The Conan O'Brien Show* (O'Brien having written for and produced *The Simpsons*), and the 1960s series of *Batman*.

An example of how *The Simpsons* uses film references can be seen in the use of *The Wizard of Oz*. These references, seen in 'The Last Temptation of Homer' and 'Rosebud,' add to the characterisation of Mr Burns. Both episodes compare Montgomery Burns to the Wicked Witch of the West, as he is the quintessentially evil character in *The Simpsons* just as she is in *The Wizard of Oz*.

The references are not merely cultural; there are also numerous political and religious themes and characters which appear in the show. Examples include 'Homer vs Lisa and the 8th Commandment,' when Lisa becomes obsessed with Homer getting cable TV without paying for it and thinks he will go to hell because of his actions, and 'Homer the Heretic,' when Homer decides that he is no longer going to attend church.

There are also humorous references to popular science, including a guest appearance by Stephen Hawking and the episode called 'Deep Space Homer'. In this episode Homer goes into orbit on the space shuttle, the show poking fun at the apparent pointlessness of some mission objectives including the idea that a colony of ants are on board in order to see if they can sort tiny screws in space.

The horribly awkward humour in the show arises in part through some of the physical comedy, predominantly those scenes of a violent nature. We often see Homer suffering eye-watering physical injuries which make us wince and sometimes squirm in response, such as in 'Bart the Lover', when he treads on a nail while trying to build a kennel for the family dog, Santa's Little Helper, or when he falls down Springfield Gorge after accidentally trying to jump across it on Bart's skateboard in 'Bart the Daredevil'.

The most obvious examples of this horrible humour can be found in the cartoon within a cartoon that is *Itchy and Scratchy*, an animation that is supposedly for children and which is shown during the *Krusty The Clown Show*. In this show within a show, which parodies the lighthearted violence of other children's cartoon shows, especially *Tom and Jerry*, the violence is both extreme and bloody. Itchy the mouse takes great glee in dispatching Scratchy the cat using ingenious, but gruesome methods.

It is, of course, the central character of *The Simpsons* who best embodies the sort of comedy addressed in this book. As we have seen with such live action characters as David Brent and Alan Partridge, their horrible awkwardness is linked to social ineptitude coupled with their egocentric nature, aspects that Homer shares.

His self-obsessive, boorish, often drunken behaviour, childishness and bad parenting make him the most unpleasant of cultural icons.

Episodes such as 'Hello Gutter, Hello Fadder', when Homer bowls a perfect game at the local bowling alley and gets so caught up in the 'glory' that he neglects his children,

or 'D'oh-in in the Wind', when in an effort to become a
hippie he stops showering, show him at his insensitive, selfish
and disgusting worst.

The fact that Homer nevertheless remains hugely popular
can be put down in part to the fact that he is an animated
character – it would be much more difficult for the audience
to laugh at a live action overweight bald man who routinely
abuses his family.

The animation, being so obviously unreal, provides enough
distance between reality and the on-screen action that *The
Simpsons* becomes bearable to watch. This strange ability
to make what would in real life be repellent amusing was
addressed in an eleventh series episode 'Behind the Laughter'
– a mockumentary on the making of *The Simpsons*.

During an interview Homer and Bart describe how the
recurring physical joke of Homer strangling his son whenever
he misbehaves came about. Homer sums it up with the phrase;
'And that horrible act of child abuse became one of our most
beloved running gags.'

'Behind the Laughter' also addresses another advantage that
animation has over live action comedy – the ability to show
far more extreme situations than would be possible in real
life. The episode depicts a more realistic aftermath of one the
show's best known jokes: the aforementioned scene in 'Bart
the Daredevil' when Homer keeps falling down the cliff. In
'Behind the Laughter', Homer is shown undergoing months
of painful medical rehabilitation after his body is seriously
damaged by the stunt – as would happen if the scene were
attempted in real life.

In fact, when examined more closely, the Springfield of
The Simpsons is revealed to be a rather miserable place to live
– not dissimilar to Royston Vasey, the Britain of *Little Britain*

or Wernham Hogg, where *The Office* is based.

The Simpsons are hardly an ideal family unit: Marge is constantly overwhelmed by her husband and family; the key thing apparently keeping Homer and Marge together as described in 'Secrets of a Successful Marriage', in Season Five, is Homer's 'complete and utter dependence' on Marge.

Lisa is a social outcast on account of her intelligence and idealism, her talents being consistently ignored by her parents and mocked by her brother.

Bart constantly misbehaves, is already overweight and is proud of his underachievements and ability to make other people's lives a living hell.

Maggie is addicted to her pacifier and constantly gets into dangerous situations.

Grandpa Simpson is starved of attention, going senile and revealed in numerous episodes to have been a terrible father to Homer.

The misery, of course, extends beyond 742 Evergreen Terrace; Springfield is populated by misfits and misanthropes. To name just a few: Moe the Bartender is chronically depressed, spiteful and ugly, Chief Wiggum and Mayor Quimby are both desperately corrupt and incompetent, Mr Burns, the most evil man in Springfield is also the richest and most powerful, Waylon Smithers, Burns' right hand man, is wracked by unrequited love for his boss, Principal Skinner and Edna Krabappel's half hearted attempts at teaching Springfield's children reflect their own unhappy personal lives, and this is not to mention characters like Gil and Hans Moleman who appear in the show simply to be the butts of cruel jokes. Even Ned Flanders was dealt a blow to his apparently perfect lifestyle when his wife Maud was killed in the eleventh season.

It is rare that an episode will have a genuinely happy ending, the broad majority obeying the rule mentioned earlier by David Mitchell that a sitcom must always return to the status quo by the end of the episode.

An excellent example of this is shown in 'Rosebud'. Here, when Mr Burns ends the episode by getting back his beloved teddy bear Homer is prompted to ask Marge 'Is this a happy ending or a sad ending?' Marge simply replies 'It's an ending, that's enough.'

In another good example: 'Simpsoncalifragilisticexpiala(Annoyed Grunt)cious', in which Shary Bobbins, a parody of Mary Poppins, tries and fails to change the family for the better, the episode ends with a song celebrating their shortcomings.

Some of the characters, especially Homer, are, however, allowed moments of redemption. For instance, when Homer realizes that he has been neglecting Maggie in 'Hello Gutter, Hello Fadder', they do eventually make up, Maggie rather implausibly saving Homer's life after he tries to teach her to swim in the sea.

These moments are comparable to the final episodes of *The Office* in which Tim and Dawn finally get together and David Brent is made to seem slightly better adjusted, or the moments of friendship shared between Mark and Jeremy on *Peep Show*.

In spite of these brief glimpses of happiness, the broad majority of *The Simpsons*' humour shares the same dark view of the world as many of the comedians already mentioned in this book.

Futurama

Matt Groening's next project in the realms of animated entertainment was *Futurama*. Part of the inspiration for this new project came from the end of the Season Five episode of *The Simpsons*, 'Rosebud', which sees both Mr Burns and Mr Smithers as heads conserved in jars atop robotic bodies at some point in the distant future.

In the commentary for that episode Groening explains, 'This actually was one of the things that inspired me to do *Futurama*. I was watching, and then I went, "Oh, cool, heads in jars." You know, "Hey, let's do that." You know? The future? I got really excited by this ending.'

> ### *Futurama* Quote
> Bender: 'Ahhh, what an awful dream. Ones and zeroes everywhere... and I thought I saw a two.'
> Fry: 'Don't worry, Bender: there's no such thing as two.'

Developed by Groening and fellow executive producer David X. Cohen, *Futurama* is set in the year 3000 and centres around the Planet Express delivery company where Fry, who was accidentally cryogenically frozen at midnight on December 31st 1999 only to wake up one thousand years later, somehow finds himself a job as a delivery boy alongside a number of strange characters.

The two people who share the majority of Fry's adventures are Bender, a lazy egocentric robot with a large dose of attitude and very light fingers, and Leela, the Planet Express ship's pilot and captain who believes she's a one-eyed alien, but later finds out she's actually a human mutant. Her voice is provided by Katey Sagal, who played Peggy Bundy in the notorious US sitcom *Married With Children*.

One of the things this series has in common with *The Simpsons* is a highly recognisable title sequence with elements that change with each episode. At the start a different statement is show beneath the show's title, including 'As

Foretold by Nostradamus' and 'Presented in Doublevision (where drunk)'. The other aspect that changes is the cartoon displayed in the advertising screen into which the Planet Express ship crashes.

The show also has a common link with *The Office*, *Extras* and *Phoenix Nights* in that it is a work-based sitcom. However, like *The Simpsons*, the fact that it is an animation allows the makers more creative possibilities than would be possible in live action comedies. This creative freedom is also helped by the fact it is set in a fictional future where space travel has become commonplace.

Futurama's humour derives in part from its ability to comment on contemporary social and cultural issues from a point in humanity's future. For example, it has plots centering around segregation, specifically of human mutants who live underground, and pollution, when garbage from the 20th Century threatens to destroy New New York (which is built on the remains of 'Old New York').

Despite being the brainchild of *The Simpsons* creator Matt Groening, *Futurama* doesn't have as many catchphrases as its predecessor. The only notable ones being Dr. Hubert Farnsworth's 'Good news everyone,' and Bender's 'Bite my shiny, metal ass.'

However, the show does contain many references to popular culture. Obviously, there are many mentions of past and contemporary science fiction writing, such as *Star Trek*, *Star Wars* and *The Outer Limits*. There are also cultural references within the narratives, which, as this chapter demonstrates, is very common in contemporary animation.

In *Futurama* these include such things as a spread called 'I Can't Believe it's Not Slug' and Slurm Ball, which is the year 3000's version of baseball. Another similarity with *The*

Simpsons is the frequent use of celebrity voices, often playing themselves and historical figures. These characters often appear as heads which have been preserved in jars, as they would obviously have died around a thousand years before the programme is set.

The series first aired in 1999 and lasted for four seasons, though four films are currently in production and will be split into a fifth season.[5]

> ### *Futurama* **Quote**
>
> Fry: 'Psst! Leela! You've got to get me out of here! It's horrible! Eating scraps; letting my waste drop wherever it falls, like an animal in a zoo!'
> Leela: 'Animals go in the corner.
> Fry: The corner! Why didn't I think of that?'

Like *The Simpsons*, it has won Emmy Awards but could never match its creator's other animated show when it came to audience ratings, partially thanks to the unfavourable position in the schedules that FOX gave it. Due to its Tuesday evening slot in the US it was often displaced by sports programming.

Much of the show's horribly awkward humour arises from the character of Bender and his extreme behaviour. For example, in one episode we see Bender make popcorn inside his body. He asks if anyone wants butter on it while pressing down on the aerial on top of his head and holding the bucket of popcorn off screen in front of his crotch, implying that the butter is oozing from a part of his metal body that you certainly wouldn't want it to ooze from.

The Season Two episode entitled 'Raging Bender' is another good example of the horribly awkward humour to be found in *Futurama*.

This is in part due to the title, which seems far from politically correct because of its association with homosexuality, but also the content. Not only is there a lot of violence because

Bender becomes an ultimate fighting robot, but there is also the theme of sexual identity. However, though the title may verge on being politically incorrect the episode satirizes lingering homophobia in society: To ensure that he is beaten by a more popular newcomer, Bender is forced to change his fighting image to become a gender bending robot in a pink tutu who challenges gender stereotypes, a guise sure to be unpopular with the ultimate fighting robot crowd.

This is just one example of how, even though narratives of this show may be set in the future, they can still successfully broach subjects relevant to contemporary society.

As well as Bender, there are other contributors to the dark humour in *Futurama*. Professor Hubert Farnsworth, who is Fry's very distant nephew, for example, can be seen in the Season Two episode entitled 'Mother's Day', naked with Mom, the owner of a global corporation. Both characters are far beyond pension age. The sight of their wrinkled, saggy bodies is enough to make anyone wince and squirm, as is the thought of them making love as we see them entwined in bed. Farnsworth later glories to great cringing effect in the dryness of his lover's skin.

Like *The Simpsons*, we find that the horribly awkward makes itself apparent in the characterisation of the show. However, there are two main characters who display the traits commonly associated with this kind of humour.

These are Fry and Bender, who are both extremely selfish and share a common bond of being rather socially inept. In the latter this is caused by rudeness and a disregard for anyone but himself, and in the former it's due to his self-absorption and stupidity.

As with characters such as David Brent, there is something both repelling and appealing about characters like this. We are repelled because we recognise an element of ourselves in their behaviour, as well as the way they treat others. At the same time their flawed natures make them endearing.

We can identify with them because of this humanity (even though one of them is a robot). Other characters in *Futurama* also have their moments, Doctor Zoidberg for example, the inept alien doctor from the planet Decapoid 10, whose crushing poverty, lack of friends and penchant for eating out of the garbage all produce cringeworthy television.

There is also Zapp Brannigan, a parody of the Captain Kirk/space adventurer figure. Brannigan is another egotistical, misogynist, idiotic character, not unlike David Brent or Alan Partridge, who abuses the various positions of responsibility in which he finds himself and often brags about his in reality limited sexual experiences. Another similarity with Alan Partridge is his fondness for extremely short shorts: there are a number of scenes with his long suffering adjutant Kiff that are similar to the 'popping out' episode in the second Alan Partridge series.

The Ren & Stimpy Show

The third animated show to be discussed is *The Ren and Stimpy Show*. This was created for the children's network Nickelodeon. The characters of Ren Hoek, an asthmatic and rather wretched Chihuahua, and Stimpson J. 'Stimpy' Cat, his idiotic friend who is extremely naïve, were created by John Kricfalusi in 1979 while he was working on low–budget cartoons.

Despite the characters' early conception, the cartoon featuring these two oddballs was not aired until 1991 and featured rather surreal and bizarre humour.[6]

The show is peppered with statements like Ren's: 'I'm

the King of Cheese and you're the Lemon Merchant,' and 'Put your hand on the TV screen and repeat after me: "I do hereby promise only to watch *The Ren and Stimpy Show*, to make underleg noises during the good scenes, and to wear unwashed lederhosen every single day for the rest of my life." That's it, you're in our secret club.' These comments typify the strange but compelling content of the show, which children enjoyed for its originality as it was totally unlike anything else on television at the time.

Although the series was cancelled in 1996, it had a brief resurrection on Spike TV and the characters have remained popular in the computer game format. They are also referenced in at least two episodes of *The Simpsons*, one of which pokes fun at the fact that Kricfalusi became notorious for not getting commissioned work completed to schedule. This is why the show's resurrection on Spike TV was very short-lived, with only three of a supposed nine episodes being completed in time, Spike TV then pulled the programme from their listings.[7]

The characters of Ren and Stimpy have continued to exist not only as part of numerous computer games, but also as a paper comic.

In 1992 Marvel Comics obtained the rights to produce comics based on programmes and characters made by Nickelodeon. Marvel initially intended to create an anthology, but the popularity of Ren and Stimpy meant that the comic became entirely dedicated to them, and forty four issues were brought out.[8]

The humour in this show arises in part through Ren's rather brutal treatment of his friend. On numerous occasions he hits Stimpy and often shouts at him for his displays of stupidity. There are also elements such as Stimpy's collection of belly button fluff and nostril pickings, and Ren's eyes popping out of his head and then bursting. It is this kind of gross content that can make us wince. It is also the kind of content that many children love, but some parents found it unsuitable, especially Ren's violent abuse of Stimpy.

This animated show differs from the other four discussed in this chapter in that it has a single writer and because it was made by a children's network specifically for a young audience. This means that there is little humour aimed directly at adults, few pop culture references and the humour is more surreal than risqué.

> ## *South Park* Quote
>
> Stan: 'You guys, I'm getting that John Elway football helmet for Christmas.'
>
> Cartman: 'How do you know?'
>
> Stan: 'Cause I looked in my parents' closet last night.'
>
> Cartman: 'Yeah, well I sneaked around my mum's closet too and saw what I'm getting. The Ultravibe Pleasure 2000.'
>
> Stan: 'What's that?'
>
> Cartman: 'I don't know but it sounds pretty sweet.'

However, one element which does challenge politically correct sensibilities and which drew a number of complaints was the fact that the main characters are depicted as smoking. This is very unusual in a contemporary children's television programme, although classic cartoons such as *Looney Tunes* and *Tom and Jerry* would occasionally show their characters smoking before the ill effects of tobacco were widely known.

South Park

Far more outrageous is *South Park*, an animated series which first aired in 1997 on Comedy Central. The show's creators, Trey Parker and Matt Stone, are contracted to continue making the programme until 2011, at which point they will have made fifteen seasons.[9]

Unlike the other US shows mentioned here, the creative process behind *South Park* is similar to UK comedy programmes, as there are only two writers who also play most of the voice roles. The pair wear their horribly awkward credentials on their sleeve. *South Park* is vulgar, crude, tackles taboo subjects, holds no regard for political correctness, and often seems to set out purely to shock.

The show's very foundations were irreverent: the first *South Park* short featured Jesus fighting with Santa for ownership of Christmas. It was this short that led to the creation of the series. Parker and Stone were commissioned by FOX executive Brian Graden to make a video Christmas card which he could send to friends and family and it proved so popular that talks were held with FOX and then Comedy Central to produce an animated series. The short went on to appear in the episode called 'A Very Crappy Christmas'[10]

The style of animation used for the creation of *South Park* differs from that of the other programmes discussed in this chapter. Inspired by Terry Gilliam's *Monty Python* work, *South Park* uses animated cut outs. The show also shares *Monty Python's* surreal sensibilities.

South Park, like both *The Simpsons* and *Futurama*, has won multiple Emmy Awards. Its four central characters are children named Stan, Cartman, Kyle and Kenny. It is partly because the characters are children that the content of the show has shocked so many people, not least because of the kind of language they use.

Kenny is a prime example of this. His words are usually indistinguishable thanks to the hood he always wears but when the scripts of *South Park* were published, his dialogue was included, much of it exemplifying the shocking use of language in the show.

In the opening credits to Seasons One and Two Kenny says, 'I love girls with big, fat titties. I love girls with deep vaginas.' For Seasons Three to Five this changed to, 'I've got a ten inch penis, use your mouth if you want to clean it.' And finally, from Seasons Seven to Ten he says, 'Some day I'll be old enough to stick my dick in Britney's butt.' The language is both horrible in its crudity and awkward in that we are made to squirm at the fact that it is a third grade child making such sexually explicit statements.

Of course, the most famous aspect of Kenny's character is his propensity to die at some point during each episode – always lamented by Kyle and Stan's 'Oh my God, they killed Kenny!', 'You bastards!' – only to return unscathed in the next.

In fact, this running joke was only kept up for the first five seasons, with Kenny apparently permanently dead in the sixth, only to return in the seventh. In later series he is only killed occasionally, Parker and Stone having got bored of the joke. Even so, Kenny's repeated death is one of the best examples of the extremely black humour that reigns in *South Park*.

Kenny is not the only character who speaks in a sexually explicit manner. The character of Chef is often musing about sex in one way or another. When talking about how to hold an American football, for example, he says, 'You've got to hold a football like you would hold your lover… Be naughty with the football. Mmmm, spank it. Ever so gently. Spank it. Oh, uh, sorry children.'

These comments are clearly inappropriate for an adult to be saying to children and highlights the fact that this show couldn't have been anything but an animation. Like the violence in *The Simpsons*, it would have been completely unacceptable for real children and adults to say the kinds of things aired in *South Park*, let alone have a character die in the way that Kenny does.

The explicit sexual content and violence are just a couple of the themes that cause controversy in the programme. No subject is beyond the *South Park* treatment, or person for that matter. Parker and Stone have made episodes that address important themes such as terrorism, gay marriage and immigration completely irreverently and almost all the personalities mentioned in the show such as Paris Hilton, Saddam Hussein, and Michael Jackson, are mocked harshly.

> ### *South Park* Quote
>
> Stan: 'You know, somebody once said, "Don't try to be a great man, just be a man."'
> Jesus: 'Who said that?'
> Stan: 'You did, Jesus.'
> Jesus: 'You're right, Stan. Thank you, boys!'
> Kyle: 'Wow, did he say that in the Bible?'
> Stan: 'Nah, I saw it on Star Trek.'

This was especially true for Barbara Streisand. She was not only shown in the episode 'Mecha-Streisand' as a crazed megalomaniac bent on changing herself into a gigantic metal dinosaur but her face was also used in the Season One's Halloween episode 'Spooky Fish' to create 'Spooky Vision'. This involved the normal picture with Streisand's face shown on all four corners of the screen.

There is also a grotesque element to the humour in *South Park*, similar in some ways to *Little Britain* and *The League of Gentleman*. Again, because the show is animated the makers can portray things which would not only be too disgusting in live action but also impossible.

Examples include the character Mr Hanky the Christmas Poo – a sentient piece of excrement who distributes presents at Christmas to children who have plenty of fibre in their diet or Kenny deciding to climb into a woman's uterus for a cable television show, the tone for such disgusting humour having been set in the pilot episode when aliens plant a satellite receiver into Cartman's anus.

South Park tends to satirise every side of a particular argument or subject, its creators feeling that nothing is beyond the bounds of ridicule, much in the same way that Chris Morris feels no subject is beyond his satirical treatment.

This is not to say that the makers of *South Park* do not use the show to air their own opinions. Their forthright belief in freedom of speech is best illustrated by an incident in the tenth season.

In reaction to the world wide controversy which took place after cartoons depicting the Prophet Muhammad had been published in Denmark, Parker and Stone decided to make two episodes called 'Cartoon Wars I' and 'Cartoon Wars II'. In 'Cartoon Wars I' it is announced that an episode of *Family Guy* which was to depict Muhammad is to be censored by The FOX Network for fear of a violent response from terrorists. (*Family Guy* will be discussed later in this chapter, and both episodes also reference *The Simpsons*, with Bart making an appearance.)

This decision incenses Kyle, who decides to travel to the network headquarters to persuade them to air the programme uncut, arguing that if the scene is censored then the terrorists have won. The plot was designed to echo real life as Comedy Central, the network behind *South Park*, decided to censor the same clip that was to be fictionally censored in 'Cartoon Wars II' for exactly the same reasons.

Although Kyle wins the day in Parker and Stone's version, in real life the clip was censored and replaced with a black screen simply stating, 'In this shot, Mohammed hands a football helmet to *Family Guy*,' and a second saying 'Comedy Central has refused to broadcast an image of Mohammed on their network.'

It is fair to assume that Parker, Stone and the other producers of the show were upset by this decision, having openly challenged Comedy Central not to 'pussy out' before the programme was aired. The strange thing about this controversy is that *South Park* had already depicted Mohammed in the Season Five episode 'Super Best Friends' to comparatively little reaction.

More controversy has been caused by *South Park*'s digs at Scientology. Though this occurred a number of times, the most notable occasion was 'Trapped in the Closet.' This Season Nine episode poked fun at both the cult and its followers, including Tom Cruise, outlining the core beliefs of Scientologists with the strapline, 'THIS IS WHAT SCIENTOLOGISTS ACTUALLY BELIEVE'

The episode was due to be repeated, but the channel took it off the schedule at the last minute. The reason for this sudden change is alleged to be a threat by Tom Cruise not to publicise his new film with Paramount, who are owned by the same parent company as Comedy Central: Viacom.[11]

It was thanks to this particular *South Park* episode that Isaac Hayes, who provided the voice for the character of Chef and was a scientologist, quit the show unexpectedly days before the episode was due to be repeated.

Family Guy

Family Guy is the fifth and final animation to be discussed in this chapter and shares much in common with the shows previously discussed, not least in its use of horribly awkward humour. Like *The Simpsons* and *Futurama*, the show was created for the FOX Network. Its creator, Seth Macfarlane, also provides a number of character voices for the programme.

As with *The Simpsons*, the central characters are all part of a dysfunctional family unit. Peter and Lois Griffin are the parents and have three children, Chris, Meg, and a super intelligent baby called Stewie who speaks perfect English in an upper-class accent and is bent on killing his mother. There is also Brian the dog, who speaks, walks on his hind legs, drinks a lot and has normal human relationships.

One of the conceits of the show is that no-one is bothered by Brian's human behaviour, another that everyone except for Brian generally (but not always) ignores Stewie's often violent and threatening rants.

Another running joke with both characters is that they occasionally revert to behaving in a more conventional manner. For instance, Brian suffers from fleas and is scared of vacuum cleaners and Stewie – in spite of being capable of building a time machine – cannot change his own diapers.

The first two seasons of *Family Guy* were made in 1999 and 2000. After the third series FOX announced its cancellation. However, thanks to an outcry from fans and a change of management at FOX, the decision to cancel was later rescinded. In 2002 the programme was again cancelled, and once again re-commisioned, becoming the first show to be resurrected thanks to the strength of its DVD sales.[12] Four more seasons were produced from 2004 to 2007.

Like the majority of the other programmes discussed in this

chapter, there is a great deal of popular culture referencing in this series. Shows mentioned or parodied include *Star Wars*, *Superman*, *Old Yellow*, *Willy Wonka and the Chocolate Factory*, *As Good as it Gets*, *Quantum Leap*, *Monty Python*, *Bugs Bunny*, *The Dukes of Hazard* and *Little House on the Prairie*.

> ### *Family Guy* **Quote**
> Peter: 'Oh my god, Brian, there's a message in my Alphabits. It says, "Oooooo."'
> Brian: 'Peter, those are Cheerios.'

Much of the humour in *Family Guy* comes from taking these staples of American culture and giving them bizarre and often cruel new twists. For example, in the *Family Guy* take on *Little House on the Prairie*, the blind girl (Mary) has tricks played on her until she is eventually made to fall out of a second floor window.

These twists are often woven into the narrative. The episode from Season Two called 'Wasted Talent',' in part a parody of the 1971 movie *Willy Wonka and the Chocolate Factory*, also contains references to movie star Cheech Marin, Coors beer, 80's TV drama *Dallas*, Dolly Parton, *The Incredible Hulk*, *The X Files*, and *Count Chocula*, and more.

Referencing creates a greater degree of audience engagement with the show, because the viewer is comfortable recognising these elements but surprised by the new angle that the writers of *Family Guy* take.

The show, like *South Park*, has no regard for political correctness. It includes taboo subjects such as paedophilia, incest, and murder, making them part of the comedy.

It also includes a great deal of sexual content, as personified by Quagmire, who is one of the Griffin's neighbours and also a sexual predator who never seems to stop having sex in ever stranger and more perverted ways. Even his car has airbags in the shape of breasts.

Some of the strangest sexual content is linked to Stewie. Despite the fact he is only a baby and still wears nappies, there are a number of occasions when his comments or actions are of a sexual nature.

These include him looking around at a number of female babies in one scene and saying

which ones he would 'do', slapping a grown woman's backside at a party he is hosting, having a Benny Hill style party with lots of semi-naked women, and waking up next to an ugly baby the morning after apparently being seriously drunk and saying 'Please tell me we didn't do it.' However there are also a number of episodes in which he reverts to a more normal juvenile stereotype by admitting that he doesn't actually know what sex is, in one speculating that it must be 'some kind of cake'.

The final episode of Season Two displays a good deal of cringeworthy humour. Called 'When You Wish upon a Weinstein,' it uses the stereotype of Jewish people being skilled in financial matters as the basis of the narrative. This unsurprisingly caused a degree of controversy, especially thanks to Peter's song: 'I Need a Jew.'

The episode also uses iconic Jewish symbols as part of the humour, something which is clearly likely to cause consternation amongst the Jewish community. However, there is no particular attack on Judaism. The episode actually undermines Jewish stereotypes by pointing out their ridiculousness through Peter's adherence to them.

Peter Griffin is like Homer, Fry and Bender. He displays the same selfishness and social ineptitude. His actions are often misguided by his ego, driving a car into the side of a house purely for the heck of it, writing a newspaper article claiming that Luke Perry is gay, or kidnapping Lois and rolling her off a pier in order to build a better relationship with Stewie. Like other such characters, he still remains endearing because of his humanity.

Family Guy uses regular insert scenes. For example, when Peter talks to Lois about being there when she needs him. This is followed by an insert of the couple in their car and Lois having guns pointed at her by a gang when she stops at a junction, Peter then getting out of the car and thanking her for the lift as if she were a stranger.

Another example can be seen when Stewie states to Meg, 'Now fess up or I'll do to you what I did to John Lennon.' The following insert then shows Stewie introducing Lennon to conceptual artist Yoko Ono.

These inserts have drawn criticism from other animators who claim they are interchangeable and could be used within any episode. These points are made in the two-part *South Park* episodes mentioned earlier; 'Cartoon Wars I and II', which mocks *Family Guy*, with the revelation that the writers are manatees who generate their ideas randomly. In response to such criticism MacFarlane states on the Season Four commentary that what had been said about the interchangeable and unrelated insert gags was completely true, even citing times when jokes meant for one particular episode were actually used for another.

However, this is only true with some of the inserts, such as the *Little House on the Prairie* segment already mentioned.

Other insert gags are clearly linked to the plot of the episode in which they appear, such as when a mention of laser surgery to fix Meg's deficient eyesight leads to an insert of Luke Skywalker using his light saber and The Force to do violently unsuccessful laser surgery on a woman.

Other criticisms which have been levelled at the programme include accusations of unoriginality – the show is often said to be too similar to *The Simpsons*. In fact, in one of The Simpsons' Halloween specials Peter Griffin is portrayed as a clone of Homer, something which clearly shows the opinion of *The Simpsons* writers.

Ren and Stimpy creator John Kricfalusi has also aimed negative comments in *Family Guy*'s direction, stating, 'the standards are extremely low.'[13] In spite of these slights, the show has also won a number of Emmys, including an award to Steve Fonti for Outstanding Individual Achievement in Animation in 2007.

As we have seen, all of the animated shows discussed have contributed to the horribly awkward pantheon of humour. They also show that the U.S. is leading the way when it comes to animation. Whichever age groups these shows are aimed at, they all have one thing in common; they've made millions of people laugh for many years and will hopefully do so for many more years to come.

ENDNOTES

1. *The Simpsons: America's First Family*, BBC, 23rd June 2000

2. Deneroff, Harvey. '*Matt Groening's Baby Turns 10*', Animation Magazine, Vol. 14, #1, January 2000

3. *It's in the dictionary, d'oh!*. BBC News (2001-06-14).

4. Simon, Jeremy. '*Wisdom from The Simpsons' 'D'ohh' boy*' (Interview), The Daily Northwestern, 1994-02-11.

5. '*Groening's Bargain to Yield Four Futurama Movies*'. Reuters January 28, 2007

6. Kricfalusi, John, '*The Ren and Stimpy History*' http://www.geocities.com/hellas_corvus13/renstimpy.htm

7. Animation Flash! Industry Newsletter, November 4th, 2003

8. http://www.toonopedia.com/renstimp.htm

9. Halbfinger, David M. '*South Park creators win ad sharing in deal*,' The New York Times, 27th August 2007

10. http://www.southparkstudios.com/behind/how.php?tab=20

11. Collins, Scott, *Clamour outside South Park Closet*, Los Angeles Times 16th March 2006

12. Levin, Gary '*Family Guy un-canceled thanks to DVD sales success*' USA Today 23rd March,2004

13. John Kricfalusi; *The John Kricfalusi Interview*, Part 2. Cartoon Brew.

11. SMILES & LAUGHTER: The World of Comedy

It has become evident that some of the most successful programmes and films which have appeared on our television and cinema screens since the first half of the 1990s have made their mark because they are tapping into a taste for the extreme, the awkward and the horrible. Learning about the talents behind this work it becomes clear how far people like Sacha Baron-Cohen and Ricky Gervais have helped shape and define this new wave of humour.

However, there are still a few other programmes and comedians we have to mention, whose popularity demands that they are given due attention, starting with the slightly surreal sitcom *Ideal,* starring Johnny Vegas. This programme is centred on the character of Moz, a small-time drug dealer played by Vegas. His policy is to only sell to friends and acquaintances, and this strange array of characters gives the sitcom its vitality when they visit Moz's flat. The small and rather grotty flat is where the majority of the action takes place, though there are rare excursions into the hallway outside and into his neighbour's flat. The neighbour, Judith, has a crush on Moz, but also has the unusual sexual habit (to put it mildly) of necrophilia.

The show's writer, Graham Duff, appears as Brian, the flamboyant gay who changes his boyfriends as often as he changes his colourful clothes – a fact not lost on Moz. Duff chose the area of Salford in Manchester as the location due to his familiarity with the area, coming from his days on the stand-up circuit.

> ### *Ideal* **Quote**
>
> Moz: 'Face it Brian, when it comes to relationships you're as shallow as a dimple.'
> Brian: 'For your information, you are talking to a mature, responsible adult. Ooh, pills. Yum, yum, yum-yum-yum.'

The first series of *Ideal* aired in 2005 and there were three further series in the following three years. There was also a Christmas special in 2005 and the show won the 'Best Comedy' award at the 2006 RTS North West Comedy Awards (which would have pleased Steve Coogan, as one of the companies involved in bringing the programme to our screens was his production outfit Baby Cow Productions.)

Another main character is Moz's girlfriend, Nicki, played by Nicola Reynolds. She becomes pregnant, but, due to the fact she is cheating on Moz, does not know who is the father. Moz and Nicki are due to get married in Series Three, but he gets very cold feet and is tempted by a string of other women, not least Judith.

Possibly the most memorable character is Cartoon Head. He never utters a word on screen, which makes his sinister nature all the more striking, and has the face of a cartoon mouse glued to his own, permanently obscuring his actual profile. Our attention is particularly drawn to his mask when Judith accidentally gets a wasp mask stuck to her face. Cartoon Head is a hit man who accompanies wanted criminal Stemroach and his right-hand man Psycho Paul on their visits to Moz, including the occasion when they go round purely to film a porno movie in his bathroom, with Moz happy to comply as long as he receives a free copy.

Ideal displays some elements of the horribly awkward. These include such things as a Christian workman being stung by a multitude of wasps and the less than comfortable interactions which take place between Moz and Judith. We squirm when we see a vision of the hole in

> **Potato Men Quote**
>
> 'If I wasn't so lazy I'd become a workaholic.' Dave

Stemroach's neck speaking and when Judith puts on the wasp mask not realising that it is covered in glue.

However, this type of action is only horribly awkward in a superficial sense. As we have seen from the programmes and characters discussed in previous chapters, horribly awkward humour at its best should have an additional depth. This is due to the use of parody, satire, exaggeration or caricature. Horribly awkward humour of the kind discussed in this book can make a pointed statement about society or elements within it, *Ideal* does not.

The 2004 movie *Sex Lives of the Potato Men* similarly displays what at first seems a shallow horribly awkward humour due to its sexual content, one that has the audience grimacing in places. It is a comedy which stars Johnny Vegas alongside Dominic Coleman, Mackenzie Crook (who played Gareth in The Office) and Mark Gatiss (one of the four members of the League of Gentlemen). These are the potato delivery men referenced in the film's title. Also starring is Lucy Davis, who played Dawn in *The Office*.

This British, male-orientated and sex-themed comedy was controversial for two reasons. Firstly, its sexual content and secondly for the large amount of lottery funding it received, allegedly around £900,000. It was due to the first point that the second became contentious.

Critics rounded on the film, saying it was crude and tasteless. It was this opinion which caused people to call into question the wisdom of the movie being partly funded by the lottery-backed UK Film Council. The controversy was such that even members of Parliament took a swipe at the film.

> **Spaced Quote**
> Tim: 'You ready, Mike?'
> Mike: 'I was born ready, Timmy'
> Tim: 'Yeah, but are you ready now?'
> Mike: 'Uhh...yeah'

Andy Humphries both wrote and directed the film, and in its defence claimed that what really offended the predominantly middle class critics was seeing average working class people having and talking about sex. He said portrayals of men in the work of writers like Nick Hornby and Richard Curtis did not ring true and so he presented a different view. He stated, 'my film was the first to truly portray the lad mag generation.'[1] He went on to point out that critics have no problem with seeing beautiful film stars having sex and so maybe they were reacting to such things as seeing the overweight Vegas enjoying a sweaty threesome.

The public reaction to the film does back-up Humphries' argument as many who went to see the film found *Sex Lives of the Potato Men* to be thoroughly amusing with more social realism than most movies in regards to the depths men can plumb when trying to 'get laid'. The movie also took over half a million within the first few days of its release, not something you'd expect from a truly tasteless flick.

The sexual, often perverse content in *Sex Lives of the Potato Men* can be seen to contain a degree of the horribly awkward, especially during the threesome scenes already mentioned, and because the portrayal of Moss is a successful caricature of a type of man evident in contemporary society. It is a comment on changes within society, on a stereotypical sports-and-sex- obsessed male who is being pandered to and reinforced by the media, largely through magazines which cater to these narrow tastes.

> ### *Shaun of the Dead* Quote
>
> Ed:'You gonna thank me then?'
>
> Shaun:'For what?'
>
> Ed:'Tidying up.'
>
> Shaun:'Doesn't look that tidy.'
>
> Ed: 'Well, I had a few beers when I finished.'

The 'potato men' characters of Dave, Ferris, Jeremy and Tolly are akin to Ali G, *Little Britain's* Vicky Pollard, Catherine Tate's Lauren Cooper, and *The League of Gentlemen's* job restart officer, Pauline; to name but a few. They are exaggerations of a contemporary cultural phenomena.

Of course, horribly awkward humour is not the only kind of comedy that has proved popular in recent years. There are programmes like Dylan Moran's *Black Books,* featuring Tamsin Greig alongside Bill Bailey, best known for his appearances on *Never Mind the Buzzcocks* and *Have I Got News For You?* as well as his experimental stand-up routines. (In fact Bailey once performed a whole set consisting entirely of punchlines, when one reviewer criticised him for not including enough jokes.)

There are 'comfortable' comedies such as *The Vicar of Dibley,* starring Dawn French, which is hardly ground breaking but clocked-up an incredible amount of viewers during its three series and the many 'Christmas specials' that the BBC aired between 1994 and 2006. Jennifer Saunders' *Absolutely Fabulous* was a phenomenal hit and she appeared in a new series *The Life and Times of Vivienne Vyle* in 2007. The *French and Saunders* show itself continues to attract viewers in their thousands although the pair have announced that the series aired in 2006 will be their last.

Perhaps it is telling that the new faces and breakthrough acts however, often do contain elements of the horribly awkward. One of the most successful of these 'new faces' is Simon Pegg, whose pop-culture riffing, film parodies and send-ups of the slacker student lifestyle have proved an immediate hit with under 30s.

As well as appearing in *24 Hour Party People*, the *Brass Eye* paedophilia special and *The League of Gentlemen's Apocalypse*, Pegg also co-wrote and co-starred in the Channel 4 sitcom *Spaced*, two series of which aired in 1999 and 2001. This cult comedy about a selection of odd friends was also written by Jessica Stevenson, who starred alongside Pegg, their characters being Tim Bisley and Daisy Steiner. Similarly to the cartoons discussed in chapter eleven, *Spaced* contained countless film and TV references. These often occured in the dialogue, a memorable example being Bisley's angry reaction to a child who goes into the comic book store where he works in the vain hope of buying a Jah-Jah Binks doll from *Star Wars: Episode I – The Phantom Menace* (1999). There are also scenes which contain brilliantly executed parodies of films like *The Matrix* (1999) and *Fight Club* (1999) which add to the humour. However, there are also a number of horribly awkward moments, and quite extreme humour. There is Brian, the strange artist who lives in the ground floor flat, and his fits of despair or Marcia, Tim and Jessica's landlady, whose alcoholism and sex drive are a continual cause for laughs, and her age and physical appearance are used to create further humour. In moments such as her reunion with Tim and Daisy after a bust-up, for example, there are some hideous shots of her moving in for a kiss which are certainly not comfortable viewing, but are all the funnier because of this.

Spaced was directed by Edgar Wright, who also appeared in the programme, along with other comic celebrities such as Bill Bailey as comic store owner Bilbo, Mark Gatiss of *The League of Gentlemen* as a *Matrix*-inspired agent hunting Daisy, fellow 'League' member Reece Shearsmith as TA soldier Dexter who has a *Robot Wars* obsession, and David Walliams as the odd conceptual artist called Vulva. With this amount of comedy talent signing up to appear on *Spaced* it would have been difficult for the show not to be successful.

The character of Tim had a talent for comic-book illustration and worked in a comic store. The influence of comic-book styles are echoed in the hyperactive, shot jumping style of the sitcom, which would often leap from one situation into an aside or flashback. Examples of these include flashes of Brian, trying various approaches to creating artwork, using concepts such as anger and fear. We also see flashbacks from the childhoods of Bisley and Nick Frost's character, who is called Mike Watt. That Pegg and Frost are such great friends gives them great on-screen chemistry. It's clear for all to see and this friendship, coupled with that of Pegg and Frost with Jessica Stevenson, creates a sense of fun and genuine warmth in *Spaced*. You can tell they had fun making the show, and this comes out well on screen.

Pegg and Frost went on to star in the 'romzomcom' *Shaun of the Dead* in 2004, which was a parody of zombie movies and romantic comedies. Pegg played the title character and Frost played his best friend, Ed. Jessica Stevenson and Matt Lucas also made cameo appearances in the film. The movie was directed and co-written by Edgar Wright, along with

Pegg himself.

Due to the success of this blood-spattered romp of the undead, to their delight both Pegg and Wright were invited to appear in cult horror director, George A. Romero's film *Land of the Dead* (2005). Romero has made some of the best-loved horror films of all time, including *Night of the Living Dead* (1968) and the film which had its title parodied by Pegg and Wright, *Dawn of the Dead* (1978).

After making *Shaun of the Dead* Pegg was asked if he would be leaving the British film industry behind and moving on to Hollywood. He replied, 'It's not like I'm going to run off and do *Mission Impossible III*,' which is exactly what he ended up doing, playing an assistant to Tom Cruise's character, Ethan Hunt.

Pegg, Wright and Frost teamed up again recently to bring another parody-fuelled comedy film to the big screen in 2007, this being the cop buddy movie *Hot Fuzz* (which, like *Shaun of the Dead* is arguably more middle of the road, less quirky, and contains less horribly awkward humour than *Spaced*.). This takes the city-based cop action hero stereotype (Pegg as Nicholas Angel) and places him in sleepy rural England. Things are not quite as sleepy as they would seem and we see the cool, shades-wearing hero in action as he rises to the challenge that his new position sets him, with his not-quite-so-cool sidekick in tow.

Though *Shaun of the Dead* and *Hot Fuzz* are clearly British, not least in the locations of both movies, Pegg is a fan of influential US sitcoms which have made it across the Atlantic to meet with huge success. These shows represent further styles of comedy beyond those which have already been discussed.

There are of course dozens of US live action shows which

meet with varying degrees of success, but *Friends* requires a mention, if for no other reason than its phenomenal success – it was a massive hit both stateside and in the UK, so much so that it is constantly repeated despite the last series having aired back in 2004. This was a warm and light-hearted comedy about six friends, something you'd only be unaware of if you'd spent the last couple of decades living on Mars. *Friends* contained themes of love, friendship and family. Ultimately, it was a feel-good show created purely for the purpose of entertainment, not to challenge, make a point, or cause us to squirm in our seats.

The same can be said for *Frasier* – though the dry wit this programme's creators display is perhaps of a more cerebral and biting kind – a spin-off from the equally brilliant *Cheers*. Both of these programmes also find themselves regularly repeated and have the same warmth at heart, which has proved of broad appeal.

This trait of much US comedy can be traced back through family favourites like *The Wonder Years, Mork and Mindy, The Cosby Show* and *Happy Days*. This warmth is always coupled with a certain degree of sentimentality, something which could make shows like *Happy Days* a little too sugary to swallow at times.

However, the general feel good factor and overall harmlessness which has made a success of so many recent US comedies is continuing in many more new productions, such as *Everybody Loves Raymond, My Name is Earl, Ugly Betty* and *Scrubs*. There is a marked difference between these and the trend towards the horribly awkward in the UK, which is in general harsher, more probing and more confrontational. It seems TV bosses have realised that there is a growing tendency amongst the British public to examine their lives critically, to laugh at themselves and the society in which they live. The emerging comedies of the US tend towards drama, more so than in the UK at the moment.

An interesting tendency of the horribly awkward in recent years is its extension into other areas of entertainment and the media. Millions can be found squirming as terrible acts audition for *The X Factor*. We writhe and wince in discomfort while entrepreneurs are grilled by the dragons in *Dragon's Den*. We feel our stomachs churn when celebrities are covered in all sorts of nasties in *I'm a Celebrity... Get Me Out of Here*.

So it is clear that it's not just comedies which exhibit this style of comedy, it is evident upon our screens and in our magazines, and it is enjoyed by many millions of people.

The Office, Little Britain, The League of Gentlemen, and the other horribly awkward works discussed in this book are deserving of a place in the pantheon of great comedy. Will these programmes leave a lasting impression? I think the answer is already a resounding 'Yes!' People are responding to this type of humour with alacrity, and repeat its catchphrases in the streets across the nation. As the trend for reality TV shows begins to decline, comedy is dominating the airwaves. This is a golden age in comedy, which will be remembered for a long time and our love of the horribly awkward looks set to continue.

ENDNOTES

1. Humphries, A. ' If it's too smutty, you're too snooty,' (*The Guardian*, 27th February 2004)

Index